New Theology No. 9

New Theology No. 9

Edited by
MARTIN E. MARTY
and DEAN G. PEERMAN

The Macmillan Company, New York, New York
Collier-Macmillan Limited, London

The Macmillan Company
866 Third Avenue, New York, N.Y. 10022
Collier-Macmillan Canada Ltd., Toronto, Ontario

Library of Congress Catalog Card Number: 64–3132

First Printing

Printed in the United States of America

Contents

V. THEOLOGICAL SYNTHESES AND PROSPECTS

Peoplehood and Particularism

NEITHER OF the two main lines of theological inquiry reproduced in the eight earlier volumes in the *New Theology* series saw fresh or significant development during the past year; the new energies and excitements come from different sources, move toward different ends, and have to be measured by different standards from those used to scrutinize "secular" and "new-religious" schools of thought.

Secular theology, a kind of worldlier-than-thou mode of writing, dominated the first four volumes in this series. That theology came to prime during the high years of the religious liberals' social-action causes. In its extreme forms it was known as radical or death-of-God thought and was colored by a kind of cool agnostic temper and an empirical style. Accommodation and conformity to some mainlines of secular tendency were called for.

Nothing has happened to expunge the note of seculariza- tion from history. Metaphysical atheism may still be rare, but most of the time people continue to act the same way whether or not God lives, and their styles of living reflect commitments other than those associated with traditional faith. But the secular mentality has been challenged and compromised, and religious thinkers are less confident than they were five years ago that they could attach theological futures to the merely worldly trends and developments. *Honest to God* and *The Secular City* already look like period pieces, and the editors of the journals on which we draw give scant attention to articles written in the manner of the mid-1960s. Fresh words need to be said about the secular, but so far as we can tell, they are not being said.

For the past four years or so the *New Theology* antholo- gies have concentrated on what might be called new-religious tendencies. At the very moment when a kind of secular syn- thesis was being announced it was also breaking apart. There were religious dimensions to the new political radicalisms, both in America and elsewhere. More important, signs were present that men and women and especially young people were turning inward in order to reach outward; cults of meditation led people through a spiritual quest to some sort of appeal to transcendence. Eastern religions have won new devotees; astrology and the cult were reexamined with new favor; the theological dimensions of various utopias were reexplored.

Nothing has happened to lead us to report that the meditational modes and spiritual quests have diminished. Indeed, they have been enhanced and transformed on occasion into some traditionally Christian molds through "the Jesus revolution" of street people and freaks, the resurgence of "civil religion" which blends conservative nationalism and Christianity, Catholic pentecostalism, and the like. But *New Theology* is not a book of reportage; it collates and reproduces theological reflection. And the Christianization of the "transcendence movements" has not yet produced much theological construction. It remains at the stage wherein people seek "the immediate experience" without much theoretical grounding or interpretation. No *Theology of Hope* or *Apology for Wonder* attracted attention during recent seasons.

No one has yet successfully accounted for the relative decline of attention being paid to traditional models of theologizing devoted to these nontraditional ways of looking at the world. Perhaps the mix was unnatural: the message of secularity or resurgent religious experience could not be adapted to the medium of theology which followed paradigms established by Greek philosophy in the format of Germanic tomes. Something had to give. Time will tell if that theory can be supported. Others might say that whatever needed to be written along these two lines has been written. People are bored and have to move on. We tend toward a third theory: that the two dominant lines of inquiry in the recent past represent apparently contradictory ways of looking at things and of "being in the world." Yet, despite the contradictions, individual people seem to live with both at the same time, and the culture as a whole tolerates a kind of religio-secular tension and ambiguity. It may be that we are on the verge of a new synthesis, or—as many observers in the schools of Theodore Roszak and Charles Reich might term it—of new break-throughs in human consciousness, housed in ever-expanding countercultures. Recent volumes in *New Theology* have tried to do justice to religious writing at the edge of such a synthesis or in a time of such contradiction. Not much that is new can be said until theological writers find better ways to state this case.

Until we read such statements, we may expect some continuing diminution of interest in conventional ways of stating unconventional theology. It is no secret that there is a bear market in serious religious writing (while things are bullish in the field of religious experience and emotional statement); that the visiting theologian rarely attracts the crowds he used to on campus or at ecumenical forums; that schools of theology suffer along with the rest of the humanities' orbit in higher academia. Meanwhile, something else is occurring in the theological realm, something not quite in continuity with either of the two main trends of the decade past. This year's anthology is devoted to that "something else"; depending on how readers look at the subject, we are either backing off and bringing matters up-to-date this year, or we are joining an advance guard and stepping far ahead.

That "something else" refers to a way of writing theology with special reference to the popular (= people) context. This setting might imply nation, race, tribe, clan, ethnic background, denominational groove, gender, or generation. In any case, it assumes that the language with which theologians work is developed in particular, not universal, communities; that the experiences on the basis of which they do their extrapolating belong to relatively exclusive groups of people; that identity is found when people come to terms with sub-communities before they take on realities like those condensed in the phrase, "the family of man."

If attention continues to be paid to "peoplehood" (a word not yet in all dictionaries, but on the verge of being added if more religious thinkers keep using it!) and particularism, this will mean a bending, stretching, cracking, and breaking of old theological molds. Few self-respecting pioneers today talk about such change without reference to Thomas S. Kuhn's *The Structure of Scientific Revolutions*. The Kuhnsians would say that Greco-Germanic paradigms are no longer adequate and that the turmoil of recent religious inquiry reflects their inadequacy and the reaching for alternatives.

The pool of possible alternatives is relatively limited, but there are historical precedents for almost any that can be dredged up or conceived. The most familiar term applied to alternatives to the historic European way of writing theology has to do with "Hebraic" models. The Hebraic derives from the experience of a people and deals with that derivation in very concrete, event-centered terms. To foresee an advance of this approach in the West is to see a return to some roots at the expense of some branches.

We as editors are anything but ready to proclaim the "death" of the theology that grows out of Greek philosophy and German metaphysics. We have seen too many revivals this side of death and resurrection to pronounce anything dead. Plato and Aristotle, to say nothing of Hegel, are too much bonded with and integrated into the experience of the Western world for us to picture more than an eclipse, life under a shadow while attention moves somewhere else for a time. But that time seems to be here, and the writing that has impressed editors of theological journals and ourselves deals with that "somewhere else."

In the definition that could be drawn from what we have read during the past year, theology would mean something like this: It is the reflection on or interpretation of the experience of a people in the light of some sort of transcendent reference. Instead of speculating about deity, inquiring about metaphysical regions, or relating ideas to ideas, it concentrates on the actions of God in history, bracketing certain ontological questions; it relates experiences to people.

Please do not read us wrong: to say that there is something Hebraic about the emerging model is not to say that there can be a simple reversion to historic experiences. In a time when people turn Eastward or inward, that model cannot be said to have the field to itself. Most of all, it would be unwise to overdo the distinction between kinds of theological experiences.

At the very least, informed theological reporters ought to know better than to wade naively into waters churned by the controversy a decade and more ago between Thorlief Bouman in *Hebrew Thought Compared with Greek* (Westminister, 1960) and James Barr in *The Semantics of Biblical Language* (Oxford, 1961). Barr's *tour de force* has led the wary to refrain from maximizing the differences. Still, Barr's work was designed not to say that there are not two different kinds of experience visible in the categories "Hebrew" and "Greek," but only to try to eliminate the semantic confusion that results from too-sharp delineations of the linguistic consequences of those experiences.

Barr reported on four conventional ways of contrasting these experiences. Greek thought was purportedly static and Hebrew dynamic; Greeks contemplated, Hebrews acted. "Movement could not be ultimate reality for the Greeks, to whom being must be distinguished from becoming, and the ultimate must be changeless. For the Israelites the true reality was action and movement, and the inactive and motionless was no reality at all" (pp. 9 f.). The dynamic showed up in the Hebrews' interest in history; their God acts in history, in their religious tradition.

The second mark noted by Barr en route to his criticism of the contrasts focused on distinctions between the abstract and the concrete. Hebrew thought dealt less with abstractions than with actual objects or situations. The third point is a contrast in the conception of man. In Greek thought man was a duality, an immortal soul imprisoned in a mortal body. In Hebrew thought "soul" and "flesh" are not separable. To the point of our collection: "The conflict of individual and collectivity . . . arises from the Greek tradition. But Hebrew life was lived in a social totality of religion and justice" (p. 13).

Finally, Barr pointed out the contrast between the "divisive, distinction-forming, analytic type of Greek thought and the totality type of Hebrew thought." Greeks allegedly split up being and becoming, reality and appearance, time and eternity, body and soul, spirit and matter, group and individual.

None of the writers in this book are involved with that against which Barr issues his strictures; at least, they do not take him on in any technical or specific sense. Some would agree with him that "a great deal of modern culture and science could not exist or progress on the basis of the classical Hebraic mode of thought alone." But most would see their work in the matrix of Hebraic thought, over against Platonic, Aristotelian, Hegelian, or other systems, and would present that work, in Barr's terms (though not necessarily with his consent), as "a live option for the present day, a mental habit which Christians or others might be practicably urged to adopt."

Jews find the Hebraic model congenial, in part because they claim never to have been completely at home with theology as it was done in the West; many of them point out that even the term "theology" includes a Greek reference and predisposition and is colored by Christian predominance in the West. Many Roman Catholics have been trying, post-Vatican II, to extricate themselves from certain specific and datable kinds of philosophical speculation which had been misread by their forebears as the *only* way Christians could think. For a variety of reasons Protestants have been coming more and more to call for dynamic, concrete, totalistic, or unitive approaches.

One is made aware of the converging of the three "denominational" clusterings on such claims and appeals, for instance, whenever there are calls for "an American theology." Sometimes these calls rise out of defensive mentalities: the Europeans have had good theology; why cannot Americans have some, too? This mentality often produces frustration over the general absence of European-style excellence in

North America or extravagant, chauvinistic claims made for mediocrities.

For all the liabilities, however, the calls go on. The Catholic Theological Society of America in June of 1971 devoted its entire meeting to the quest for an American theology; numerous anthologies on the subject have recently been published. A few serious books, some of them directly and some accidentally related to this theme, have appeared. One thinks, for example, of what turned out to be a kind of trilogy from Harper and Row: theologian Herbert Richardson's *Toward an American Theology*; James Sellers' ethicist work, *Public Ethics: American Manners and Morals*; historian William Clebsch's *From Sacred to Profane America*. However these differed from each other, they were in accord in their suggestion that theological reflection does and should grow up and draw strength from the experience of a particular people.

Theology related to the experience of a people will tend to be dynamic, concrete, unitive, totalist—and it may be dangerous. When a transcendent reference is related to tribe, clan, race, people, or nation—whether the appeal is made to Yahweh or Allah, the God of Our Fathers or the God of Battles—the dangers of messianism, destructive missionism, and pride are all present. Yet at certain moments in history, men feel that the dangers and risks must be borne (and somehow checked and qualified) in the interests of other benefits. In the modern circumstances the benefits that are advertised are the potential overcoming of *anomie*, of a sense of hopelessness or personal worthlessness, of the loss of identity. It is argued that we are not persons in general but part of a people in particular; that somehow unless one comes to terms with the dignity of that particularity he will be lost; that some sort of ultimate reference and ceremonial reinforcement should be associated with it.

Theologians in this tradition argue for what we call "public theology," a term which can be taken as referring to critical reflection on the positives and negatives of what is often denominated "civil religion." Civil (or folk or generalized or societal or lay) religion is frequently isolated as a phenomenon which runs parallel to or even encompasses the particular denominational religions in a pluralist society such as America's is. It is a kind of religion which sanctions the life of a nation, and is supported by public officials and enhanced by the prayers of nationalist-minded clerics. Left to itself it may indeed lead to an exaggeration of all the risks mentioned above. Qualified by a "public theology," its benefits may survive but its faults can be minimized.

In America, it can be argued, there is considerable precedent for such popular, dynamic, concrete theology. Jonathan Edwards, perhaps the most notable theological mind the continent has known, was certainly schooled in the Greek styles of thinking. But his love of religious experience led him to enlarge on the cosmic meaning of revivals in his hometown, which became a kind of *axis mundi*; his love of the empirical led him to ask what divine purpose there was for his colony and his people. His love of divine sovereignty led him to call all human ventures into question.

An equally obvious example, drawn from the civil and not the ecclesiastical realm, would be Abraham Lincoln. On one hand he is remembered as a theological critic of the pride and pretense of North and South and nation and nations; he seemed to begin with reference to the mysteriousness of divine will. Yet he directed his reflections to the validity of the experience of America as the world's "last, best hope," and—artfully balancing adverb and adjective—could speak of his own as an "almost chosen people."

It can be argued that Horace Bushnell did something similar in his theology, though he kept less Protestant-prophetic distance than did Lincoln; social gospel leader Walter Rauschenbusch, in his view of the Christianizing of social orders, stood in this tradition, though a metaphysics of progress colored his view; Reinhold Niebuhr certainly reflected on the divine meaning of the experience of his people, though even more than Lincoln he dealt with their tradition in ironic terms as a qualification against devotion to manifest destiny and expressions of *hybris*. The variations are seemingly endless; to point to them is to suggest that America has had a theological tradition informed by the Greeks and the Europeans but directed to different subjects and experiences and transmuted by the American experience.

New Theology No. 9 is *not* an anthology on "toward an American theology." Only two or three of its essays could be construed as such, even in the broadest and most qualified of terms. William Clebsch concentrates on the churches as particularist elements inside the American environment, as traducers of the larger tradition; Robert Michaelsen ponders the problems associated with the task of dealing with America as "a people" while it is so manifestly pluralistic, of seeing the people's record theologically, when so much of it appears to be secular or even profane. William J. Scheick provides a needed historical accent as he compares and contrasts the nation's most intact theological tradition from the remote past with the intentions and understandings of the New Left, which has been at the center of so much recent controversy and which at first glance seems to be so far from the tradition.

The rest of the book is devoted to parallel readings; some of the readings center on Americans (blacks, youth, Indians, women, Jews), but they either see these as part of larger peoples (*all* blacks, *all* women) or further subdivide the Americans' experience in pursuit of identity (*some* Americans who are Indians, etc.). A few of the essays (especially the one dealing with Latin America) have little North American reference at all. These demonstrate that theology of peoplehood and particularism is developing elsewhere and serve as useful checks against the equation of the idea of peoplehood with the reality of American people or peoples.

The case of Judaism is most instructive. If a public theology somehow derives from or is reminiscent of Hebraic experiences, it is natural for Jews to be at the center of this drama. And so they are. Standing off, as we noted above, from much of Western theologizing—and reluctant participants when they participated at all in the framework of Christian questions-and-answers—they have pioneered in the effort to instruct Westerners about the varieties of modes of religious reflection, particularly as these relate to the life of a people. For that reason, after Owen Thomas' introductory and inclusive essay, our attention turns to Judaism.

Modern Jews have been bewildered at the difficulty they have experienced communicating to Christians the theological importance of Auschwitz and the Holocaust as "death"-events and the rise of modern Israel as "birth" or "resurrection." Many Christians and their secular cousins regarded the sacred drama as having ended with the completion of the biblical canon; subsequent history was not revelatory, was nothing but profane. Jews have largely said, No! Here a new chapter in the divine dealing with a people is being written. Participation in that drama is somehow revelatory and redemptive.

Not all Jews agree on a single interpretation, however. Walter Kaufmann, generally agnostic about theological interpretation, questions whether a religious reading can ever again bond Israelis and Jews: too much of the structure of Israel is simply secular, and Jewish observance has been too attenuated or neglected to issue in anything that can be called a theological version elsewhere. Jews must look to other sources and records for their integrity and survival. Samuel E. Karff disagrees; a moderate, he is not nearly as nationalistic or—to non-Israeli eyes—as chauvinist as more extreme spokesmen are, and he wishes to call attention to the religious meaning of Jewish peoplehood.

Some of the impetus for our thematic selection this year came from the International Colloquium on Religion, Peoplehood, Nation and Land held in Jerusalem in November 1970. Professor Zwi Werblowsky of Hebrew University discussed that colloquium in a paper published in *Christian News from Israel* (Spring 1971, pp. 18 ff.). He noted that theological interest actually predominated over the more obvious or natural historical, sociological, and political concerns over peoplehood. The colloquium recognized the presence of nationalism in the orbit of the United Nations and especially in the Third World. "Movements that like to call themselves revolutionary, socialist, radical, and the rest, and which pretend to be in the vanguard of a new universalist humanism, nevertheless encourage, affirm and identify with national liberation movements as a step toward total revolutionary liberation." On the other hand, "it is equally obvious that we are living in a period of revulsion from nationalism. There is a yearning for a new humanism and new structures of societal living . . . and the concepts of peoplehood, nationhood and statehood may well deserve careful examination." (Peoplehood, he stresses, is not identical with nationhood or statehood.)

Werblowsky urged religious people to take seriously the question of peoplehood. "For religions, too, have been viewing themselves, and have been viewed by others, in terms of the contrast universality-particularity." What is the attitude of the great religions to the historical facts of peoplehood? Do religions consider them religiously irrelevant? Are they part of the natural order, the order of creation? "Or can a religion consider the fate, history and destiny of a people as its immediate subject (as in some interpretations of Judaism)? Are peoples (i.e., nations) bearers of a religiously significant vocation, or are 'people' (i.e., individuals, and not peoples) the only relevant subject of religion?" Is peoplehood an anachronistic category in the world of haves and have-nots? Are nationalisms romantic miasma, or a transitional phase? "Is Man at home everywhere? If so, is this not tantamount to saying that he is at home nowhere?"

Werblowsky points out that "the people of God" in the Christian church is used purely metaphorically; the Moslem *umma* is a societal but transnational or supranational concept. The Buddhist *sangha* is certainly not a people, but it can involve itself profoundly in national movements. The "mystical" bond to earth and to land may be foolishness to progressive rationalists and a scandal to spiritual religionists. "But the bond exists not only in African sensibility or in the Jewish tradition, but in other parts of the world as well."

So religions today have to deal with two versions of the universal/particular problem: one is in religion, the other in society and history. The matter of pluralism has to be faced in new ways; the United States' experience is not universally translatable and applicable.

Werblowsky's comments on the Jerusalem colloquium admirably pose questions faced by most of the other writers in *New Theology No. 9.* He referred to the African sensibility; in the United States (to say nothing of Africa itself) that sensibility has caused new concentration on "peoplehood" as a result of various movements for black identity, dignity, power, and purpose. This is not the first year in which this series has presented items dealing with the black experience or calls for "black theology," but this year it presents them in a larger context.

Black theology seems to many to be a retrogression from ecumenical, universalizing, and integrative appeals and tendencies. It arose at the time when "integration" as a simple pattern was being called into question in the mid-1960s. Integration, articulate blacks said, meant submersion of identity in an amorphous white whole; Negro Americans could be absorbed only on someone else's terms. In religious thought, many of them pointed to Joseph Washington's *Black Religion* as the last book of "the old school." It expressed the hurt and the anger with which later blacks associated themselves, but these appeared in tandem with what looked like envy of white (and, apparently, specifically Barthian continental) theologizing. In the process it seemed to be embarrassed about elements of the black religious experience on which later spokesmen have drawn.

A number of gifted spokesmen for a black theology have come to prominence: Vincent Harding, James Cone, Preston Williams, and Albert Cleage are among them. At times they deal with demonstrable historical events and at other times they deal with the mythical as they stress Afro-American ties, intact black experiences untainted by slavelords or segregationist whites. Many of them have felt it valid to purge the biblical tradition of its translations into the white pattern by erecting shrines of the black Madonna, claiming that God is black and that Christ is black; many whites have accepted these transformations as valid correctives against white Anglo-Saxon Protestant versions or perversions of Jesus' Jewishness. They have been less cheered when black theology takes on not merely particularism but also exclusivism. Thus when James Cone has argued that theology is the witness of the oppressed; that blacks are the oppressed of the modern world; that only blacks, then, can properly "do" theology, they do not know how seriously or literally to take the spokesman.

Enough returns are now in to indicate that the salutary features of black theology have begun to emerge: it does contribute to the sense of manhood, dignity, and worth needed by any people who are on the move, who share a revolutionary spirit. It is not yet clear how seriously the exclusivist claims (as opposed to particularist appeals) should be taken. This is not the occasion for a critique; we are interested in representing what is going on in black theological circles. Lawrence Jones's essay is a narrative; narrative "belongs" in a book which deals with Hebraic-event-centered theology. Robert A. Bennett does what most thinkers dealing with "peoplehood" have to do in the Christian tradition. He reckons with the biblical witness—the Bible being, as we like to think of it, a kind of "genetic programming" in the Westerners' religious experience.

The Third World, made up of nations not committed either to Russian or to American orbits of influence, is full of people struggling to assert themselves over against old colonialist influences. Many of their nationalist strivings have been associated with historic religious resurgences. Some of the developing nations have had long associations with Christianity; this is particularly true in Africa and in Latin America. Latin American thought has become well known in the United States in recent years, particularly in radical political circles. Roman Catholic leaders, among them Dom Helder Câmara, or heroes, such as the late Camilo Torres, have been studied and extolled around the Christian world. A number of theologians have begun to translate the anticolonialist mentality of developing nations in the light of religious references. One of the better known of these translators is Rubem Alves, who in thetical form outlines some of the implications of Third World realities for the future of theological language.

Not much has yet been done outside black America to deal with the colonializing record in theological terms, but beginnings are present in both Chicano and American Indian circles. Vine Deloria, Jr., author of *Custer Died for Your Sins* and *We Talk—You Listen*, has had theological training but is generally and quite understandably critical of ecclesiastical life and formal theology. Yet in the latter chapters of his second book he does discuss some aspects of tribal thinking which he believes have a bearing on larger American life. Carl F. Starkloff in the example in this book looks from without at the Indian community and regards very positively the mutual benefits that would accrue should Christians become empathic about Indian traditions.

The above all deal with race or nation as elements in "peoplehood"; but theology as a reflection on the life of a people has also been associated with sex and generations. The celebrated "women's liberation" movements have some of their roots and many of their articulators in religious groups. Some of the speakers for the "feminine principle" in theology, among them Mary Daly, have gone so far as to ask for a complete reworking of Christian theological terminology— even to the point of doing away with masculine pronouns in addressing deity—as a step toward developing a new consciousness among women as "a people of God." The selection by Margaret N. Maxey is representative of the attempts being made to see women as "a people" in a religious framework.

Similarly the youth counterculture has worked hard to develop styles of community and to pursue the quest for identity, often in religious terms. To develop this subject in detail would carry us far from the general intention of the book, but the essay by Douglas H. Heath shows how similar youthful subgroups are in their asking the questions associated with peoplehood elsewhere in the book; inclusion of this subject is another example of the ways in which theology can deal with the problems of peoples without simple resort to nation or race.

Not represented here because we found as yet no serious theological essays on the theme are the many associations between "ethnic America" and divine purpose. These associations developed in part out of a sense of backlash against black and Chicano assertiveness, and reside in what is often condescendingly referred to as Middle America, the Silent Majority, and the like. The same problems of identity and dignity seem to be represented here as in other peoples; the ties with Christianity are many and deep, however ambiguous. It is to be expected that before long what is now largely "theology on bumper stickers," in slogans or in sermons, will be rendered more formally by spokesmen for ethnic America.

The reader unfamiliar with the kind of literature represented here may be surprised at its variety and quality. Right under the noses of thoughtful people in the "ecumenical century," apparently contra-ecumenical trends have developed. We anticipate that before long an anthology or symposium could be put together devoted to the theme, "The New Particularism as a Problem for Ecumenism." Given the recall of the warfare and chaos engendered by nationalism over the past two or three centuries and the racial strife which tears the world apart, men and women of good will have devoted much energy in the twentieth century to discern the expressions of the universal, of world integration, even of religious synthesis. Most serious philosophers of religion have advocated some coming to terms with universalism and overcoming of exclusivism and particularity. The United Nations was "secular ecumenism's" chief symbol and the World Council of Churches and Vatican Council II were Christian ecumenical ideals. Ironically, the U.N. came to prominence during the quarter-century of neo-nationalist and assertively racial tendencies; and Christian ecumenical organizations found that even as they began to overcome old religious particularities new national, racial, or interest-group divisions developed.

It would be hard to look at particularism and peoplehood with equanimity, especially when they are associated with divine appeals. If racism and nationalism can be ugly without the claim that "God wills this or that," they can be even more menacing when ultimate concern and liturgical trappings are associated with them. It would seem that tomorrow's theologians, even as they deal with the question of peoplehood, will have to find ways to temper the identifications of religion and people. They may find that the new accent represents a temporary retreat as people "get things together" and find themselves, their power and their voice. Peoplehood and particularism would, then, represent penultimate, temporary, or strategic retreats, while the ultimate religious word would remain reconciliation and unity. How masses of people will be led to such sophisticated and balanced apprehensions of reality so that they can assert the theological validity of their own experience without doing so at the expense of others is a problem for the theology of tomorrow. It raises questions more fateful than many with which recent theologians have dealt. Theology may be changing in mode, structure, and intention; far from falling into decline, it may come into new and practical if not urgent prominence but in surprising patterns.

The accent on race, people, and nation in recent theology can both be glamorous and problematic: glamorous, because conventional religious scholarship pales by comparison; problematic, because this newer accent runs counter to so much that has become commonplace and normative in mainline twentieth-century Christian theology. For that reason we have chosen two essays to suggest some of the adapting or accommodating that is possible in that mainline; these are by men who typify the liturgical, biblical, and ecumenical renewal of our decades. What does the talk about "the peoples of God" do to the concept of the people of God, to ecclesiology as it has been known?

While J. Robert Nelson's essay includes, in its last half, general comment on ecclesial problems of polity, leadership, and sacraments, his opening half relates to the newer theological themes with astonishing forthrightness. First, there is an accent on the concrete character of historical existence in the Christian drama. Nelson stresses the tensions between universality of intention and the particularity of a people, tracing the concept of "peoplehood" in both the Old Testament and the modern church. Next he moves to the connection between the corporate concepts and the popular expressions of the church as God's own people, and he talks about the laity as a "people."

Rather than cover the same ground in a second responsive essay, we have chosen Paul Minear's piece on communications because it sets forth so clearly (especially in its discussion of "Type Seven") the problems Christians have conversing across subcommunity lines. It is often stated that "integration" and "reconciliation" are ultimate ideals in the Christian community, even if penultimately and for strategic reasons one must settle for some particularity and even temporary separation. But such separation can become separatism; subcommunities of Christians can conclude by talking only to themselves unless they all take great care about the problems of addressing each other. We consider Minear's article to be a frank confrontation of those problems rather than a direct illustration of the concern for race or ethnicity in theology today.

In the course of the eight previous years we have had occasion to give thanks to authors of 109 articles and scores of journals for making their writing available in this form to us and to a larger and more diverse audience. Now again we have occasion to acknowledge our indebtedness to that fraternity (and sorority) which year after year assures the public of high standards in theological and religious writings through journals. These thanks are personalized in connection with the individual essays here. Librarians, chiefly at Chicago-area universities and seminaries, have again been of much help as has, of course, Mrs. Joanne Younggren—who sooner or later should be identified as the real "producer" of these productions.

D. G. P. and M. E. M.

I. The General and the Particular

Where Are We in Theology?

O. C. Thomas

Writing with refreshing candor, O. C. Thomas takes on the question of the current status of theology. He finds that much of what passes for theology nowadays is not theology at all, but "a mixture of confession and prophecy." The locus of theological reflection, he maintains, should be "simply the questions, the issues, and the problems which arise in the lives and work of Christians and in their communal life in the church." As to how this reflection should proceed, contemporary theology, says Dr. Thomas, offers little help; however, the "new hermeneuts"—who seek to translate creatively the meaning of biblical texts into terms appropriate to present-day situations—are on the right track. Professor of Theology at Episcopal Theological School, Cambridge, Massachusetts, Dr. Thomas is the author of *Science Challenges Faith* and *William Temple's Philosophy of Religion.* His essay originally appeared in the April 1971 issue of *Anglican Theological Review.**

IN THIS ESSAY I want to comment on the current scene in theology and to suggest some directions which I believe will be fruitful for the future. In spite of a great deal of recent writing about the nature of theology and its method and function, these seem to be the points at which theology today is most confused. I believe that what we find in a great deal of theological writing today is a mixture of confession and prophecy which is not theology at all.

Let us look, for example, at the so-called new, secular, or radical theology, much of which was inspired by the later writings of Bonhoeffer. A typical sample of this writing moves through the following stages: (1) what I cannot or do

* 600 Haven St., Evanston, Ill. 60201.

not believe any longer; (2) because no modern secular, pragmatic, urban, technological man believes that or could possibly believe it; (3) what I do still in fact believe; (4) which is what Jesus and/or the Bible really means anyway.

I suggest that this is a mixture of confession of unbelief, a groundless universalizing of the same, an occasional sample of authentic prophecy, and an exercise in doing theology backwards. Let me explain. (1) The winsome character of John Robinson's *Honest to God* rests in the honesty and humility of his confession of unbelief in the traditional ways of understanding God, prayer, ethics, etc. (2) Paul van Buren argues that the cognitive use of religious language is impossible because modern, secular, empirical man cannot understand any reference to transcendent reality. And Harvey Cox argues (or used to argue) that modern secular pragmatic man is not concerned anymore with religious questions about the meaning of life. These are apparently empirical assertions about the attitudes and beliefs of the majority of modern people. But they are mere assertions which have no basis in sociological research. They might be supported by such research, but as presented they are hunches or guesses with no grounds given. I am suggesting that what is involved here is the projection of the theologian's beliefs and doubts upon "modern man," the universalizing of the personal situation of the writer. I am fascinated with what my old friends do not believe anymore and I am interested in what they think everyone else can or cannot believe, but I am not persuaded that this is theology and I am very surprised that they think it is.

(3) I am also eager to hear what my old friends do in fact believe, perhaps because it does seem to change rather rapidly. But again I am not so foolish as to confuse this with theology. I suppose it might be called a new type of empirical theology with the empirical field reduced to one person, namely, the author. But that, of course, is just bad empiricism. On the other hand, what they do believe may occasionally take the form of authentic prophecy, and I will return to that.

(4) Finally, the new secular, or radical, theologians attempt to demonstrate that what they in fact do believe is really the central message of the prophets and apostles, the heart of the teaching of Jesus, and the kernel of the gospel, e.g., "Yahweh is mobile," "Jesus is pragmatic," "The Apostles were truly secular men," etc. And none of them, of course, was religious. They have not been able to bring themselves to assert that Jesus was urban or technological, but he was perhaps proto-urban or paleo-technological. The result is that Jesus comes out looking like Bob Dylan, Mark Rudd, Bobby Seale, or an assistant professor at M.I.T.

I would like to describe this last move as doing theology backwards. That is, these theologians do not begin with a problem and then apply specific methods, procedures, and criteria in order to reach a solution to the problem. Rather, they begin with a problem whose solution they have already reached by some unknown means which I shall call intuition or perhaps prophecy, and then they attempt to give it some semblance of theological justification by a highly selective mining of scripture and tradition. Now I do not want to run this down as a theological method, for it may be more widespread than we are aware. In fact, it may be the main theological method in the history of Christian theology.

Very few theologians have indicated to us in their writings how they actually arrived at the conclusions they present. What they usually present is the way they would like us to think they arrived at their conclusions, which may or may not have any connection with the way they actually arrived at them. The closest approach to an explicit description of the actual procedure in arriving at theological conclusions has perhaps occurred in the form of dialogues or autobiographical confessions. Justin's *Dialogue with the Jew Trypho* and Anselm's *Cur Deus Homo?* are rather artificial; but Irenaeus' *Against the Heresies*, Origen's *Against Celsus*, and Augustine's *Confessions* are closer to what I have in mind. Even those contemporary theologians who make the most explicit claim to be following a specific theological method, for example, Tillich and Bultmann, may in fact be doing theology backwards.

So doing theology backwards may not be so unusual, but this raises the intriguing question as to whether or not it is ever really done forward, whether the work of carrying out a theological method ever really affects the theological judgment rather than simply supplying window dressing for a judgment made in some other way. This leads us to the even more intriguing question of how theological judgments are really made, what really determines their outcome.

These reflections raise sharply the distinction between making a judgment that a particular theological assertion is "true doctrine" or a valid part of the content of Christian faith, and believing or affirming this assertion. Much of the writing of the new theologians may be the result of a rediscovery of this distinction or of the closely related distinction between understanding and affirming some particular theological doctrine. In the heyday of neo-orthodoxy many of us overlooked these distinctions. We thought that when we came to understand Barth's Chalcedonianism, for example, and concluded that it was "true doctrine," we had also affirmed it as true for us and made it our own. Now, however, these distinctions have been perceived clearly again, and many former Barthians, such as Paul van Buren and William Hamilton, following the example of Bonhoeffer, have begun to concentrate their attention on what they themselves actually believe and do not believe, rather than on what they might conclude to be true by applying some theological method.

It may be, however, that what the new theologians have to say about what they believe may occasionally constitute authentic prophecy. Let us define prophecy as the discerning of the signs of the times, the perceiving of the hand of God in contemporary history, and the announcing of the meaning of current intellectual, artistic, social, and political movements and events in the light of Christian faith. The writings of the last generation of Christian theologians included much authentic prophecy, especially those of Barth, Tillich, and

Niebuhr. And I believe that Christian prophecy is alive today in the works of William Hamilton, Harvey Cox, and Herbert Richardson, for example. So in authentic Christian prophecy today we have the sketching of new visions of the fulfillment of man, of the mission of Christians and the church, or a new intuition of the reality of God.

My point is, however, that prophecy is not theology. That is not a derogation of prophecy, of course, since prophecy stands much higher on the scale of spiritual gifts than theology. But this paper is about theology, and I am simply suggesting that good prophecy may make bad theology. The converse of this statement is too obvious to point out. Prophecy must be waited upon. It can be prepared for but it cannot be produced. Theology, on the other hand, although at best it may involve inspiration, is a more straightforward intellectual task. Part of its task is the critical testing, refining, systematic relating, and elaborating of a prophetic vision or intuition. "The task of prophecy is to illumine contemporary history, to clarify the crucial options, and to summon man to the responsible stewardship of his world. The task of theology is to guide, criticize, and deepen prophecy."[1]

Of course, there is more on the current theological scene than the secular theologians, and I will return to other aspects of that scene in connection with some more constructive suggestions later. But now let us return to the question with which we began, namely, where are we in theology?

The first question I would like to raise is a preliminary and formal one, but a radical one. I have often had the impression in the past few years as I have read theological books and journals that theology was simply an intellectual or academic game without serious purpose or serious effect upon the thinking and action of anyone, in particular Christians and the church. To be sure it is a fascinating game and supplies many of us with a living, but it claims to be more than that, and the question is, Can it maintain this claim? Is there any real point in theology? Is there any necessity for it? Can we avoid it? Let us honestly try to apply a version of

Occam's razor and the law of parsimony to theology. More specifically, what is the true locus of theology? Where does it need to be done, not as a game but of necessity?

I would suggest that the primary locus of theology is the life of Christians, both their private and family lives, and their public lives as citizens, workers, professionals, etc. For whom else is it of vital concern to get clear on what is involved in the Christian faith and life and what is not involved? For whom else is it a matter of the most intense interest how they are to understand from a Christian point of view the complex problems and rapid changes of life today?

Thus I would argue that the fundamental beginning point of all theology is simply the questions, the issues, and the problems which arise in the lives and work of Christians and in their communal life in the church. This is where theology becomes a necessity and not merely an avocation, hobby, or luxury. Has it not always been so? Was this not the case for Paul and John, for the author of Luke-Acts, for Ignatius and Clement of Rome, for Justin and Irenaeus, and so on? Sometimes these problems took the lowly form of how to deal with food offered to idols, with the Jewish law, with Gentile converts, with the governing authorities, with the instruction of converts, with marriage and divorce, with ecstatic phenomena. Sometimes they took the form of alleged distortions of the apostolic gospel, or of attacks upon Christians and their faith and life by pagans. Read the New Testament and the apostolic fathers and make your own list.

The task of instruction and the explication of the developing rule of faith led naturally into the treatment of more speculative issues which were also being raised by the contemporary Middle Platonist philosophers. This issued in works such as Origen's *On First Principles*, later in the medieval summae, and ultimately in the massive dogmatic theologies of the 17th to 20th centuries. This type of work which was in such vogue until recently had two results. The first was to tend to hide the original impetus to theological reflection in the issues in the lives of Christians. The second was to turn the study of theology into the study of these great systems, that is, toward the study of the *results* of theological reflection rather than the method and actual carrying out of theological reflection itself. To be sure the study of the great systems supplied a framework with which specific issues could be approached, but it did not offer a method for dealing with these issues.

One of the striking aspects of contemporary writing about theological method is that most of it deals either with the method of interpreting biblical texts or with the method of developing a theological system, and very little if any of it deals with how to detect, clarify, and resolve a particular theological issue. This is one reason why much occasional writing on specific issues is based on intuition, or an anachronistic mining of scripture and tradition, or on doing theology backwards. This is also why I have been driven in the teaching of theology to the investigation of the case or problem method as it is used in other graduate professional schools such as law, business, medicine, and education. The case method has been used widely in theological education in such areas as ethics and pastoral care, but not in theology, yet history tells us that theology began that way.

An interesting possibility in regard to the use of the case method in teaching theology is that it might indicate that certain theological loci are not operational, i.e., certain theological topics may never be brought into consideration by actual cases. What would this mean? It might mean that these loci were the historical result of speculation or intellectual game-playing rather than the result of treating and resolving actual issues. It might also mean that we had not pushed the consideration of cases back far enough toward first principles. This incidentally is one of the main disadvantages of the case method in theology: it usually does not allow enough time for the thorough analysis of all the issues raised. For example, a case may raise the issue of the relation of sin, grace, and freedom. But there would probably not be time to pursue these themes thoroughly in Paul, Augustine and Pelagius, Luther and Erasmus, etc. Thus the use of cases would have to be backed up by independent historical study.

But the failure of some theological loci to come into operation in the treatment of cases might also mean that these topics of theology were the result not of concrete problems of the past but of the impetus toward coherence, consistency, and comprehensiveness. They might be the result of pursuing the question about the implications and interconnections of what had been already affirmed. Thus we find here both the historical origin and the reason for being of the systems of theology. The only mistake would be to consider the systems themselves to be at the center of attention in theological study rather than the problems and issues of the Christian life.

Now if I have correctly determined the locus of theological reflection, then how should this reflection proceed? I have already noted that we receive very little help on this question from contemporary theology. Most of the current discussion of theological method is either too abstract ("Listen to the Word of God") or is concerned with the method of developing a system rather than with resolving specific issues. But there is one area of contemporary theological writing which comes closest to offering help here, and that is the discussion of hermeneutics and the writings of the "new hermeneuts" in particular. I believe that they are on the right track in regard to the method for the resolution of specific theological issues. It might seem that they would be of very little help because of their concentration on the task of proclamation, the question of the translation of meaning from the biblical text to the sermon. But this seems to me to be the underlying issue in the treatment of theological problems.

The history-of-religions school of biblical criticism has successfully established the great cultural distance between the biblical texts and the 20th century. This problem of distance has been suppressed by the liberal theologians and the new theologians through the perilous modernizing of Jesus. It was suppressed by the neo-orthodox through a process of archaizing ourselves, that is, through the adoption of the alleged thought forms of the first century. But the establishment of the cultural distance has posed sharply the hermeneutical problem, namely, the question of how you go about translating what a text meant then to what it might mean today.

At this point two questions arise: Why a biblical text? and How will the translation of the meaning of a biblical text or all biblical texts help us in the solution of theological issues today? It would seem that the irreducible minimum in any theology which could call itself Christian is that its focus should in some way be on Jesus of Nazareth. If the focus were upon the transcendent creator, the immanent spirit, the universal consciousness, the historical process, or something else, then it could be argued that it was not essentially a Christian theology. Thus, for example, it could be argued that the theological transformation attempted by Paul van Buren in *The Secular Meaning of the Gospel*[2] is essentially Christian, whereas that attempted by H. N. Wieman in *Religious Inquiry*[3] is not.

Now what does it mean to focus on Jesus? I would suggest that it means concentrating on the historical reality of Jesus, his actions and teaching, as these are available to us through historical research. This would have to take into account the various interpretations of the significance of Jesus by the first Christians.[4]

The primary documents for this historical reality and its significance are the writings collected in the New Testament. The Old Testament should also be included among the primary documents, but the distinctions and relationships are so complex that this issue must be passed over here. Focussing on Jesus in this sense would mean treating the historical reality of Jesus as the prime locus for the disclosure of the true reality of man, history, nature, and God. It is the concentration of the new hermeneutics on just these issues which makes it the most likely source of help in theological method.

But how will the translation of the meaning of biblical texts help us in the solution of theological issues? In particular how will the new hermeneutical concentration on the movement from a biblical text to a sermon be of any assistance? It can help us in the resolution of theological issues only if it is seen as an item of theological interpretation which must be related in a systematic way to innumerable other items.

An example may help to clarify this point. Suppose we are confronted with the problem of what a Christian congregation and its members are called to be and do in relation to a confrontation by a representative of the Black Manifesto. This is obviously not a purely theological problem, because other kinds of issues are ensnarled here: political, economic, legal, moral, factual, psychological, historical, etc. But it is also quite clear that a number of theological issues are also involved, and one of them is the fundamental purpose, function, and calling of the church and its members. In the light of what I have said above, one prerequisite in the clarification and resolution of this issue is to understand what the biblical authors have to say about this, to understand what they meant when they spoke about the church. Needless to say, consideration must also be given to the theological tradition as well. This will involve the interpretation of a great many texts by many different authors. If this means an irreducible plurality of points of view, then the theologian is faced with the tricky problem of selection among them, as well as the problem of translation.

But Krister Stendahl, for example, argues that what he calls the descriptive task of biblical theology, which is to render the meaning of the original in its own terms, does not present us with a conglomeration of diverse and unrelated ideas but rather with "an organic unity," a "highly developed" theology comparable to that of Aquinas and Calvin. He concludes that the task of systematic theology is that of translation from one pattern of thought into another.[5]

Now it is quite clear that the descriptive task of biblical theology has not been completed, although stabs at a complete picture have been made, especially by Bultmann, Stauffer, Grant, and Conzelmann. And other stabs and more than stabs at the task of creative translation have been made by Bultmann, Tillich, and many others. In short, enough has been and is being done to tackle specific theological issues such as the calling of the church in the face of the Black Manifesto.

This raises the question, however, of whether or not a theological translation can be made of the biblical theology of the church apart from making a translation of the biblical theology of God, man, Christ, world, etc.; without, that is, making a total translation of biblical theology. The alleged organic character of the unity of both biblical theology and its translation would seem to indicate that a piecemeal translation would distort the pieces translated. At the very least each bit of translation would have to be related consistently to all the other bits available. This may imply the necessity of an overall framework of categories to be employed in each bit of translation. In recent years classical, existentialist, and process ontologies have been used for this purpose. But since the philosophical framework may distort some of the intention of the biblical authors, a dialectic must be maintained between the two.

This same point can be approached in a somewhat different way. Under the phrase "creative translation" is hidden a very complex and mysterious business. On the one hand we have, hopefully, the description of the meaning of the original texts, the description of the intentions of the authors in their own terms, patterns of thought, and cultural context. On the other hand we have the terms, patterns of thought, and cultural context of the present issue and the theologian facing it. Now the question is, What would the original intention and meaning of the authors look like when translated, transferred, transported into this present situation? This is a task demanding the highest type of imagination and creativity and thus one which is open to the maximum of self-deception and reading back into the original. For all that can be said in criticism of Bultmann, his attempt is a perfect type of the kind of imaginative translations we are seeking.

More needs to be said, however, about the contemporary end of this task. Stendahl implies that there is some kind of unity in the pattern of thought of the biblical authors. That is a problem for the historians. What about the present situation? Can we use the singular? Is there one set of terms, one pattern of thought, one cultural context in the present, in America, or in the church? It is fashionable today to stress all kinds of pluralism everywhere. But an ultimate pluralism is logically unperceivable, even as universal change is logically unperceivable. So there must be at least a minimal sharing of terms, pattern of thought, and cultural context, or else communication is impossible. Now should the theologian work with this minimal common text of translation or should he seize upon some very specific set of terms, pattern of thought, and cultural context as the locus of his theological translation? Presumably the preacher and instructor must work with the latter, but the theologian must use some kind of compromise.

Now various patterns of thought have been chosen by recent theologians. I suppose that classical ontology, existentialist and process philosophy are in some ways compromises between least common denominators and very specific and localized patterns of thought. If this is where we are in theology, then our work is cut out for us.

Notes

1. Harvey Cox, in *Frontline Theology*, ed. by Dean Peerman (Richmond, Va.: John Knox Press, 1967), p. 149.
2. (New York: Macmillan, 1963).
3. (Boston: Beacon Press, 1968).
4. See the excellent analysis of these issues in V. A. Harvey, *The Historian and the Believer* (New York: Macmillan, 1966), pp. 265 ff.
5. *Interpreter's Dictionary of the Bible* (New York: Abingdon Press, 1962), I, 425 ff.

II. The Debate over Historic
Judaism's Contributions

The Future of Jewish Identity

Walter Kaufmann

The search for Jewish identity has accelerated in recent years, and one who has shared in that search is Walter Kaufmann, Professor of Philosophy at Princeton University. Dr. Kaufmann presents what many will regard as a highly personal—and therefore controversial—definition of Judaism or Jewishness. He does not affirm the religious dimensions of Judaism; instead, he contends that the essence of Judaism lies in its concern for social justice, music and literature, and learning. He also argues strongly that Israel should strive to "build an exemplary pluralistic society." Dr. Kaufmann is the author of *Nietzsche, Critique of Religion and Philosophy, From Shakespeare to Existentialism, The Faith of a Heretic, Cain and Other Poems, Hegel,* and *Tragedy and Philosophy,* all of which are available in paperback. His most recent book is tentatively titled *Beyond Justice and Equality.* He has also translated Goethe's *Faust,* Martin Buber's *I and Thou,* and ten of Nietzsche's major works. The present article, which appeared in the Summer 1970 issue of *Conservative Judaism,** is based on a paper which Dr. Kaufmann read at the American-Israel Dialogue sponsored by the American Jewish Congress, and held in Haifa, in July 1969.

TIME WAS when a convertible, a glamorous girl friend, and membership in some fraternities or clubs were status symbols among American students. In the late sixties, however, they became symbols of a way of life despised by *avant-garde* students. No single set of symbols took their place: neither beards, drugs, and Yoga, nor civil-rights work, demonstrations, and occupying buildings. Trying some of this, like reading Hermann Hesse and talking about existen-

* 3080 Broadway, New York, N.Y. 10027.

tialism, is part of a search, a quest, a crisis. And this is the new status symbol. It even has a name: *the identity crisis*.

You can be "with it" without a beard and without taking drugs, and you certainly do not have to occupy a building; but if you are not concerned about your identity you are really "out of it."

This way of putting it may seem not merely nasty but downright wrong. For the identity crisis is not acquired like a car, or membership in a club, or a glamorous girl friend; it may involve sleepless nights and despair. So, of course, may a glamorous girl friend. But in the case of the girl, suffering is incidental, while an identity crisis is painful through and through. Still, that does not mean that it cannot be a status symbol. The duelling scars that German fraternity students used to sport were no mere side effect of duelling; often salt was rubbed into the gash to make sure that the scar would become huge and highly visible. The parallel to the identity crisis is palpable. Here, too, it is fashionable to rub salt into the wound.

I find this practice rather distasteful. The irritation of a grain of sand may prompt an oyster to produce a pearl, but men are not oysters, and it is highly questionable whether making so much of one's worries about one's identity is very often fruitful. Such worries may be a part of growing up and to some extent inevitable; but if an adult has not resolved them we do not expect him to publicize that fact. If he is a good writer, he may deal with his identity crisis in an illuminating manner, not necessarily in the context of adolescence. He may show us, as Tolstoy does in *The Death of Ivan Ilyitch*, how an incurably sick man, about to die, looks back on a futile life, and asks himself what and who he really is.

If the Jewish people were either very young, or incurably sick and about to die after a pointless life, it would be fitting for us to worry about Jewish identity. But our people is much more than three thousand years old, our life has not been futilely frittered away on trivialities, and prophets of our impending death have been proved wrong so often that it seems more fitting for us to continue to do worthwhile things rather than worry a great deal about our identity.

Consideration of the future of Jewish identity poses an additional problem. An active, healthy person does not try to predict his own future. He creates it, knowing that sudden, unforeseen, capricious events are almost certain to make the result quite different from his dreams. He therefore does not dream too much but acts, finding an element of fascination in the never-ceasing challenge of the unexpected. The same is true of an active, healthy people.

By these criteria, the men and women of Israel are a paradigm of an active and healthy people. Nobody needs to tell them about the unexpected and the unpredictable. Nobody needs to tell them that it is fruitless to keep talking and worrying about the future. Nobody needs to tell them about the fascination of challenges, about courage, about action.

If the question of Jewish identity is incomparably more acute in the United States than it is in Israel, this is not merely because America is the home of the identity crisis, or because American students and blacks make so much of their concern with their identity. The intellectual climate in the United States accounts for the formulation of the problem in terms of identity, but the basic concern is older. Assimilation calls into question the *future* of Jewish identity, and the decline of religion raises the problem of the *nature* of Jewish identity.

Indeed, a surprising number of Jews in Israel are worried about Jewish identity. They are much less likely to think of the problem in terms of "identity," but large numbers of Israelis wonder about their relationship to the Jews abroad. What is it that they have in common? What constitutes Jewishness? (Meanwhile many Egyptians debate whether they are, above all, Arabs or Egyptians.)

The concerns that lead to such questioning and discussion among Jews both in the Diaspora and in Israel are perfectly understandable. But discourses on "Jewishness" and the frequent use of the term "un-Jewish" bring to mind the House

Committee on Un-American Activities. The concept of "un-American activities" became so odious to so many Americans that the committee eventually changed its name; but liberal Jews who for years criticized the notion of "un-American activities" have no qualms at all about branding all sorts of conduct and ideas as "un-Jewish." What would they think of equally prolonged discussions about Polishness and what is un-Polish, Russianism and what is un-Russian, or what is truly German and un-German?

Such terms may seem descriptive, but the discussion is rarely about facts. The terms are evaluative, and what we are offered are persuasive definitions, prescriptions, exhortations, and denunciations. Even as anti-Semites use the word "Jewish" as an opprobrium, many Jews use "Jewish" as an encomium and "un-Jewish" as a term of censure. Therefore most discussions of this sort are quite as sterile as disputes about what is "un-Christian." From a multitude of rich traditions many Jews and Christians distill what they strongly favor and call it "Jewish" or "Christian." What they fervently dislike becomes "un-Jewish" and "un-Christian"—precisely if it is something that is done by many Jews or Christians.

As long as terms are used this way, no dialogue is possible. As long as each discussant feels free to ignore change and development, and to freeze as the norm certain favored elements from the tradition, Orthodox, Conservative, and Reform Jews will disagree as predictably as Calvinists, Catholics, and liberal Protestants.

In sum, we should try to discuss the future of Jewish identity without getting caught in the semantic pitfalls of "Jewishness."

Identity as Shared Fate

In biblical times a Jew was distinguished from other men by his beliefs—and even more by his disbeliefs—his way of life, his language, his traditions. After the emergence of Christianity and the destruction of the Temple, being a Jew became primarily a matter of religion. But it never was *only* that. Ever since the days of Ruth, a person becoming a Jew did not merely embrace another religion but also cast his lot with the Jewish people. *Amech ami, v'elohayich elohai, ba'asher tamuti amut*—your people is my people, your God my God, and where you die I shall die.

For roughly three thousand years the words of Ruth have summed up the meaning of being a Jew or choosing to be a Jew: membership in a people, in a religion, and in a *Schicksalsgemeinschaft*—a community that shares a common fate.

The erosion of religion in the modern world calls the traditional meaning of "Jewishness" into question. Both the beliefs and the disbeliefs that at one time distinguished Jews are widely shared by non-Jews; and many Jews have lost all religious beliefs. The way of life governed by the 613 do's and don't's of traditional Judaism has been abandoned by millions of Jews, while millions more pick and choose a few of the traditions, giving up others. Many feel that what they keep is genuine "Jewishness," and that what others choose to perpetuate are mere frills. Differences abound even among those who call themselves Orthodox. For centuries, being a Jew meant primarily that one adhered to the Jewish religion. In the twentieth century that is becoming the exception rather than the rule.

Nor is it clear that being a Jew still means membership in a *Schicksalsgemeinschaft*. When I formally left the Lutheran church into which I had been baptized (although my mother and all of my grandparents were Jewish) and chose to become a Jew, in Berlin in 1933, I seemed to choose not only a religion but a common fate. *Amech ami, v'elohayich elohai, ba'asher tamuti amut*. But where *they* died, *we* did not die. We did *not* share their fate.

Still we share the fate of being survivors. For some of us that is a large part of the meaning of our being Jews—an experience at the very core of our existence, with which we keep trying to cope.

Yet it is a small number of Jews with whom we share this bond. Most American Jews and a large number of Israelis did not share this fate either, and the experience of the rapidly growing majority of Jewry—those born since World War II—is different from ours. The fate of the Jews in the United States and in the Soviet Union is not at all the same, and neither of these two large communities has shared the hardships and the hazards of the Jews in Israel, any more than most Israelis have shared the miseries of Soviet Jewry. Being a Jew no longer involves sharing a common fate.

Did it ever? The fate of Judah was not that of Israel, and the Jews who returned to Jerusalem after the Babylonian Exile did not share the fate of those who remained in Mesopotamia. The fate of the Jews in Alexandria was not that of the Jews in Palestine, and later the Sephardim and the Ashkenazim went their separate ways. Even in Germany in 1933, the fate I chose was that of half-a-million German Jews, not that of the vast majority of Jews abroad.

Our common fate exists only in memory and apprehension. Talk of a *Schicksalsgemeinschaft* suggests that, given a long enough span of time, we can always count on persecution and destruction, and that only a remnant will survive. Talk of a community of fate involves a degree of fatalism.

In the mid-thirties we had a newspaper in Berlin that was called *C-V Zeitung*. The full name of the *C-V* was *Central-verein deutscher Staatsbürger jüdischen Glaubens*, Central Association of German Citizens of the Jewish Faith. That organization and its anti-Zionist spirit quickly became dated by events. But many Israelis wonder whether American Jewry does not look upon itself the same way—as American citizens of the Jewish faith. One important difference, however, is that many of us have given up the Jewish faith, the Jewish religion; for us the Jews are a people. And the Americans are not a people in the same sense as the German or Italian people. The United States is a pluralistic country in which many citizens take pride in their Italian, German, Irish, or Jewish background. In the American framework one may try to preserve or develop a Jewish sub-culture. But it is far from clear what its distinctive content might be, apart from either religion or such highly dispensable folkways as eating *gefilte* fish. And you don't have to be Jewish to eat Jewish foods, which are now available in supermarkets.

Jewish Nationalism

For the past two thousand years Jewish identity depended on the twin pillars of religion and persecution. With both of them disappearing, what remains? There is a deep reluctance to face up to this crucial question. Many Israelis take refuge in the fancy that there is a great deal of anti-Semitism and discrimination against Jews in the United States. If there were, American Jews would not have to worry about the future of Jewish identity. In fact, it is extraordinary that the provocations of the S.D.S., among whose widely publicized leaders there have been so many Jews, have not elicited a wave of anti-Semitism in the press, on Capitol Hill, and among grass root politicians. That American Jewry may nevertheless eventually suffer something like the fate of Spanish or German Jewry is possible. But instead of defining Jewish identity in terms of this possibility, it makes more sense to exert oneself to prevent such a catastrophe.

Many Israelis insist that *all* Jews ought to come to Israel. This would not only turn the whole country into one vast Tel Aviv; it would also deprive Israel of crucial financial and political support. The United States and England would then cease to sell arms to Israel, and would give their full support to the Arab countries. After the events of 1967, Israel's feeling that she cannot depend on other countries is fully understandable—and yet her survival depends on at least half-hearted support from some countries with large Jewish populations.

Some Jews prefer to doubt the effects of the erosion of religion. Certainly, one can grant that it was, in large measure, the Jewish religion that kept the Jewish people alive after the destruction of the Second Temple; but if the survival of Jewry in the future should depend on religion, only a very small remnant would survive, while those engaged in the most creative and promising work, both in Israel and in the Diaspora, would be lost.

In my *Critique of Religion and Philosophy* (1958), in which I dealt at length with Judaism and Christianity, I expressed a profound sympathy for Orthodox Judaism, although I doubted the future of religion. But the behavior of the Orthodox in Israel toward the un-Orthodox fills me with revulsion, and the idolatry of the Western Wall is an abomination that brings to mind Isaiah's and Jeremiah's protests.

What remains if neither religion nor the community of fate can vouchsafe the future of the Jewish people? Nationalism.

My opposition to nationalism does not entail any hostility towards Israel. In the years before, during and after World War II, Zion ceased to be an ideological question. The rest of the world did not receive the Jewish refugees with open arms as it later accepted Gentile fugitives from Hungary; even the survivors of the war were sent back to D.P. camps in Germany. One did not have to be a nationalist to feel that this was intolerable. After the state of Israel was proclaimed, I could have wished for it to become a model to the nations in some ways in which it did not; for example, in its treatment of minorities. To say that there were extenuating circumstances would be a gross understatement. Nonetheless, I wish that Israel were less nationalistic—and I know that many Israelis feel the same way, although mine is, as usual, a minority view.

"Nationalism" is not a univocal term. In the course of its history it has been applied to different things, and I do not abhor everything that has ever been called by this name. The kind of nationalism that might be invoked to guarantee the future of the Jewish people—and that I reject—can be sketched rapidly. It consists of the demand for a nation-state, with one language, in which minorities are treated as outsiders and in some ways as second-class citizens. Often nationalism of this kind is accompanied by a feeling of superiority to other peoples and by irredentism.

Nationalism of this sort represents one powerful tendency in the modern world; internationalism represents another.

Millions of Europeans and North Americans have come to look upon nationalism as a nineteenth-century disease of which humanity might yet perish; the Common Market, the United States, and the relationship between the United States and Canada are harbingers of internationalism.

"Internationalism" can also mean many things. What I mean is the lowering of barriers to travel and trade, the willingness of people who speak different languages to work together on an equal basis, and the habit of seeing others first of all not as Jews, Arabs, Negroes, Indians, Mexicans, Germans, or Frenchmen, but as human beings. That the United States still has a long way to go in this direction is obvious, but growing numbers of Americans, including the majority of American Jews, recognize this ideal. I am not alone in my wish to be recognized as a human being and an individual—as me—instead of being stereotyped as an American, a Jew, a professor, one of those over thirty, or whatever other category may serve to dehumanize me.

One can be against nationalism and love Israel. The future of Israel—whether it develops along nationalistic lines or not—is a great issue. Most of my friends in Israel oppose nationalism as I do, and they need the help of their friends in the Diaspora.

It is a disgrace when Jews who are non-observant at home not only suddenly sprout skull caps when they visit Israel but sentimentally condone religious compulsion. And it is inhuman when Jews who insist that Negroes are first of all human beings and must not be reduced to second-class citizenship in the United States do not extend the same consideration to the Arabs in Israel.

As long as the Arab countries refuse to discuss peace with Israel, the treatment of the Arabs in Israel poses special problems, the differences between the Jews in Israel will continue to be dwarfed by an intense feeling of solidarity, and Jews all over the world will go on identifying with Israel. But if peace came and persecution ceased, what might then be the future of Jewish identity? It is a large "if," and the condition may not be fulfilled in our lifetime. But should the whole point of being a Jew be limited to defiance, refusal to bow out in the face of overwhelming odds, the proud determination to survive one's persecutors? Growing numbers of Jews in Israel and abroad feel that this is not enough. But what else is there?

I have argued that it is pointless to define Jewishness. An accurate description of what has been Jewish in the past would have to include much that we have no wish to preserve. But what many reject, others prize. Persuasive definitions of Jewishness make dialogue impossible and get us nowhere. What remains? The question whether a non-religious and non-nationalistic selection from our heritage is viable.

For twenty-five centuries, since the destruction of the First Temple which might well have spelled the end of a brief but glorious history, generations of Jews have endured exile, persecution, war, and martyrdom—for what? Are we content to say that the finest hour of our people lies a few thousand years back? Are we satisfied to be a living anticlimax?

Of course not. Our achievements in the twentieth century need not fear comparison with those of any other people during the same period. We have no reason to be obsessed by the question of who or what we are. The most crucial question that confronts us is what to do next. But in a quiet moment we may also ask if there is any continuity between our accomplishments in modern and in biblical times.

Sense of History

There is, but before we come to that, it is worth noting that a Jew's attitude toward time is apt to be distinctive. More and more Americans are fascinated by "antiques," meaning anything that is a hundred years old and sometimes even a mere fifty or sixty. Englishmen may expect you to feel impressed if they live in an eighteenth-century house or when they mention that New College at Oxford was founded in the fourteenth century. Roman Catholics boast of the antiquity of their church. For me, Moses, David, and the pre-exilic prophets are early, and everything Hellenistic and Roman is late.

If my historical perspective, which is so different from the unhistorical outlook of many English-speaking thinkers, owes something to German philosophy, especially to Hegel, it is nevertheless rooted in the Bible. There we find genuinely historical thinking centuries before Thucydides.

Contrasts between the Greeks and the time-conscious and history-minded Hebrews have been attempted by Leo Baeck, Hans Kohn, and Erich Auerbach. This is not the place to reflect on the significance of either Greek sculpture or Plato's denial of the reality of time. It is undeniable that in the Bible we find a striking concern with time, development, and history, and that this is one of the major distinctions between ancient Judaism on the one hand and the religions of the Greeks, the Chinese, and the Indians, on the other. Similarly, what distinguishes Marx from previous economists, and Freud from earlier psychologists, is their preoccupation with time, development, and history. Perhaps one could say something similar of Einstein.

It would be absurd to claim that an interest in development is a Jewish trait, or to speak of "Jewishness" and "un-Jewish" in this connection. But here is an element in the Jewish tradition that is worth preserving and developing.

What Jewish identity comes to in the end is the acceptance of the history of the Jewish people as one's own. And if anyone accepts that, it is inhuman to refuse to consider him a Jew merely because his mother was not Jewish.

Anyone concerned with the future of Jewish identity should above all else see to it that young Jews learn Jewish history, including the Bible and Jewish literature. The feeling that many of us have for the land of Israel and for Jerusalem comes of that; it is not religious faith, but thousands of associations that make our skin creep.

The teaching of Jewish history in America is as disgraceful as the religious instruction in most Christian Sunday schools. If Jewish identity survives in spite of that, it will be a miracle.

Jewish survival has always depended to some extent on miracles, but it is not decent to rely on them. Those who speak and write so much about Jewish identity ought to know what they can do to preserve it.

Claims about the essence of Jewishness or Judaism that are not based on the study of Jewish history and literature can hardly be taken seriously. But even intensive research cannot reveal this essence. Leo Baeck wrote a very remarkable book on the essence of Judaism (*Das Wesen des Judentums*), prompted by Adolf von Harnack's influential lectures on the essence of Christianity (*Das Wesen des Christentums*); but neither Judaism nor Christianity has an essence. Both have a rich history and literature—and it is up to us to determine what strands in our traditions we choose to develop. Study has to come first, but eventually a decision is required. As long as we are alive, our character is not fixed.

The choice we have to make is not between life and death, good and evil, or black and white. We are confronted by a wealth of possibilities. There are various versions of Orthodox Judaism, there is a great variety of more recent models, and we can also opt for one of many secular paths. Here is *my* way; and I might add, like Nietzsche's Zarathustra: Where is yours?

The Kaufmann Syndrome

Jews are heirs to a tradition marked by three fierce concerns that are very far from entailing each other: a concern with *social justice*, with *music and literature*, and with *learning*. This combination is highly unusual. Nowhere else have all *three* been cultivated.

The first concern—with social justice—is the most distinctive. Nothing like it is to be found in the scriptures of the other major religions. Love of learning is found in many religions and cultures—as the province of a small élite; as an almost universal concern of the whole community it remained, until recent times, a distinctive trait of Jewry. Love of music and literature is found in many places, but not in the Upanishads or in the Dhammapada, in the Book of Tao or in the New Testament.

Being used to all three concerns, we are prone to overlook the singularity of their conjunction. In other cultures, concern with social justice is quite apt to lead to some impatience with music and literature, and even with learning. Conversely, those interested in scholarship often have no time for music or for a social conscience. The Jewish tradition is distinguished by the fusion of these three intense concerns. A name may help to focus attention on this unusual combination: Let us call it the *Kaufmann syndrome*.

The persistent concern with social justice from the Law of Moses and the Hebrew prophets down to the twentieth century, the disproportionate presence of Jews in movements of social reform, and the central place of philanthropy in the Jewish tradition are not likely to be questioned. But is there really any continuity between the biblical injunction "You shall be unto Me a people of priests," and the staggering number of Jews among twentieth-century scientists? Surely, the kind of learning cultivated in the ghettos of Eastern Europe and the training required to become a leading physicist or mathematician are utterly different. (Freud's interpretation of dreams and parapraxes is not that different from the traditional approach to Scripture.) The ancient insistence that no Jew should remain illiterate, and the medieval love of learning, bore abundant fruit whenever opportunities arose—in Spain during the age of Maimonides, and then again after the emancipation. In utterly disproportionate numbers, Jews crowded into colleges and universities, obtained professorships and Nobel Prizes, and made their mark in almost every field of learning. Such an explosion was possible only because there was such a pent-up force that had been cultivated for thousands of years.

It is precisely the same with the love of music and literature. There are not so many names of the first rank in these fields—Mendelssohn-Bartholdy, Heine, Kafka—but there are legions of distinguished Jewish writers and musicians who are not quite of that order. The point is not how we should rank this composer or that novelist. Rather consider the world's major violinists and ask yourself why most of them are Jews. And why so many of the better writers in Germany and Austria during the first third of the century, and in the United States during the second third, have been Jews. And why you see so many Jews when you go to a concert; and why in Israel you can scarcely get into a concert hall unless you have held a series subscription for years.

Jews have not been equally outstanding in all fields. They have not produced major composers as the Germans and Austrians have, or painters as the Dutch and Italians have. Painting and sculpture have not been part of the Kaufmann syndrome, no doubt owing to the Mosaic prohibition. It is a delightful surprise that so many beautiful mosaics have been found in the ruins of ancient synagogues under the sands in Israel. Many of them are exceptionally lovely, and to my mind Jacob Epstein was the greatest sculptor of our time; but it is nevertheless plain that painting and sculpture have not been cultivated persistently by Jews since biblical times.

A traveling Van Gogh exhibition in Warsaw, October 1962, found the museum all but empty and the intellectuals of Warsaw largely unaware and unconcerned, while at a similar Van Gogh exhibition held three months later in Tel Aviv one could hardly see the pictures for the people who thronged in to see them, although the doors were open until midnight. The syndrome is not a static thing that is given once and for all, but is capable of development and expansion.

Being a Jew means having the good fortune to have such a background. One deserves no blame or credit for one's parents, but one can feel grateful or hateful. It is the same with the tradition out of which one comes. What I feel is love and gratitude. If I were about to be born and could choose what people to be born into, I'd say, feeling that the wish was presumptuous and that I could not expect its fulfillment but that after all I had been asked to indicate my first choice: I should like to be a Jew.

To have such a history is marvelous. To have such ancestors is unbelievable. And to have ready access to such a tradition and such a syndrome is a great blessing.

In Poland one is struck by the great effort that has gone into the reconstruction of palaces and other buildings that are a few centuries old. In a country that is far from rich this vast expense of wealth and labor testifies to an intense desire to establish a national past. But to how much high culture does a Pole have first-hand access? . . . To much more than most people do—even if he should only speak Polish.

Not all national heritages are equally rich. Not every nation has a great literature. And if an Israeli spoke only Hebrew and always stayed in Israel . . .

I am glad I am a Jew. But I am also grateful that I grew up in Germany, speak German, and have the kind of easy access to German literature and philosophy that anyone with a different upbringing must work for years to achieve. And it is my good fortune that I can write English, a language that hundreds of millions of men can read; that I can easily read what is written in that language; and that I live in a large country that abounds in interesting men and women, splendid libraries and museums, and magnificent scenery—a country in which I can travel freely and have a sense of space and freedom—and where if one does not like it in one place it is easy to go to another.

I do not mean to give the impression that life is wonderful. Where they died we did not die; Israel is embattled; and poverty, starvation, misery, injustice, and despair abound—also in the United States. But upon mentioning what one loves in the Jewish tradition one may be suspected, unjustly, of being a chauvinist. Actually, the Kaufmann syndrome should be seen in perspective. The Jews certainly do not have a monopoly on everything good. But the sense of history and the syndrome I have described are worth preserving and developing.

The stones of religion and nationalism that I reject may nevertheless remain the cornerstone of "Jewishness." Still there is the question of what might happen if my wishes came true. My own outlook is never likely to be shared by very large numbers of people; it is very personal though far from unique.

We Jews are a family. We often irritate each other, we dislike some of our relatives, and there are many people outside the family whom we like far better. Being always with each other makes for a great deal of tension, and it is quite possible that some of us are more creative and work better in the Diaspora.

New Dimensions of Identity

No discussion of the future of Jewish identity should concentrate exclusively on preservation and transmission. From the start of the Zionist movement it was part of the dream that new dimensions might be added to Jewish identity. In the *kibbutzim* the traditional concern with social justice, music and literature, and learning was to be developed into a new life style. High hopes were also centered in the creation of the Hebrew University. We should ask to what extent these hopes have been realized.

It is my impression—but I should love to be convinced that I am wrong—that the younger generation is less fiercely intellectual than were the founders, that the three-pronged tradition of which I have spoken is in danger, and that the scarcely credible linguistic versatility of the older generation is now dying out. If so, the *kibbutzim* will not enrich the meaning of Jewishness as much as they might have, and the universities, though they may be excellent for a tiny country, will not, in time to come, hold their own with the best schools elsewhere. To that end the students would have to be at least effectively bilingual. But there are degrees of perfection, and even now Israel has already added immensely to the meaning of Jewish identity.

There is always the unexpected, and the armed forces of Israel are more unique than her universities. It may be here more than anywhere else that a truly new style has been developed—a style, to be sure, that owes much to the *kib-*

butzim. It is doubly impressive that such a highly effective army and air force should have succeeded to such an extent in avoiding both authoritarianism and militarism. This is due partly to the palpable dangers that make such effective armed forces necessary, and partly to the true universality of service which extends to women, too.

The spirit in the top echelons of Israel's government is also striking. There is a directness, an authenticity, and a lack of formality, evasiveness, and airs that sharply distinguishes Ben-Gurion, Golda Meir, Moshe Dayan, and Yigal Allon from the leading statesmen or politicians of other countries. They listen and speak man-to-man, without fancying that their high office makes them different. This is a rare quality among famous men: Einstein possessed it in the highest degree. Its presence at the top level of government may be unique. It certainly has no precedent either among the kings of ancient Israel or among the *tsadikim* of the Hasidim. Ben-Gurion deserves a great deal of credit for having set this tone when he became the first Prime Minister of Israel.

Confronted with so much creativity and so many innovations, we should not look blindly to the past as if our only problem were to guard our precious heirlooms. Giving up orthodoxy is not a negative thing; it liberates us to concentrate on the future.

The Jews gave the world monotheism. Let us now work for pluralism, both in the countries of the Diaspora and in Israel. Let us continue to work for the rights of minorities—not only of Jews but also of Negroes, American Indians, and Israeli Arabs. Let us not embody in the state of Israel those features of nationalism which were the bane of our existence when we lived in nation-states. Let us build an exemplary pluralistic society.

If Israel could prove to the world that Jews can excel as farmers and soldiers and pilots, if it could triumph over all odds in 1967, it cannot be content to plead extenuating circumstances for its treatment of the Arabs in Israel and in the occupied territories. Of course, there *are* extenuating circumstances, and it is maddening that most of mankind continues to apply a double standard to Jews and Arabs—for example, by expressing much concern about the treatment of the Arabs by Israel but hardly any, if any, about the treatment of Jews in the Arab countries. But if Israelis had failed as farmers, there would have been extenuating circumstances, too. And had Israel lost in 1967, there would have been extenuating circumstances. And if the Jews had produced no Nobel Prize winners, there would have been extenuating circumstances. And if there had been no more prophets after Micah and Isaiah, there would have been extenuating circumstances. And if no more books worthy of inclusion in the Bible had been written after the return from Babylon, there would have been extenuating circumstances. It was by never settling for the justified excuse of extenuating circumstances that the Jews became a light to the nations.

Nobody has any right to ask the Jews to go on demanding more of themselves than other nations do—nobody, except a Jew.

Jewish Peoplehood—A Signal of Transcendence

Samuel E. Karff

Unlike Walter Kaufmann—author of the preceding essay—Samuel E. Karff relates Jewish peoplehood and particularity to a transcendent vision and to covenant-boundness. In Rabbi Karff's view, "even when the contemporary Jew has positively and fervently affirmed the covenant on a manifestly secular level we may discern in this gesture an echo of God's traditional call and Israel's traditional response." For the rabbi, Israel's rebirth is a sign of divine grace, "an intimation of God's abiding and redemptive presence in history." Israel's theological significance could not be fully grasped, however, until Jews "came to grips with the awesome dimensions of the Holocaust." Rabbi Karff—spiritual leader of Sinai Congregation, Chicago—concludes with some instructive comments in the direction of Christian-Jewish rapprochement. His article first appeared in the April 1971 number of *CCAR Journal**—the publication of the Central Conference of American Rabbis, on whose theology committee he serves as chairman. He also serves as lecturer in Jewish Thought and American Culture at the University of Chicago Divinity School.

SPECULATION ABOUNDS on the future of the rabbinate. Among the many variables to which that future remains mortgaged none is more decisive than the prospect for *homo religiosus* himself. Some sociologists have proclaimed eloquently the dawn of post-religious man. Such a man will reduce his physical and emotional pain through drugs, extend his mortal span by the conquest of disease and by means of artificial organs, and pass his leisure hours bemused by a dazzling array of distractions. So armed, post-

* 790 Madison Ave., New York, N.Y. 10021.

religious man will exclaim: Let us eat, drink, love, work, play and, if we must, die.

Philip Rieff, one of the most impressive creators of such a scenario, identifies the decline of religious man with the "triumph of the therapeutic." Post-Freudian man, no longer gulled by illusions of traditional piety nor sustained by trust in a transcendent order of meaning, will now invest all his energies "wittingly in techniques that are . . . 'therapeutic' with nothing at stake beyond a manipulable sense of well-being. This is the unreligion of the age and its master, science."[1]

Dissenting voices are also heard which insist that man is quintessentially religious—that by his very nature man is captive to a realm of being and meaning which transcends the empirical world. The cultural matrix may encourage or discourage formal structures of faith but no human culture is likely to divest man of his spiritual patrimony.

Peter Berger, a sociologist of religion, is among the subscribers to this view. In a recent volume (*A Rumor of Angels*) Berger argues that by exploring the ordinary experience of secular man it is possible to discover "signals of transcendence." Man's tendency to structure his existence "is grounded in the faith or trust that ultimately reality is in order . . . (and) in this fundamental sense every ordering gesture is a signal of transcendence."[2] Man's propensity for play, his delight in entering a different time (game time), Berger takes as a symbolic awareness of eternity. Similarly, man remains hostage to hope and is a creator of humor, by which gestures he celebrates his ultimate triumph over the dehumanizing aspects of his finite life. This style of theologizing insists that man is more religious than he realizes or may be able to express comfortably in a culture which does not encourage the language of faith.

But how shall these universal signs of transcendence ("general revelation") be related to the particular faith claims of the historic traditions? Berger replies that considerations of economy and humility dictate a serious encounter with the spiritual discoveries of the past. By this encounter and openness to all traditions man's religious alternatives will be clarified. Such an encounter with the available options will prompt these questions: "What is being said here? What is the human experience out of which these statements come . . . to what extent and in what way may we see here genuine discoveries of transcendent truths?"[3] In concluding his volume Berger applies this method of correlation to his own tradition and seems reasonably content with the place he has found for himself in the Christian community—especially with that tradition's power to erect upon the foundations of Judaism a sense of "the redeeming presence of God within the anguish of human experience."

Berger introduces his chapter on "Confronting the Traditions" with this word of methodological caution:

The traditions must not be confronted because they have some mysterious but irresistible claim to our loyalty. Such notions have a curious persistence even among intellectuals who have largely emancipated themselves from their respective backgrounds but who nevertheless view the respective traditions as somehow part of the individual's being, an inner reality that he must confront. *In the Western world such an attitude is most frequently found among Jews for historically understandable reasons.*[4] (italics mine)

In this brief aside Berger unwittingly reveals a curious blind spot which impairs his understanding of Judaism or the contemporary Jew. That "gesture" which he empirically observes to be especially prevalent among Jews may itself be revelatory—at least for the Jew. If he is prepared to take seriously such gestures as man's propensity to order, play, humor—finding in them signals of transcendence, why not regard the particular gestures of the Jew, i.e., his persistent covenant-boundness—as a signal of transcendence? May it betoken an intuitive awareness of a primordial claim which he, the Jew, is not free to reject?

Those who search for traces of *homo religiosus* in the ordinary gestures of human life—whether under the tutelage of Peter Berger, Langdon Gilkey, or Schubert Ogden *inter alios*—might fruitfully consider the value of this theological method for an understanding of the contemporary Jew in his concrete particularity.[5]

*   *   *

One of the central symbols in the classic Jewish theological consensus is the peoplehood of Israel. The Jew felt himself part of a people singled out by God for a particular destiny. The Jew was called to persist as a Jew and accept the burdens of the covenant even at times when he felt least disposed to do so. His was a destiny not easily rejected. (At the foot of Sinai his reluctance impels God to suspend the mountain over his head and exclaim: "Either you be My people or here will be your burial place.")[6] That destiny was linked by a sacred bond to the land of Israel. This people was called to bear witness to God by the quality of its life. It was not permitted to become "like all the nations," to "normalize" its existence, and it must be prepared to endure some hostility—Sinai= *seenah*, or hostility—until its vocation is fulfilled.[7]

Peoplehood is the primary aspect of Jewish self-consciousness in the modern world. Even the Jew who has difficulty affirming belief in God and feels awkward in speaking of Torah may speak of this people's claim upon him. We suggest that this "mysterious but irresistible claim" and the "gestures" it evokes may contain peculiarly Jewish "signals of transcendence." These gestures bear further investigation by any one in search of fragments of faith within the contemporary "non-religious" Jew.

What evidence exists for the Jew's covenant-boundness? Analyst Ernest Van den Haag suggests that a Jew finds it more difficult casually to shed his Jewishness than a Christian his Christianity. He categorizes the "Jewish mystique" in these terms:

Jews may call themselves humanists or atheists, socialists or communists, they may indifferently or passionately repudiate any reason whatsoever for remaining Jews, they may even dislike Jewishness and feel it—to use an apt metaphor—as a cross they have to bear. They may deny its existence in scientific terms . . . (but) they won't give up being Jewish even when they consciously try to. When they change names, intermarry and do everything they can to deny Jewishness. Yet they remain aware of it and though repudiating it they cling to it. They may repress it but do act it out symptomatically. Their awareness of their Jewishness is shared by others simply because the denial is always ambivalent. Unconscious or not at least some part of every Jew does not want to give up its Jewishness.[8]

Some no doubt would argue that this syndrome is confined to a generation over thirty or even over forty. Campus Jews, for example, seem much less bound by such elemental claims. Has not a small but highly conspicuous group found it possible to identify itself at this juncture in history with an Arab liberation movement aimed at destroying the State of Israel? One may counter that this phenomenon signifies not a casual indifference to Jewish destiny but a classic instance of Jewish self-hate—the yearning to be cool toward, to escape from, that which insistently presses its claim.

Perhaps a more valid symptom of covenant casualness may be found among those campus Jews who contemplate intermarriage with little apparent concern for the future of Judaism or the Jewish people. Nathan Glazer has pointed to parents who do not oppose intermarriage and young people who undertake such a step neither goaded by escapist impulses nor inhibited by traditional restraints. The parents simply value their children's right to freedom of choice in such matters and the children embark upon such a step as "the natural concomitant of life in a certain cultural milieu, for example the university community."[9] But such casualness, however genuine, does not presently embrace most Jews on campus, and the breakdown of the classical liberal model of a color-blind, religiously and ethnically neutral society—dramatized by the new affirmation of ethnic pride among Blacks—is compelling many campus Jews to reexamine their own particularity.

One may, of course, grant that covenant-boundness—the sense of an inalienable Jewish claim—is felt by most Jews, but interpret this phenomenon as a "negative identity," simply the byproduct of a not yet fully open society. Berger himself suggests as much when he speaks of "historically understandable reasons" which appear to bind even religiously emancipated Jews to the covenant. He alludes no doubt to the traditional hostility, the lingering barriers by which the non-Jewish world invites the Jews to keep his distance. This reductionism finds its classic formulation in the writings of Sartre when he argues that the non-Jewish world essentially defines the Jew.

Such reductionism is not our only option. The rabbis also posit a relation between Sinai and *seenah*. The world's hostility remains both the response to and confirmation of the covenant's undischarged mandate. On the day when being Jewish no longer exposes one to special hazards anywhere in the world, the covenant may lose its primordial claim for on that day "the Lord shall be One and His name One."

*   *   *

Even when the contemporary Jew has positively and fervently affirmed the covenant on a manifestly secular level we may discern in his gesture an echo of God's traditional call and Israel's traditional response. This insight has been expressed elegantly in the recent writings of Emil Fackenheim. Referring to the remarkable renaissance of commitment to Jewish survival among Jews after Auschwitz, Fackenheim observes:

Jews throughout the world—rich and poor, learned and ignorant, believer and unbeliever—were already responding to Auschwitz and in some measure have been doing so all along. Faced with the radical threat of extinction they were stubbornly defying it, committing themselves, if to nothing more, to the survival of themselves and their children as Jews. . . . In the age of Auschwitz it is in itself a monumental act of faithfulness as well as a monumental albeit fragmentary act of faith. To be a Jew after Auschwitz is to confront the demons of Auschwitz and to bear witness against them in all their guises. It is to believe that they will not prevail and to stake on that belief one's life and those of one's children's children.[10]

Fackenheim avers that by his very existence the Jew counters and confounds the demonic faith of Hitler; and by resolutely committing himself to Jewish survival the Jew is faithful to his covenant in a deeper sense than he may consciously realize. His covenant-boundness, warmly and determinedly embraced after Auschwitz, becomes a "signal of transcendence"—a "fragmentary act of faith."

* * *

Christian theologians (and some Jewish thinks, especially in the 1950s) have been prone to desacralize the phenomenon of Israel reborn and the feelings it has inspired among "non-religious" Jews. Political Zionism has been invidiously contrasted with a full-bodied faith in God, Torah, and Israel. Yet here too it may be fruitful to look for signals of transcendence.

There is first the land itself. No one can deny the centrality of that land in Jewish religious consciousness for the two thousand years of the *galut*. The special sense of home which this land evokes in the Jewish pilgrim today and the fascination, nay reverence, with which Israelis archaeologically explore their people's roots in this land are not purely "secular" gestures.

The classic covenant speaks of this people's obligation to bear witness to God by the quality of its existence. That witness assumed special dimension and was to attain its choicest fruit in the land of Israel. There alone could certain of the Commandments be fulfilled. There would Israel's witness signal the dawn of God's hope for man and history's fulfillment be proclaimed.

Zionism for all its secular impulse and its yearning for the normalization of Jewish existence did not forsake this transcendent vision. David ben Gurion, an avowedly "non-religious" Jew, once placed the return to Israel in this historic context:

Ours was a tiny nation inhabiting a small country and there have been many tiny nations and many small countries but ours was a tiny nation possessed of a great spirit, an inspired people that believed in its pioneering mission to all men, in the mission that had been preached by the prophets of Israel. This people gave the world great and eternal moral truths and commandments. This people rose to prophetic visions of the unity of the Creator with His creation, of the dignity and infinite worth of the individual (because every man is created in the divine image), of social justice, universal peace and love. . . . This people was the first to prophesy about 'the end of days,' the first to see the vision of a new human society.[11]

The ferment among Israeli youth in the "non-religious" kibbutzim recorded in published dialogues reveals an unslaked yearning to relate their life as Israelis to the values and dreams of a living past. They ponder and seek to understand the "mystery of the existence of the Jewish people." They do feel singled out for a precarious existence. They relate this vulnerability to the historic destiny of the people Israel and they wonder why and to what end.[12]

*   *   *

The God of the traditional covenant is the God of history. Events in the life of the people were received as signs of God's redemptive grace, fruits of divine wrath, or manifestations of divine hiddenness. The exodus from Egypt, the settlement in Canaan, the exile, and the return were all revelatory events illuminating God's relation to Israel and the world. The Jew has been schooled to search for "signals of transcendence" in current events. Jewish faith has been most bitterly strained and most exaltingly confirmed by history.

No event more virulently strained the traditional faith than the Holocaust. We hesitated to confront its horror fully until the sixties (the Eichmann trial may have marked the turning point), perhaps because, as Fackenheim suggests, we realized the magnitude of the threat to our sense of transcendent meaning and stepped back with trepidation. Yet only one major theological voice (Richard Rubenstein) has drawn the "logical" conclusion and proclaimed the death of the God of history. Significantly some who had direct experience with the role of victim (Fackenheim, Wiesel) have been most unwilling to recite Kaddish for the traditional God of the covenant. Whatever our particular theodicy—whether we speak of a God who is hidden or finite—even Auschwitz did not lead us to renounce Him who acts in history. This is not to suggest that we were spared the anguished question: Where is a sign of God's redemptive power? Is being Jewish a tragic absurdity after all?

In this context the theological significance of Israel must be assessed and our trembling response to the events of June 1967 understood. Israel's rebirth as a *sign of divine grace*, as an intimation of God's abiding and redemptive presence in history was only fully comprehended *after* we came to grips with the awesome dimensions of the Holocaust. When in 1967, seven years after the Eichmann trial, we heard Arab rhetoric promise a new Holocaust our response testified that we understood—many for the first time—how deeply revelatory Israel's rebirth had been in 1948 and how crucial Israel's survival was now to our elemental confidence in the meaning of our life and our covenant.

The secular Jew acted out his quest for this confirmation of faith. The theologian dared articulate the meaning of what we feared, waited for, and hoped for during those fateful days. Let Fackenheim speak for some of us:

On a public occasion in March 1967 I asked the following question: Would we (like Job) be able to say that the question of God at Auschwitz will be answered in any sense whatever in case the eclipse of God were ended and He appeared to us? Less than three months later this purely hypothetical question became actual. When at Jerusalem the threat of total annihilation gave way to sudden salvation . . . precisely and only because of the connection with Auschwitz was there a radical astonishment which gave a military victory . . . an inescapable religious dimension.[13]

* * *

I would suggest that Christian theologians, or sociologists of religion who find intimations of transcendence within the ordinary experience of secular man and then relate these to the affirmations of Christian faith, might extend their theological method in order to understand the peculiar covenant-boundness of "non-religious" Jews. Such a method may reveal that the Jew who is gripped by the "irresistible claim" of the covenant people Israel may, by implication if not affirmation, be gripped by faith in the God of the covenant.

Such a method may be especially fruitful in dialogues on the Christian response to Israel's political rebirth. (Why do some Christian activists who have invested Black nationalism with theological significance scruple to find God active in the renaissance of "Jewish power"?) The value of such an approach should be especially apparent to those Christians who, mindful of the tragic dimensions in the historic relation between our peoples, seek a new ground for the affirmation of both covenants. Significantly the rebirth of a political Zion, the termination of the Wandering Jew syndrome, mocks those Christians who continue to see in Jewish homelessness the price the Jew pays for having rejected him who "came unto his own and his own received him not." Israel's rebirth cannot be dismissed as a purely secular phenomenon. By its very existence Israel disputes the church's traditional concept of the Jewish role in salvation history.

He who seeks a theological ground for affirming the integrity of both covenants under God must at some point come to terms with the rebirth of Jewish sovereignty in the land of Zion. Such a purportedly non-religious "gesture" by Christians is fraught with the deepest theological overtones—for the Christian cannot acknowledge the abiding legitimacy of Israel's election without first acknowledging "signals of transcendence" within Jewish peoplehood. Here is perhaps one of the most important applications of the theological method which insists that man is more "religious" than he seems or may himself recognize.

Notes

1. P. Rieff, *The Triumph of the Therapeutic,* New York: Harper & Row, 1966, p. 13.

2. P. Berger, *A Rumor of Angels*, New York: Doubleday, 1969, p. 70.
3. Ibid., p. 105.
4. Ibid., p. 96 f.
5. See Schubert Ogden, *The Reality of God*. New York: Harper & Row, 1966. L. Gilkey, *Naming the Whirlwind*. Indianapolis: Bobbs-Merrill, 1969.
6. b. Shabbat 88a.
7. Ibid., 89a.
8. E. Van den Haag, *The Jewish Mystique*, New York: Stein & Day, 1969, p. 52 f.
9. N. Glazer, "The Function of the Rabbi." *CCAR Yearbook*, 1967, p. 132.
10. E. Fackenheim, *Quest for Past and Future*. Bloomington: Indiana U. Press, p. 19–20. cf. E. Fackenheim, *God's Presence in History*. New York: NYU Press, 1970, Ch. III.
11. David ben Gurion, "The Imperatives of the Jewish Revolution," in *The Zionist Idea*, A. Hertzberg, ed. New York: Harper Torchbook, 1966, p. 607.
12. *Bayn Tzeerim* ("Among the Young"), Am Oved, Israel, 1970.
13. E. Fackenheim, *Quest for Past and Future,* op. cit., pp. 25 f.

III. American People

American Churches as Traducers of Tradition

William A. Clebsch

Ambivalence toward Christian tradition and church traditions, says William A. Clebsch, has been a distinctive
characteristic of American churches; they have engaged in
both revolt against and renewal of tradition. The "American
churches have betrayed the Christian tradition in that their
common unity springs rather more from their shared Americanness than from a self-conscious participation in the historic identifying marks of Christianity itself. But at the same
time they have educed and transmitted the Christian tradition in a new form as their evangelical emphasis prompted
them to live for the world and as they exhibited a readiness
to seek unity and even Christianness more as a gift from
the future than as a *traditum* from the past." In tracing the
historical reasons for this ambivalence Dr. Clebsch gives
special attention to his own denomination, the Episcopal
Church. The author of such books as *Contemporary Perspectives on Word, World, and Sacraments*; *From Sacred to
Profane: The Role of Religion in American History*; and
Christian Interpretations of the Civil War, Dr. Clebsch is
Professor of Religion and Humanities and Chairman of
Humanities Special Programs at Stanford University. His
article is from the January 1971 issue of *Anglican Theological
Review*.*

THE WAYS IN WHICH Christian churches in the
United States of America have betrayed the Christian tradition and the church traditions from which they sprang have
been remarked upon by a considerable recent literature, most
of it strongly influenced by neo-orthodox theology. Writings
by Will Herberg, Gibson Winter, Reinhold Niebuhr, Martin

* 600 Haven St., Evanston, Ill. 60201.

Marty, Theodore Wedel, Peter Berger, and Harvey Cox, to name a few, have scored a variety of American churches for their cultural accommodations and their religious neologisms that, according to these writers, betray the faith once delivered to the saints.

At the same time other students were showing how the same churches have brought forth and transmitted important and long-neglected aspects of the Christian tradition and, indeed, of individual church traditions. These writers, largely of historical orientation, include Sidney E. Mead, Sydney Ahlstrom, Daniel Day Williams, H. Richard Niebuhr, and John Tracy Ellis.

Behind this debate lies long practice in the American churches of both betraying and renewing religious tradition. Since the word "traducer" originally bore rather opposite meanings denoting both betrayal and bringing forth or transmitting, it appropriately describes the force and power of traditions in the older, more typical churches of the United States. They have "traduced"—in both senses—the specific traditions of the European churches from which they derived (*traditiones interpretivae*) and they have "traduced"—again in both senses—certain historical identifying marks of Christianity itself (*traditiones constitutivae*). But with all this "traducing" they also have evinced and transmitted something of the Christian tradition that is distinctly their own and that is the corollary, even the product, of their betrayals.

Ecumenical encounters during the present century increased the American churches' ambivalence toward tradition in both its meanings. On the one hand, a new awareness of these churches' derivation from European ecclesiastical ancestors arose from their participation in omni-denominational efforts and organizations. But on the other hand, ecumenical encounters at home and abroad have revealed a kinship with the so-called "younger churches" of Asia, Africa, and Latin America, whose experience indicates that not only in the United States are the typical attitudes, aspirations, and answers of old European Christendom rank anachronisms. In American churches as keenly as anywhere there is sensed the post-Christendom (which is not necessarily to say post-Christian) character of the present age.

I. Novus Ordo Seclorum

The ambivalence of American Christians toward Christian tradition and church traditions dates back to the formative years of the nation and its typical churches, to the threescore years during which the religious and ecclesiastical implications of the spirit embodied in the Declaration of Independence and the Constitution became explicit. During that time good wine aged from must that began fermenting during the colonial period; there was a sense that a new age dawning in and for America would yield a newer and truer Christianity than Europe had known. Down to our own time this pervasive sense of novelty as not inimical to Christianity lent to these churches a common history "longer, larger and richer than any of our separate histories in our divided churches"— to put to unintended use a key phrase of the Lund Conference on Faith and Order. The denominations that shared the American experience of circa 1776-1837, and indeed also the more recent denominations insofar as they became autochthonous in the new world, engaged in a major rearranging and a selective discarding of church traditions brought over from Europe. The sense of their own novelty that these churches received as part of the grace of their baptism into American history has been and continues to be an enabling means to their participating in the current ecumenical movement, to their reappropriating certain values of the various *traditiones interpretivae*, and to their search for new expressions of the *traditiones constitutivae*.

From the beginning of the American War for Independence, and especially during the early decades of national life, the older American churches sought to actualize and symbolize their independence from the European religious traditions out of which they derived. The new nation itself was doing the same thing with respect to European culture, especially and repeatedly during the decades that elapsed between the colonies' Declaration of Independence and the "declaration of intellectual independence" proclaimed by Ralph Waldo Emerson in his famous 1837 Phi Beta Kappa address on "The American Scholar." An early incident in national politics aptly illustrates this spirit of independence and modernity. In 1776 the ardent newworlder, Thomas Jefferson, prepared a design for the Great Seal of the United States on commission from the Continental Congress. He devised an arms composed of emblems representing the eight "countries from which the States have been peopled," as he wrote, and bearing Jefferson's own personal motto, "Rebellion to Tyrants is Obedience to God." The design depicting America as derivative from Europe and obedient to deity was rejected. Only after six years of debating various alternatives did the Congress adopt a wholly different seal carrying symbols that refer exclusively to the new nation and its newness, and bearing on the reverse the mottoes, *Annuit Coeptis* and *Novus Ordo Seclorum.*

The ardor of the country's founding fathers for ushering in an epoch distinct from the era during which the *corpus christianum* had unified Europe's societies found its match in the ardor of the denominations' founding fathers for a religion that was at once voluntary, plural, and indigenous. Any religious establishment was explicitly made forbidden fruit for the new nation by its Constitution. Although the states were not directly affected by that proviso, the principle of establishment was severely weakened and placed (as Lincoln said of slavery) in the course of ultimate extinction on a local basis; its last traces in individual states had disappeared from the New England scene by the time Emerson delivered the above mentioned oration. Church leaders and members welcomed the prohibition on both religious and social grounds; in fact, religious voluntaryism fused elements of separatist and enlightenment thought. The memorial passed by "The first Church judicatory in America openly to recognize the Declaration of Independence"—the Hanover, Virginia, Presbytery, on 24 October 1776—is notable "for the fact that its arguments are not derived from the Westminster Divines [much less from the Bible], but from the same eighteenth century political philosophers who influenced Thomas Jefferson."[1] This official Presbyterian endorsement of the new religious and secular order originated a series of similar declarations by most of the American denominations, including the Roman Catholic clergy, during the next generation; in spirit all the churches approved.

European church traditions to the contrary notwithstanding, this approbation of *novus ordo seclorum* sprang at once from the regnant social thought and from a conviction that the true expression of Christianity, like that of other human ideals, loomed more as a possible *actus tradendi* of the future than as an actual *traditum* of the past. Understandably enough, ecclesiastical cousins in Europe thought that American religion drifted aimlessly when loosed from the old anchors of church life; but American Christians gloried in the fact that their religion had parted moorings to Caesaropapism in order to float on human liberty's swelling tide. If the Americans were idealistic, the Europeans were cynical. For the new country allowed old sectarian groups like the Baptists to flourish into great denominations, stirred complacent groups like the Episcopalians (who had enjoyed widespread establishment in the colonies) into fervid evangelistic action, and removed encumbrances that had hindered groups like the Roman Catholics. All joined in applauding the new order in which each flourished. And all felt quite at home in this heady atmosphere after the War of 1812 demonstrated that America's revolution would not be as revolting as France's seemed to most religionists.

Consistently since the nation's inception its churches have shared a common history not of their own making, a history that augured for them a better future than did the hard principles of their own separate histories as divided churches. The unitive force operating within and between them was no sense of their own common history as once undivided Christians. Rather it was mankind's pursuit—proudly paced by Americans—of human freedom, the enlargement of life's prospect, a cultivation of the mind uncabined by dogmas, the building of a government that served rather than bound the people, and an acceptance of religious practice or belief unconstrained and unrestrained by that government. While in the strictest sense this unitive force was not religious in content, it exhibited a dedication that was religious and certainly not untheological in form. It arose more as an aspiration for the future than as a celebration or conservation of antiquity. It found articulation more readily in patriotism than in ecclesiasticism. Its universalizing tendencies derided exclusivism of doctrinal, sacramental, ecclesiastical, social, ethnic, and even —throughout the period under consideration—racial bases. It embodied and was interpreted as Christian values and themes —liberty, justice among men, renewal, kingdom of God on earth, hope, and the like—even as it left behind or implicitly contradicted other such values and themes, like sin, repentance, dependence on God. It was full of a destiny that derived mythically from Daniel's fourth empire and the westward-movement theme but actually aspired to occupy its own empire and live out its own westward movement. In terms of religious unity, its achievement has been, as Jerald C. Brauer noted, "that all the Protestant Churches in America exhibited a certain spirit and embodied certain practices which made them closer to each other than to their European counterparts."[2] (With appropriate qualifications, Catholicism might have been included in Brauer's statement.) Moreover, it prompted and permitted American churches to disconnect themselves from the European church judicatories under which, in colonial times, most of them had haltingly been nurtured. While it is true that Catholicism's jurisdictional ties to Europe were never really severed, this spirit of newness inspired early American Catholics and earned them limited independence as a national church that found various expressions during the remainder of the nineteenth century and still prevails in covert defiance of Leo XIII's letter, *Testem Benevolentiae* (22 January 1899), condemning "Americanism." Each in its own way, but all in some way, the American churches became partners in the American enterprise, and in doing so erected the durable fraternity of American Christianity.

II. Patterns of Change

After the Revolution the American churches lived through and reacted to decisive events that endowed them with a common history in action as well as in attitude. Each church faced problems of reorganizing itself in the wake of national independence and ecclesiastical disestablishment. For Episcopalians the difficulties that rose in this connection proved barely surmountable; the Church of England was loath to provide a continuous ministry, the politics and economics of the loss of public support in a half-dozen states proved debilitating, and the divergent sectional attitudes that grew during the colonial period were divisive. At the other extreme, the Quakers' connections with the London Yearly Meeting had long been little more than tenuous, and their problems of reorganization meant adjusting their minimal polity to their insignificant shift from the status of British subjects to that of American citizens. Between these two extremes fell the predicaments of other denominations.

But another common enterprise was more important than that of reorganization. Each of the American churches, suddenly thrown on its own local resources, undertook to evangelize the people of the new nation. This expansion shattered the previous social and geographical identities of most churches. The most prominent exceptions in the Federal period were the Congregationalists of New England who, under the 1801 Plan of Union, in effect turned over domestic evangelistic efforts to Presbyterians. Yet Congregationalists settled the Western Reserve and later played a prominent part in evangelizing settlers in Oregon. All denominations had some experience of moving to the western wilderness where adherents, members, and leaders lived by an inventiveness that was hardly customary in the eastern states. While President Jefferson was wondering whether the vast territory acquired under his administration by the Louisiana Purchase of 1803 would call into being a sister, trans-Appalachian republic, the Eastern churches confidently opened revival campaigns in the populated portions of that expanse and thereby united folk on both sides of the mountains into one God-fearing, hard-praying, right-living, Bible-reading, church-going people who lived, as they thought, under a Providence who would continue to smile on their undertakings.

Although each denomination, to be sure, assumed that the message it bore was indeed the true Christian gospel, and that conversion under its auspices initiated true Christian life, people (as distinct from denominational polemicists) became primarily Christians and only secondarily churchmen. Correspondence between church leaders of the period blithely identified the entire Christian cause with the fortunes of their particular denomination. As long as interdenominational confrontation was rare denominational rivalries were few; sermons and apologetical tracts assumed that a given denomination represented the Christian tradition in its purity and entirety. Yet many records of ministerial vocation indicate that typical men were called to the ministry and the question of denominational identification was either automatic, perfunctory, or else deliberate and of secondary importance. Theological seminaries planted, cultivated, and harvested crops of preachers, not of dogmas; many ministers thought of themselves foremost as converting persons to Christ and only afterwards as recruiting for their denominations.

All the denominations after the Revolution had the common experiences of Americanizing the Christian churches and of Christianizing the American people. In so doing they gave individual expression to their common Americanness, and this effort led the major churches generally to rearrange and selectively to discard important aspects of the European church traditions that comprised their legacies. Only the numerically minor ones kept names that would identify their European origin, and these remained ethnically homogeneous in their constituencies. In every case, recognizable if not drastic changes came to be involved in remaking the old ecclesiastical entities. Individual cases illustrate the importance and the variety of these rearrangements and discardings, but a somewhat general pattern can be discerned.

The traditionary process of Americanizing the churches drove distinctions between constituent aspects of church life that in Europe and in the colonies had nicely cohered. Traditionally, polity had been a direct explication of one's theory of ministerial order in the churches of post-Reformation Europe. Scottish, Rhenish, and Dutch churches maintained orders of presbyters and were presbyterially governed by synods or classes. In the Church of England insistence upon continuity of episcopal ordination during Reformation and Civil War, Restoration and Revolution, and even through the eighteenth century reflected the royal preference for episcopal government that James I succinctly voiced when he told the 1604 conference at Hampton Court, "No bishops, no king." Worship, furthermore, typically cohered with order and with polity in Europe; episcopalism issued in prescribed liturgical uniformity administered vicarially by priests; presbyterialism yielded structured but regionally-varied and variable liturgies; congregationalism expressed itself in spontaneous, free worship. In Europe, Reformation movements both Protestant and catholic produced regional or universal confessions of doctrine subscribed by clergy, whether these confessions were authorized by crown and bishops as in Elizabethan England, by bishops and pope as at Trent, by theologians and princes as at Augsburg, by members of the congregation as at Scrooby, or by assemblies of presbyters as at Basel, Paris, Antwerp, Edinburgh, and Westminster. In each instance the authors of doctrine were chief functionaries in polity and order. Also, each of these facets of church life reflected in Europe a tradition's leading theological light, perhaps absolute church authority, perhaps justification by faith alone, perhaps the gathered-church idea, perhaps the divine right of kings.

Except for such native denominations as Mormons, Christian Scientists, and Disciples of Christ, each major American denomination emerged out of one or another major European church tradition. The rearrangement and re-emphasizing of the features of those traditions—doctrine, polity, worship, order, organization—that the early American experience prompted are appropriately seen as equipping these churches to participate in the *novus ordo seclorum*. It is of course impossible in brief compass to describe such changes as took place in each denomination.

The ambivalence toward tradition that prevailed in all instances may be illustrated by reference to exemplary cases. An exemplary case is that of the denomination which at the outbreak of the Revolution was the most widely-established under law, the most conformist to patterns of its European mother church, the most dependent upon its distant judicatory, and the one that had the longest and widest experience in the American colonies.

When American Episcopalians reshaped their inherited church traditions in order to exist in the independent United States, Anglican Christianity was a purely British phenomenon. Nowhere in Christendom since the days of the Emperor Theodosius I had episcopacy maintained itself quite apart from monarchy; since 1534 English episcopacy had been the dutiful instrument (and in 1688 a major determinant) of royal headship over the church. The Church of England enjoyed establishment in the southern colonies, including Maryland, and in parts of New York. Other Anglicans in the new world—especially in Connecticut and Massachusetts—had learned to live as legal dissenters against the congregational establishment or as one denomination amongst many in the middle colonies. The erection and federation of independent Episcopal churches in the various states in the Union meant that the dissenting experience in New England taught disestablished southern Episcopalians how to organize their church life around the voluntary principle. Meanwhile the New Englanders learned from the southerners something about provincial church organization free from supervision by the (now foreign) Society for the Propagation of the Gospel in Foreign Parts. Thus there emerged in the new denomination a new polity blending presbyterial features with a basic congregationalism that limited bishops (when there were any) to strictly spiritual functions. As events would prove, the denomination's central problem was one of church order, not polity. A strong party rallied around a plan to exist temporarily—and, if necessary, permanently—without bishops, simply by investing in an elected presbyter the functions of regional presidency and the power of ordination. Another party prized episcopacy so highly that it could accept a bishop ordained by Scottish nonjurors who, from the standpoint of the Church of England, were in schism. Both these plans of action had in common a determination to maintain the cherished tradition of worship, but both also resolved to repudiate ecclesiastical royalism even if that meant, on the one hand, schismatic church order or, on the other, radical departure from traditional episcopalian order. English archbishops and crown finally relented and allowed bishops to be consecrated for dioceses of the Protestant Episcopal Church without taking the oath of royal supremacy that had attended all Anglican consecrations since that of Matthew Parker in 1559.

Except for the imitation of some eucharistic formulae held dear by Scottish Episcopalians, traditional Anglican worship was adopted by American Episcopalians with a single revisionary principle: the repudiation of royalism. Thus the preface to the denomination's 1789 Book of Common Prayer (which remained unchanged by revisions in 1892 and 1928) decreed:

The attention of this Church was in the first place drawn to those alterations in the Liturgy which became necessary in the prayers for our Civil Rulers, in consequence of the Revolution. And the principal care herein was to make them conformable to what ought to be the proper end of all such prayers, namely, that "Rulers may have grace, wisdom, and understanding to execute justice, and to maintain truth"; and that the people "may lead quiet and peaceable lives, in all godliness and honesty."

Only in 1801 did the American Episcopalians decide whether and how traditional Anglican doctrine should bind their new church. In that year the XXXIX Articles of Religion of the Church of England were "established by the Bishops, the Clergy, and the Laity," as the American Prayer Book puts it. Doctrine was "established" simply by making the Articles, divested of royalism, an appendix to the Prayer Book. The Anglican practice of requiring ordinands to subscribe the Articles was brushed aside, and, in fact, among American Episcopalians the Articles have been regarded merely as describing the Elizabethan church's reaction to Roman Catholic claims and rarely as a confession of faith. The two books of *Homilies* of the Church of England, which explicate that church's doctrine, were nominally accepted by the Episcopal Church in the United States; a commission was appointed at an early General Convention to revise these instruments for *de jure* adoption, but the commission never reported and the *Homilies* have been virtually unknown since the demise of the first generation of Episcopalian clergy.

Traditional worship is what the American Episcopalians of the first generation wanted to preserve at all costs, but they were ready to alter it where it reflected the traditional royalist polity under which it had come into being and by which it had been protected against repeated Puritan attacks. Traditional church order they also prized, but the Puritans had so taught them to desire an episcopacy (if any) of simply spiritual authority that they were willing to undo the entire church-political tradition in which they stood in order to achieve it. Traditional doctrinal formularies of the Church of England, themselves the creatures of crown and bishops serving as civil officers, they dismissed as virtually irrelevant to the new order in which they lived.

With this difficult process of rearrangement and selective discarding of English church traditions completed, the Protestant Episcopal Church after 1811 launched into frontier American life in an unaccustomed burst of evangelistic fervor. Leaders who had dominated during the revolutionary period opposed enthusiasm but chose as assistants and successors men who thought the newly-organized church was called to a missionary endeavor to evangelize the populace of the continent. By 1835 these younger men had won their point, and, in a step that broke completely from Church of England missionary patterns, the entire membership of the Episcopal Church was formed into a Domestic and Foreign Missionary Society. The purgation of Anglican church tradition enabled these Episcopalians in America to look forward to a day when the new church might achieve and receive anew the Christian tradition of evangelism and therefore of distinctly American types of religiousness.

Striking parallels are to be found in the experiences of other major American churches. American Presbyterians held tenaciously to the polity of the reformed tradition, and preserved many features of old-world presbyterial church order. But advocates of strict subscription to doctrinal formularies had lost their cause to the principle by which local presbyteries interpreted doctrine, and the ordered worship of Europeans gave way to a freedom and spontaneity of worship that centered on evangelistic preaching. Synods and general assemblies became appellate judicatories and federative legislatures, while the main business of church administration fell to the sessions of strong congregations or to presbyteries.[3]

Methodists in the early 1780's felt keenly the need to organize an autonomous American church and did so by rejecting the order and worship of both the mother Church of England and their own founder's preference. Doctrinal statements fashioned by Wesley out of traditional Anglican formularies, however, were accepted by the American Methodists, and, interestingly enough, have remained intact until today. But free worship, authoritarian polity, and a self-generated episcopal order combined with Arminian doctrine and radically evangelistic patterns of church life to make Methodism by the 1830's the largest cohesive American denomination and the most typically American church.

Baptists, who during colonial times stayed in close contact with parent societies in London, had always stressed the congregational determination of polity and order, even to the extent that there was no European judicatory for them to renounce. Yet the early American experience drew them into a new and common religious tradition as missionary and educational endeavors linked their congregations into associations and conventions that stamped on the Baptist movement most marks of a full-fledged denomination.

Roman Catholics, as mentioned above, were granted a "this-one-time only" dispensation to have their superior chosen by American priests after the Vicar Apostolic in London announced that the success of the Revolution had terminated his supervision of Catholics in the United States. The spirit of independence that thus earned exceptional rights for the Roman clergy carried over to the laity during the period under consideration in the form of trusteeism, a stubborn assertion of congregational rights according fully with the denominational pattern in America. Although after 1840 Catholicism centered mainly in the cities of America, before that time the evangelistic spirit motivated it to spread itself from a restricted base in the middle colonies into all the new states. It was more the function of mid-century immigration than of some internal change of mind that made Roman Catholicism seem to many Protestants at least un-American and at worst anti-American. But before that happened, Catholics had shared the typical American experience and had become partners in American Christianity.

III. Orientation to the Future

Many of these features of the American churches' revolt against European church traditions—in the interest of appropriating the American enterprise—have been interpreted long ago as instances of the recovery of a true Christian tradition. Philip Schaff, the first professionally-trained church historian to examine Christianity in America, noted that prominent among these features was an orientation toward the future as the age in which the fulness of Christianity would come into being in the churches. In 1854, early in his career, Schaff explained American religion and culture to European audiences in Berlin and Frankfurt-am-Main, insisting that with regard to religion and the churches, America was the "Phenix-grave of Europe."[1] What Schaff perceived was that the typical church traditions of European Christendom tended to die in the American denominations, but that this death led in these denominations to a resurrection of a wholeness of Christianity that compared favorably with anything Europe had known.

To Schaff as to some of his contemporaries such as his early colleague, John Williamson Nevin, to a circle of Episcopalians gathered around William Augustus Muhlenberg, and to the disciples of Samuel Schmucker, the divisiveness of American Christianity constituted an unnecessary scandal that might be overcome at least in part by the efforts of the Evangelical Alliance and other ecumenical endeavors. These early heralds of the ecumenical movement wanted to expunge from American Christianity neither pluralism nor variety of religious expression but rather rancor and enmity between denominations.[5] Their manifestation of ecumenism, presaged as it had been by the Campbells and other founders of unitive denominations, finally matured in the American call for a Faith and Order Movement that should aim at church unity not as a synthesis of existing church traditions, nor even as a rediscovery and re-embodiment of some archaic Christian tradition, but rather as a reaching out to receive a new unitive grace that would heal divisions between denominations and communions. As a matter of fact these early ecumenical endeavors in America, such as Schaff promoted, had to reckon with an exclusivism that developed in the American churches mostly after the first third of the nineteenth century, partly in the wake of new waves of immigration from Europe. To be sure, engagement in evangelizing the burgeoning country produced denominational rivalries that in many cases drew the attention of American churchmen back to the traditional claims of parent churches in England. For example, many American Episcopalians read the Oxford Movement's assertion that Church of England clergy were spiritually independent from the state, and, without realizing that such independence had already been achieved in full in America,

turned these claims into a sectarian exclusivism partaking of
the spirit that nourished new American sects such as the
Mormons and the Adventists. But this re-Europeanization of
American Christianity after 1840 did not strip it of its expec-
tation that the future, not the past, was the great era of the
Christian tradition—a tradition that included unity.

When American churches more recently were drawn into
ecumenical discussions, they found themselves aligned with
their European cousins as fellow-Lutherans, fellow-Method-
ists, fellow-Anglicans, fellow-Presbyterians, or even (as
American Catholics increasingly say of themselves) as
Roman Catholics. Again they were reminded of the specific
church traditions that they in fact somewhat falteringly
represented. Earnestly and perhaps naively there arose a
yearning to utilize these church traditions as the basis for par-
ticularizing Christianity—for restoring sharp corners to the
four-square Gospel. Some American delegates to international
ecumenical meetings may not realize that the Europeans to
whom they warm as fellow-confessionalists may perceive how
much American Christians of different denominations hold in
common with one another. In spite of reasserted traditionalisms that loomed large in American churches during the
twentieth century, these denominations still share a common
Americanness and a common orientation toward the future
that prompt them to hold traditionalisms and traditions under
the judgment of a Christian criterion that is yet to be received
by the churches. From pan-denominationalism has arisen in
America a keen interest in *traditiones interpretivae*. From
broader ecumenical participation has been generated a new
appreciation for *traditiones constitutivae*. Yet in many respects it remains the typical posture of the American
churches to await an *actus tradendi* that may overcome inherited traditions by drawing them into a unity accommodating the pluralism and valuing the voluntaryism that are appropriate to modern religion.

With regard to specific church traditions, the major American denominations have been "traducers" in both senses of
the term. By rearrangement, re-emphasis, and selective dis-

cardings they have betrayed the integrity and wholeness of these traditions. But as this process has brought these churches into meaningful encounter with modern society, the denominations have brought forth and transmitted these traditions to a new age. The American churches have betrayed the Christian tradition in that their common unity springs rather more from their shared Americanness than from a self-conscious participation in the historic identifying marks of Christianity itself. But at the same time they have educed and transmitted the Christian tradition in a new form as their evangelical emphasis prompted them to live for the world and as they exhibited a readiness to seek unity and even Christianness more as a gift from the future than as a *traditum* from the past.

The distinct characteristic of Christianity in the United States, as represented by the mainline denominations, is the sense of novelty that looks forward to the churches' becoming what they should be by appreciative engagement with the creativity of culture and history. It is surely enigmatic and perhaps paradoxical that as these denominations become increasingly international in self-consciousness, they also became narrower in their adherence to the faith and order of parent traditions and thereby became also isolated from one another. Their common Americanness nevertheless holds them open to a new future even while their world-wide confessionalism binds them to a past that is dying in Europe and is already dead everywhere else. The eschatological sensitivity that is warmly advocated by theologians pleading for Christian particularity is perhaps a corollary of the accommodation to American culture that is so hotly condemned by the same theologians. For the very betrayal of church traditions has always been the primary agent of the American churches' achievement of the Christian tradition.

Notes

1. Maurice W. Armstrong, Lefferts A. Loetscher, and Charles A. Anderson, eds., *The Presbyterian Enterprise, Sources of American Presbyterian History* (Philadelphia, Westminster Press, 1956), p. 89.
2. Jerald C. Brauer, *Protestantism in America, A Narrative History* (Philadelphia, Westminster Press, 1953; revised edn., 1966), p. 8.
3. For an original and incisive study of American Presbyterianism as largely a new-world phenomenon, see Leonard J. Trinterud, *The Forming of an American Tradition, A Re-Examination of Colonial Presbyterianism* (Philadelphia, Westminster Press, 1949).
4. Philip Schaff, *America. A Sketch of the Political, Social, and Religious Character of the United States of America* . . . (New York, C. Scribner, 1855; reprinted with introduction by Perry Miller, The John Harvard Library, Cambridge, Mass., The Belknap Press of Harvard University Press, 1961), p. 104.
5. Accounts of this early American ecumenism are found in numerous articles, among which see Lefferts A. Loetscher, "The Problem of Christian Unity in Early Nineteenth-Century America," *Church History*, XXXII (March 1963), 3–16.

Americanization: Sacred or Profane Phenomenon?

Robert Michaelsen

"Let neither the individual nor his group make such exclusive claims for his sanctities that he is led to do injury to others. And let no one, especially no public official, assume that he has been especially called to define what is orthodox Americanism." Such is the plea of Robert Michaelsen as he first analyzes the unique process that is Americanization and then issues a caveat against the kind of orthodoxy in American religion that could deny the very essence of a democratic culture. Dr. Michaelsen is Professor of Religious Studies and Chairman of the Department of Religious Studies at the University of California, Santa Barbara. Among his numerous publications: *The Study of Religion in American Universities* and *Piety in the Public School*. His essay—portions of which were read at the annual meeting of the American Academy of Religion, October 1969—is from the May 7, 1971, issue of *Reconstructionist*,* a journal published by the Jewish Reconstructionist Foundation, Inc.

IT IS THE PURPOSE of this paper to use the categories of the sacred and the profane to examine Americanization. By Americanization I mean the process of "making a nation out of nations," of transforming peoples from a variety of lands into a people. It is a process unique to the United States, as G. K. Chesterton pointed out in his perceptive essay, "What is America?"[1] In using the categories of the sacred and the profane I am following the lead of some historians and sociologists of religion, especially Emile Durkheim and Mircea Eliade. I understand "sacred" as having to do with "being, meaning and truth,"[2] with power and iden-

* 15 W. 86th St., New York, N.Y. 10024. Reprinted by permission.

tity, as existentially understood and appropriated. And I use "existential" in a social as well as a personal sense, following Durkheim and H. Richard Niebuhr.[3] "Profane" is used to designate the opposite of the sacred, that which is not decisively significant in terms of meaning and identity.

Finding the Sacred in Consciousness

There are, of course, some assumptions about man in this analysis. I understand that man does not live by bread or by reason alone. With Eliade I assume that "the 'sacred' is an element in the structure of consciousness, not a stage in the history of consciousness."[4] Hence it remains in the consciousness of modern, secularized man. The trick is to find ways of discerning evidences of the sacred in that consciousness. Eliade suggests that we must turn to modern man's existential, private world, to his imaginary universe, as the chief locus of the sacred. I think it might also be useful to turn to those realms of experience where the private and the public meet, where the personally existential and the socially existential overlap. Americanization is this type of experience.

I propose to develop the theme of this paper under five headings: (1) eschatology; (2) separation; (3) secularization; (4) resacralization; and (5) toward a desacralized and pluralistic nation.

I. ESCHATOLOGY

The "discovery and colonization of the new world took place under the sign of eschatology."[5] This was the place where all things would be made new. This was the land of promise, promise of the fulfillment of human hope—or divine destiny. Articulate Christians, such as the Puritans and the Quakers, came to the American colonies to build Biblical commonwealths or to restore primitive Christianity, and in either case to do what could not be done in Europe. Men with less obvious religious commitments saw this new land as the end product of what Western man had long sought. Here, said Hector St. John de Crevecoeur, the "western pilgrims" would "finish the great circle." Here men of all nations would be transformed into "a new race of men."[6]

New Society for a New Epoch

The founding fathers embodied this eschatological hope in the Great Seal of the United States with the words *novus ordo seclorum*. Here in this new land they were establishing a new society for a new epoch in human history. This new society would produce a new human nature. The period following the American Revolution, observed Horace Mann, formed "a new era" on the stage of human history. Men were now "placed . . . in circumstances so different from any [they] had ever before occupied" that "we must expect a new series of developments in human nature and conduct."[7]

Eschatological hope continued to live more than a century after the launching of the *novus ordo seclorum*. Woodrow Wilson foresaw the emerging in this new society of a new man who would be "purged of the more debased and selfish elements of human ambition."[8] And Israel Zangwill, the most eloquent singer of the melting pot theory after Crevecoeur, saw America as "God's crucible" where "all the races of Europe" were "melting and re-forming" into a new man. This new man, this "real American" had "not yet arrived." He was still in the crucible. When he did arrive he would be "the fusion of all races, perhaps the coming superman."[9]

The promise of newness, change, fulfillment, exerted an enormous pull upon Europeans. Some thirty-five million of them made their way across the Atlantic, most of them sailing with hope in the bow and trying to leave fear and despair astern. "The immigrant's arrival in his new home," said one immigrant—Abraham Cahan—through the lead character in *The Rise of David Levinsky*, "is like a second birth to him. Imagine a new-born babe in possession of a fully developed intellect. Would it ever forget its entry into the world? Neither does the immigrant ever forget his entry into the country which is to him, a new world in the profoundest sense of the term . . ."[10] Another immigrant novelist, the Norwegian Ole Rølvaag, wrote in *Giants in the Earth* of the near madness which had seized these "western pilgrims" in their relentless pursuit of the promised but elusive Eden. "Here on the trackless plains, the thousand year old hunger of the poor after human happiness had been unloosed."[11]

Understand Out of the Past, Live Out of the Future

"We live out of the future . . . ," says the philosopher of religion, Ray Hart, in his massive work on the human imagination.[12] America epitomized and capitalized upon this future orientation. It was much easier to Americanize by pointing to the future than by trying to improve the past, observed a perceptive first generation American, Carol Aronovici.[13] A German-American reported his discovery that while "every other people has some culture, some civilization, handed down from the past . . ." America was different because it derived "its inspiration from the future."[14]

2. SEPARATION

But, while we live out of the future, "we understand out of the past."[15] And the immigrant was cut off from much of his past. Oscar Handlin, one of the best known of the historians of the immigrants in America, entitled his major work on this subject, *The Uprooted*. From the standpoint of the immigrant, the one who left his homeland to come to America, "the history of immigration is a history of alienation and its consequences," Handlin concludes. From the moment the emigrant made his decision to leave home he was confronted almost daily with decisions for which his previous cosmos had done little to prepare him. He found the new world to be a very different place from the old. "Strangers, the immigrants could not locate themselves; they had lost the polestar that gave them their bearings." Nearly all aspects of the new world, including Americanization efforts and crusades, deepened the immigrant's "consciousness of separateness," Handlin maintains. "I am in America and I do not even know whether it is America," one immigrant confessed in bewilderment.[16] In this context, one might well understand that becoming "Americanized" was often for the immigrant "nothing but a treaty of peace with society," as Marcus Lee Hansen put it.[17]

Finding a New Past

The lure of the future led the immigrant away from his homeland, across the Atlantic to the new world. But the process forced upon him a kind of lobotomy in which he was severed from much of his past. Now he must find a new past, new ways of understanding, or be left to wander about aimlessly in an alien world.

Actually there appears to have been a double movement within the soul of the immigrant—toward an assertion of individuality which tended to cut him off from his anchorage in a traditional society and cast him adrift in the new world, and a counter movement toward reestablishing in the new world as many elements of the old as possible. The very decision to leave home usually involved an assertion of individuality. Whether out of despair or hope, whether in careful calculation or in almost sheer caprice, the decision to emigrate was a momentous one which transformed the emigrant's life. That decision set in motion a centrifugal force which tended to war with the gravitational pull of the traditional cosmos. (These countervailing pulls were evident within families as well as within individuals. Note, e.g., the sharp contrast in orientation between Per Hansa and his wife, Beret, in Rølvaag's *Giants in the Earth*. For Beret Americanization was profane, even obscene, and it seemed to lead only to madness.)

Identity was inextricably tied up with the old world. The immigrant usually sought out his own people, established his own press, his own native societies, etc. Handlin points out that the first concern of the immigrant self-help societies was death.[18] In the old world this critical time of passage was securely ritualized. To counteract the dark threat of ultimate meaninglessness it was necessary to reestablish this protective shield as soon as possible.

The double movement within the immigrant's soul had varying effects. Some were quite literally pulled apart. Some returned to the motherland. Others struck some kind of equilibrium between the two pulls within them. Marcus Lee Hansen points out that the immigrant father, who compromised most willingly with the outside world for job purposes, still generally insisted upon the old ways within the home.

The Yankeeized American

3. SECULARIZATION

Some immigrants put on new faces. By a combination of the forces of circumstance and will old masks were torn off and new ones put on. This kind of Americanization seems to have involved more than an ordinary amount of suppression of subconscious elements. Often the result was a kind of rationalized, secularized man, seen more clearly perhaps in the second generation than in the first. There occurred a decrease in emotional sensibility, "a fading of emotional tones," as one immigrant put it. "I forgot for some years that birds sing, flowers have odor, stars shine." Emotion was replaced by calculation. "I did not think of what I liked or disliked, but of what was advantageous or disadvantageous. There was a decided shifting from emotional to rational motives."[19] The development of this kind of rationalized persona is illustrated well in one classic story of successful Americanization: *The Americanization of Edward Bok*.

"Nothing was more Yankee," Hansen comments, "than a Yankeeized person of foreign descent."[20]

"A Man Apart From Place and Station"

The second generation was caught between the gravitational pulls of the two worlds and sought to escape the old as soon as possible. Hansen reminds us that the son wanted to forget everything about the father and the old world. He found his identity in the school, in his job, in his marriage, in his country. Handlin points out that marriage, for example, was often regarded as a process of liberation by which one cast off family ties and expressed himself as a person "through the power to love."[21] Horace M. Kallen commented critically that the son learned "life, the expression of emotion and the realization of desire, from the yellow press . . ."[22] Actually the second generation carried further a process begun with the first. In his story of *The Rise of David Levinsky*, the Talmudic student who emigrated from Poland to America where he became a successful businessman, Abraham Cahan emphasized the role that romantic love and sexual attraction played in secularizing this very orthodox young man. John Higham points out that Cahan was really commenting on his own experience. Exposure to romantic love began the process of Americanization even before Cahan had left his native Poland.[23]

Emigration, then, increased pressures toward individuation and secularization. It was one significant tributary to that accelerating current which has, seemingly, been carrying Western man farther and farther from the temple. In America, this "land of separated men," one discovered what it meant to be an individual, "a man apart from place and station,"[24] from sacred space and sacred time. The experience was a painful one, as leaving the securities of old ways always is. But it could also be exhilarating and liberating. Arthur Meier Schlesinger, in an essay on "The American—A

New Man," stresses the importance of what might be called the secular virtues in this new world—industry, ingenuity, mobility, individualism, optimism about human and especially one's own potential.[25] This was a potent package. From Crevecoeur to Andrew Carnegie it made for men who were masters of their world. Here truly was the *novus ordo seclorum* populated by the *novus homo seclorum*.

Making a People Out of Peoples

4. RESACRALIZATION

One might leave it at that with the second, third, fourth, and subsequent generations being born, working, marrying, and even dying outside the temple, each a happy new man in this brave new world. But that is not quite the picture. Americanization often involved a re- as well as a desacralization. It is true that the new American was encouraged to sever old world ties and to assume a rationalized approach to the world. At the same time, however, he was also exposed to the myths of the promised land and sacred peoplehood. Even the rationalized world of the secularized American was supported by a nether world of Edenic promise or mystic tribal superiority. Here one might acknowledge, with Eliade, that "the 'total man' is never completely desacralized . . ."[26] And, going beyond Eliade, one might suggest that sacred themes are evident not only in the private, existential world of modern secularized man, but also in his social, existential world, the world of group identity, or group "inner history,"[27] where myth and history meet.

Americanization came to mean nationalization, the making of a nation out of nations, a people out of peoples. The motifs of initiation, sacred history, racial or national superiority appeared more and more in American self-understanding. Focus shifted from the future to the past, from eschatology to sacred history, from the new to the old; the melting pot, from which there was yet to emerge a new man, was

replaced by the transmuting pot in which aliens and strangers
—foreigners—were converted into Americans, after the likeness of the "old" Americans.

"Land Where Our Fathers Died"?

In the early 1920's Henry Ford arranged a pageant which
illustrated this emerging understanding of Americanization.
Ford ordered a large pot constructed outside his factory. "On
the day of the pageant groups of immigrants, dressed in the
colorful costumes of their native lands, marched and danced"
toward the pot.

When the group at the front of the procession reached the
enormous pot it sang and danced one final chorus of its song
and then disappeared inside. One by one the various groups
followed the first.

From the other side of the . . . pot there began to emerge
people dressed alike in the current American fashion.
Forming ranks, they began to sing in clear English "The
Star Spangled Banner." Weaker and weaker grew the re-
frains of the tarantellas, polkas, and kolos as more and more
people emerged from the pot to swell the chorus of the
national anthem. At last the foreign tunes and words were
heard no more; the final flash of color disappeared into the
pot. All that could now be seen was a mass of people dressed
alike and marching together. All that was heard was one
song and one language.[28]

Ford meant his pageant to illustrate the "melting pot" theory,
but his pot was more a "transmuting pot" than a melting pot.
Immigrants were changed into the likeness of native Americans and Ford knew quite well who was an American; he had
only to look into a mirror.

The immigrant was still to become a new man, but now
there was a pattern. The focus shifted from the future to the
past, and someone else's past at that. When Mary Antin,
Russian-born Jewish-American author, proudly sang of this
"land where our fathers died," she was jeered at by "old"

Americans.[29] Miss Antin evidently had not gone far enough in conforming to the pattern. And it was clear that in the minds of some "old" Americans she could never share their past.

Radical Americanists

Park and Miller compared the radical Americanists with the radical anarchists. They wished to destroy the immigrant's past, to remove him roots and all from one soil and transplant him in another.[30] "Broadly speaking, we mean" by Americanization, declared the Superintendent of the New York City public schools in 1917, "an appreciation of the institutions of this country [and] absolute forgetfulness of all obligations or connections with other countries."[31] In reaction to this kind of pressured Americanization one "new American" sadly observed "we are submerged beneath a conquest so complete that the very name of us means something not ourselves . . . I feel as I should think an Indian might feel, in the face of ourselves that were."[32]

This pressure toward sacred peoplehood reached a high point during World War I. The declaration of war in April 1917 "ushered in a new ideology," John Higham observes.[33] When President Wilson delivered his war message to Congress "almost every member of the excited audience before him was waving or wearing an American flag. . . ." Americanization had come to be understood in terms of the slogan popularized by Teddy Roosevelt: "100 percent Americanism." What was demanded was "complete identification with the nation—a sense of identification so all-embracing as to permeate and stabilize the rest of (the individual's) thinking and behavior." The essential duty consisted in "right thinking, i.e., the enthusiastic cultivation of obedience and conformity."[34]

Society's Idea of Itself

Native-born Americans had participated in the Americanization movement since early in the century out of two different motives: (1) an "idealistic" and service-oriented motivation, directed toward helping the immigrant to adapt to the new environment; and (2) a "patriotic" motivation, directed toward rooting out the un-American. Hope played a large role in the former, fear in the latter. With the entry into the war the latter gained ascendancy. "An intense patriotism and devotion to all things 'American' gripped the nation, while a suspicion of all things alien in nature . . . began to grow in intensity. . . . The time was ripe for a campaign of crusading proportions to win over the nation to the necessity for concerted action along the lines of assimilation or Americanization" in order to "mold the immigrant into a full-fledged American with undivided loyalties."[35]

A society, observed Emile Durkheim, "is not made up merely of the mass of individuals who compose it, the ground which they occupy, the things which they use and the movements they perform, but above all is the idea which it forms of itself." Hence a society must periodically "assemble and concentrate itself" in order "to become conscious of itself." This "white heat of concentration" gives off "a set of ideal conceptions" which portray "the new life thus awakened." A new consciousness emerges which exerts a powerful influence upon the individual. As the "collective life" reaches "a certain degree of intensity . . . it brings about a state of effervescence which changes the conditions of psychic activity. Vital energies are over-excited, passions more active, sensations stronger . . . A man does not recognize himself; he feels transformed and consequently he transforms the environment which surrounds him."[36] The period of American participation in the First World War was such a time in America. There are grounds for maintaining that it was the most important single event in shaping and focusing national consciousness.

Ferreting Out "Un-Americans"

The new national consciousness demanded of the immigrant a frantic affirmation of loyalty to the nation in word and deed and a suppression of all elements of "difference" in his speech, manner, clothing, and ideals. Public officials from court house to White House joined in or led the parade toward national uniformity. The governor of Iowa issued a proclamation banning any language except English in all schools, church services, conversations in public places, or over the telephone. "You cannot become thorough Americans if you think of yourselves in groups," President Wilson told a gathering of newly naturalized immigrants. Having "once entered into this sacred relationship" newcomers "are bound to be loyal whether they are pleased or not . . . ," he asserted at an Americanization conference.[37]

The native-born American was afforded the opportunity to demonstrate his unalloyed loyalty in a host of ways, including the ferreting out of un-American elements. Governmental authorities from the President down encouraged citizens to report and discourage instances of disloyalty. For one dollar a person could obtain membership in the American Protective League and thereby gain the authority "with the approval of the Department of Justice to make investigations under the title 'Secret Service.' " It is estimated that this American Protective League "brought to judgment three million cases of disloyalty." The Attorney General of the United States declared in 1918: "It is safe to say that never in its history has this country been so thoroughly policed."[38]

The Secret Society

This period of high intensity left a lasting legacy. It precipitated a new level of consciousness of what the radical Americanist Gino Speranza called "the nation-spiritual," by which he meant the nation suffused by what were understood to be the moral and spiritual values of the "old" Americans.[39] To such self-appointed guardians of that "nation-spiritual" Americanization was "a thing of the spirit, a purpose and a point of view that only came through instinctive racial understanding . . ."[40] And few "aliens" could understand that spirit. This narrow understanding of Americanization was formalized in restrictive immigration and other forms of legislation enacted in what Higham calls "the tribal twenties."[41] It was also expressed in thousands of less formal ways as the high and low priests of tribalism put their fellow citizens to a variety of loyalty tests.

On this view, then, Americanization was a sacred phenomenon; it involved an initiation into a sacred society, membership in which took on spiritual dimensions and gave a fundamental raison d'être to the life of the initiate.

5. TOWARD A DESACRALIZED AND PLURALISTIC NATION

Obviously an understanding of Americanization as a sacred phenomenon creates problems. The sacred peoplehood notion is narrow and restrictive, forcing radical change upon immigrants and tending to exclude racial and religious minorities from the tribe. Marcus Garvey urged that the only viable option it left open to Blacks was emigration. Horace M. Kallen argued vigorously against it, pointing out that there is no such thing as an "American race" or an "American religion" and calling for a pluralistic society, "a great republic consisting of a federation or commonwealth of nationalities."[42] The caustic critic of war-time patriotism, Randolph S. Bourne, praised the excluded minorities for "keeping us from being swept into a terrible national engine" which might easily roll over all dissent, smooth out all differences, and become a terror to the world.[43]

How To Avoid Becoming a "Terrible National Engine"

The earlier, eschatological emphasis at least had the advantage of stressing the future. This emphasis contributed toward an openness in society. The pattern was not yet firmly established. Americanization, as Hartley Burr Alexander affirmed in 1919, was "yet to be created."[44] But there are problems in stressing the future, especially if this is done in a utopian fashion. Camus called hope man's greatest enemy because it is often built upon illusions—of utopia, of heaven, of promised land, of eternal fulfillment. The hint that these might be illusions can turn a man into a fanatic in defense of their reality. At the same time, hope disappointed gives over not only to despair but to bitterness.

This would argue for a desacralized version of Americanization, and especially for a desacralization of politics. Let politics deal with the realities of bread. And if men need more than bread, as apparently we do, let them find it in soul music or in identity and practice as a Jew, a Catholic, or a Protestant, or in the visions of the Apocalypse, or in Satori. But let neither the individual nor his group make such exclusive claims for his sanctities that he is led to do injury to others. And let no one, especially no public official, assume that he has been especially called to define what is orthodox Americanism. It is well to recall those magnificent words of Justice Jackson, writing for the U.S. Supreme Court in 1943 in the second Jehovah's Witnesses flag salute case: "If there is any fixed star in our constitutional constellation, it is that no official, high or petty, can prescribe what shall be orthodox in politics, nationalism, religion, or other matters of opinion or force citizens to confess by word or act their faith therein."[45]

"Multiplicity is of the essence of democracy," Sidney E. Mead rightly affirms, and it "must be maintained."[46] If we are thinking of the deeper aspects of "being, meaning and truth," we might wish to make a slight change in the motto on the Great Seal of the United States: from *E pluribus unum* to *In pluribus unum*. Pluralism is tested daily in American experience. It is a changing reality which needs constantly to be affirmed against those who would make us into a monolithic and "terrible national engine."

Notes

1. In *The Man Who Was Chesterton*, Raymond T. Bond, ed. (New York: Dodd, Mead & Co., 1937), pp. 183–97, especially 193.
2. Eliade, *The Quest: History and Meaning in Religion* (Chicago: University of Chicago Press, 1969), Preface.
3. Durkheim, *The Elementary Forms of Religious Life*, Conclusion, and H. R. Niebuhr, *Christ and Culture* (New York: Harper & Bros., 1956), the section on "social existentialism," pp. 241–49.
4. Eliade, *The Quest*, Preface.
5. *Ibid.*, p. 89.
6. "What Is an American?" in *Letters from an American Farmer*, Letter #III. Quotations from the Everyman's Library edition (London & New York, 1912, 1951), pp. 40 ff.
7. *Life and Works of Horace Mann* (Boston: Lee & Shepard; New York: C. T. Billingham, 1891), II, 14 ff., IV, 8 ff.
8. *The Public Papers of Woodrow Wilson*, ed. Ray Stannard Baker and William E. Dodd, 6 vols. (New York: Harper & Bros., 1925–27), III, 132.
9. Quoted by Andre Siegfried, *America Comes of Age* (New York: Harcourt, Brace & Co., 1927), p. 145.
10. Quoted from the Harper Torchbook edition, New York, 1960, pp. 86–87.
11. (New York: Harper & Row, 1964), p. 227.
12. *Unfinished Man and the Imagination* (New York: Herder & Herder, 1968), p. 11.
13. *Americanization* (St. Paul: Keller, 1919), p. 47. Aronovici was a social worker and chairman of the Minnesota Committee on Americanization.
14. As quoted in Gino Speranza, *Race or Nation: A Conflict of Divided Loyalties* (Indianapolis: Bobbs-Merrill, 1925), p. 114.
15. Hart, *Unfinished Man and the Imagination, op. cit.*
16. *The Uprooted* (New York: Grosset & Dunlap, 1951), pp. 4, 94, 169.
17. "The Third Generation" in *Children of the Uprooted*, Oscar Handlin, ed. (New York: George Braziller, 1966), pp. 256–57.
18. *The Uprooted*, p. 173.
19. As quoted by Robert E. Park and Herbert A. Miller, *Old World Traits Transplanted* (New York: Harper & Bros., 1921), pp. 54–55.
20. "The Third Generation" in *Children of the Uprooted*, Handlin, ed., p. 259.
21. Handlin, *The Uprooted*, p. 256.
22. "Democracy Versus the Melting-Pot," *The Nation*, C (1915), 194.

23. In the Introduction to the Harper Torchbook edition.
24. Handlin, *The Uprooted,* p. 305.
25. In *Children of the Uprooted,* Handlin, ed., pp. 193–216.
26. *The Quest,* Preface. See also the last chapter of *The Sacred and the Profane.*
27. See H. Richard Niebuhr, *The Meaning of Revelation* (New York: Macmillan, 1941).
28. Edmund Traverson, *Immigration: A Study in American Values* (Boston: D. C. Heath & Co., 1964), p. 75.
29. See Randolph Bourne, "Trans-National America" in *War and the Intellectuals;* Collected Essays, 1915-1919, Carl Resek, ed. (New York: Harper & Row, 1964), p. 107.
30. *Old World Traits Transplanted,* p. 281.
31. *Ibid.*
32. As reported in Horace M. Kallen, "Democracy Versus the Melting Pot; A Study of American Nationality," *The Nation,* C (1915), 194.
33. *Strangers in the Land* (New York: Atheneum, 1963), p. 204.
34. *Ibid.,* pp. 204–5.
35. Edward George Hartmann, *The Movement to Americanize the Immigrant* (New York: AMS Press, 1967), pp. 105–7. Hartmann offers a systematic and well-documented treatment of his subject.
36. *The Elementary Forms of the Religious Life* (New York: The Free Press, 1965), pp. 469–70.
37. *The Public Papers of Woodrow Wilson,* III, 423–25, IV, 251–52. Higham, *Strangers in the Land,* pp. 200, 248. Wilson's remarks were made before American entry into the war, but they were of a piece with the kind of rhetoric he used to justify that entry and to attain 100 per cent support of the national cause.
38. Horace C. Peterson and Gilbert C. Fite, *Opponents of War,* 1917-18 (Madison: University of Wisconsin Press, 1957), pp. 19–20.
39. Speranza in *Race or Nation.*
40. Preston William Slosson, *The Great Crusade and After, 1914-1928* (New York: Macmillan, 1930), p. 307, referring to the KKK.
41. *Strangers in the Land,* Chapter X.
42. Kallen's views are succinctly put in his two-part series on "Democracy Versus the Melting-Pot; A Study of American Nationality," *The Nation,* C (1915), 190–94.
43. "The Jew and Trans-National America" in *War and the Intellectuals,* pp. 125–26.
44. "Americanization," *The Nation,* CIX (September 13, 1919), 367.
45. *West Virginia State Bd. of Education* v. *Barnette* 319 U.S. 624, 642.
46. *The Lively Experiment: The Shaping of Christianity in America* (New York: Harper & Row, 1963), p. 83.

Agencies of Historic Change: New England Puritanism and the New Left

William J. Scheick

At first glance a comparison between the New Left and Puritanism suggests a venture in futility, if not absurdity; the two seem diametric opposites. Nonetheless, argues William J. Scheick, in the writings of the New Left one finds several images and a moral intensity which unwittingly have as their foundation various New England Puritan traditions. "The New Left sees itself, as did the Puritans, as both the vanguard and the final force for life and truth at the close of history. For them time is short and the future is now." Dr. Scheick is Assistant Professor of English at the University of Texas at Austin. New England Puritanism is his specialty, and he is the author of two books on Puritan writers: *The Will and the Word: The Quest for Conversion in the Poetry of Edward Taylor* and *Jonathan Edwards*. He is also the co-author of *H. G. Wells: An Annotated Bibliography of Writings about Him*. His article is reprinted from the March 1971 issue of *Thought*,* the Fordham University quarterly review.

I

A CONSIDERATION OF THE EMERGENCE of the New Left invites a number of historical analogies, not all of which are flattering as evidenced in at least one description of its members as the New Barbarians who "are no less rude, wild, and uncivilized than if they came from the land of the Visigoths or the Vandals."[1] Still, when some of the smoke of the rhetorical and sometimes lamentably actual barrages discharged by the Left as well as by its opponents clears somewhat, it is possible to perceive certain genuine relationships between the Movement, as the New Left is often called, and

* 441 E. Fordham Rd., Bronx, N.Y. 10458.

the past. To be sure, its most intimate link is to Marxism; but there exists an equally apparent tie to the Lockean notions of the American forefathers, especially regarding the right to dissent and the nature of revolution. However, it is not impossible to see that several roots of this relation to the American past extend further than the Revolutionary period. In terms of its increased fervor and intensity over the years, the New Left would seem to have a less obvious or expected connection to New England Puritanism.

Even though the rise of Puritanism has been interpreted as a radical political movement,[2] comparing it to the emergence of the New Left at first sounds ludicrous. The two seem diametric opposites. Nor is this initial impression completely mistaken, for several significant inversions of Puritan thought prevail in the views of the New Left. In place of total submission to religious and civil law, for instance, the Left elevates freedom and, in some cases, anarchy to the highest of principles; instead of renouncing the human body, in its fallen condition, as readily prone to sin, the Left embraces it and its desires as essential in the realization or fulfillment of the self; and even more indicative (with the notable exception of such men as the Berrigans), in lieu of God, mankind, his social and political nature, becomes the ultimate end of human endeavors. This last inversion, however, actually disguises a subtle connection between these two revolutionary forces; what has occurred is that the Puritan's politics of religion has been transformed into the New Left's religion of politics, while the animating zeal behind both of them has remained nearly the same.

In any discussion in which such an analogy provides the framework, there exist inevitable difficulties. The sixteenth and the twentieth centuries are not identical and will not meaningfully yield to any elaborate comparison. Among others, one problem encountered in such a discussion concerns the very terms "Puritanism" and "New Left." The former can be said to include such extremes as the Pilgrims and the Quakers,[3] whereas the latter may be thought to range from the violent Weathermen to university-oriented civil-rights activists, not to mention the entire black revolution which in many respects differs from the mainstream of the white Left. In this article, therefore, I shall avoid those particulars which tend to fragment these two forces into various splinter groups. What is of value for my purpose is not their numerous differences but certain broad and underlying concepts which relate to all the various factions and which also provide for a general analogy between New England Puritanism and the New Left. Nowhere, however, do I mean to suggest that this correspondence in any way defines the quintessence of the Movement; rather it is intended to shed light on the New Left by ascertaining another degree to which it is very much in the American grain. Specifically what I find in the writings of the New Left are several images and a moral intensity which unwittingly have as their foundation various New England Puritan traditions. As the following argument will attempt to demonstrate, this inheritance is best considered in regard to two areas: the Left's views of the individual and of his relation to history.

II

Although, properly speaking, the Movement is existential at heart in that it tends to endorse a permanent revisionism, there nevertheless persists beneath the surface of this sense of the relative significance of everything a still deeper feeling for something absolute, for something as firm as the faith of the Puritans. Exactly what comprises this absolute remains vague even to the Left, but it is intimately joined to the concept that man "must grow toward an ideal"[4]: "we need a vision of what we are working toward—one based on transcendental human needs and not limited by the reality we are so far stuck with."[5] Put another way, the Left requires a "sense of realizing an ideal born in the realm of pure spirit and not in *current* historical experience."[6] The informing energy of this belief is, on the emotional level at least, akin to that derived from some absolute principle or theological tenet.

This attitude partially explains the dogmatic assurance with which members of the Left so readily polarize; there is at the center of their commitment a faith as strong and as encompassing as that found in Puritan culture, and sometimes with similar results. The Puritans are well known, of course, for their religiously motivated lack of tolerance: "He that is willing to tolerate any unsound Opinion, that his own may also be tolerated, though never so sound, will for a need hang Gods Bible at the Devills girdle."[7] Likewise for the Left tolerance, even neutrality, represents opposition to faith in their ideal; it is paramount in their view that one speak out and act for what is "right" at all costs, with the consequence that "If you were *not with* us, you were *against* us."[8] How else should they respond? Like the Puritans before them, they claim to bear witness to some radical truth, to some ideal rooted in "transcendental human needs." They, similar to the Puritans, also find it necessary to view the temporal world with suspicion, seeing themselves engaged in "a movement of negation toward the existing world."[9] It is not surprising, therefore, that just as the Puritans saw themselves as divinely called to an errand into the wilderness of the New World,[10] the Movement envisages itself as the vanguard of truth as it seeks a place "out in the wilderness" where its members might "ponder basics and exercise . . . freedoms."[11]

This Puritan-like sense of mission to awaken and enlighten the world lies at the core of the New Left's concept of the individual. The Puritans and the Left both prove paradoxical concerning this matter: on the one hand, both stress the importance and value of the private self; on the other hand, both equally tend to negate this sense of self for a more collective goal. It was perfectly clear to the Puritans that each man was divinely endowed with special talents which he was to exert in some earthly vocation in order to better himself spiritually as well as materially.[12] Yet Puritan divines simultaneously argued from the beginning that the sincerest Christian learns to reject this image of self-sufficiency, that he discovers, as did Anne Bradstreet, how "the finest bread hath the least bran, the purest honey the least wax, and the sincerest Christian the least self-love."[13] According to Puritan thought the self was to renounce its selfishness and seek identity in something beyond itself—in God, ultimately; in the church-state, temporally. It is this concept which underlay the Pilgrims' attempt to own property jointly, the failure of which William Bradford, in *Of Plymouth Plantation*, cannot help but construe as a deep flaw in the very foundation of their religious experiment.

The New Left likewise stresses the importance of fulfilling the individual self—in noncapitalistic terms, of course. But overriding this idea is the importance of defining one's personal fulfillment in regard to "the cause," so that, as with the Puritans, the Left entertains an ideal of a community in which everyone will endeavor to seek his individual needs within a collective self.[14] There is, spokesmen for the Left claim, a "need to develop a communal life style which is continually sensitizing people to the larger task they are about in the society as a whole—a philosophy which leads the people to intentionally build toward the larger task."[15] The result of this effort will, they hope, produce a proper balance between the individual and the community, a situation wherein one can be "free to actualize his potentialities" and at the same time "identify with larger values that transcend himself."[16]

This aim, however secular, is treated by the Movement with the same religiosity as that manifested by the Puritans in response to their tenets of belief. Indeed, as is quite obvious at this point, in both instances we are dealing with something transcendent. But on the more mundane and practical level we will find that both equally subscribe to a necessary discipline which is contingent to this religiosity. For the Puritan this discipline entailed the surrender of his natural freedom (by which instinctively "men grow more evil") for civil liberty (by which men form "politic covenants and constitutions").[17] For the Movement, albeit in a somewhat different context, some similar renunciation is required, as, for example, when we are told: "where all are life-dedicated to a task, discipline becomes the question of how to organize ourselves toward that goal"; "discipline is a problem in the movement because most of us personally rebelled against the perversity of authoritarian families and schools where discipline was punishment or a means to get us to someone else's end. Now that self-discipline is required to free us further from this societal quagmire, we flounder. But the fact is that in the years ahead we must study and work much harder than we have to this point."[18]

As this last passage also makes clear, the union of the private and collective self as well as the need for personal discipline are founded on another Puritan-like notion: the role of the individual as an agent of truth. The Puritans were fond of finding examples of how God made use of human agency; at times even what one spoke proved to be, as Richard Mather remarked, "such words of truth and soberness as the Lord put into my mouth."[19] The Movement, for the most part, discerns no deity operating behind certain individual voices; yet time and again its members see themselves as conveyers of transcendent truth and, consequently, as "real live agencies of historic change."[20]

A person is called to play a part in this agency through a very personal and almost private experience, one that influences his entire being. In Puritanism this is the drama of conversion, an awakening to "a true sense of the divine excellency of the things revealed in the word of God, and a conviction of the truth and reality of them."[21] For the New Left this experience is the process of radicalization, a new intense and very personal commitment—hence the Left's penchant for a "language of political conversion."[22]

It is not surprising, furthermore, that just as the Puritans described this encounter as a "New Birth" producing a "New Creature,"[23] the Movement also presents the outcome of political conversion in identical terms: "The goal is a new social dispensation and a New Man."[24] Instead of the Puritan concept of an elect, of imitable visible saints who provide paragons of virtue, the Movement offers the "ideal political man," who "puts himself where he is needed; [who] gets his rewards only from the movement; [who] is pure of all material and personal needs that cannot be met by the movement."[25] Moreover, just as the Puritan saint was to be in but not of the world, so likewise the ideal political man must be willing to work within a social context while avoiding "an orientation toward professional 'success' "; above all else he must eschew the debasement of money: "What we need is a formal means of getting our money to the Movement before we get used to spending it and become corrupted."[26]

Like money, the world in which it circulates is a fallen, imperfect arena in which the political-saint must struggle. For the Puritans, of course, Adam's fall from grace was the source of the depraved condition of men and the world, as Edward Taylor, speaking as Adam, laments in the following poem:

> But as a Chrystall Glass, I broke, and lost
> That Grace, and Glory I was fashion'd in
> And cast this Rosy World with all its Cost
> Into a Dunghill Pit, and Puddle Sin.[27]

As a consequence of Original Sin, evil stains and permeates everything in the natural world. For the Left the world is in an equally deplorable condition; and, without intending a facetious analogy, I see in their descriptions of the Viet Nam war overtones recalling the Puritan doctrine of Original Sin. Consider, for instance, the imagery and meaning of the following passage on the American involvement in the war in Southeast Asia: "How can we think that in performing this, which even our apologists characterize as a cruel and *dirty* war, that our actions will not stain through our whole consciousness and benumb and degenerate us in our wholeness and make us act toward ourselves as we do toward others?"[28] In this fallen world the political-saint "can count on suffering" and he must recognize "that if we are taking casualties—even though we're not hurting anyone on the other side—it doesn't mean that something is going wrong. This is battle."[29]

III

Not only do Puritanism and the New Left share certain views of the individual, they also reflect a mutual regard for that individual's relation to history. The elect, according to the Puritans, were to strive to complete the Reformation, to ring in the Kingdom of Christ. They were to perfect themselves insofar as they could and then convert their families, the New England colonies, and finally the entire world. More than mere vestiges of this idea survive in New Left thought. Thus the Movement explains that although their "actions may lead to nothing except changing ourselves," they aim for actions which "may also explode," actions which "will change this country and change the world."[30] As their members "widen their circle the hope and spirit of their vision will be unmistakably transmitted."[31] It is this aspect of their thought which lends reinforcement to their sense of collective identity and their communal ethic. The revolutionary community may start small, like those few settlers in Plymouth, but ultimately it may convert the entire world.

Though this vision is necessarily forward-looking, it actually emphasizes the now of experience for both of these political forces. If one were to attempt to reduce the countless Puritan sermons into some single message, he might arrive at the indispensableness of being awake and alert in order to perceive God's hidden design or will, of being ready to receive grace were God to bestow it upon you. This is also suggested in their numerous diaries, journals, and meditations which reveal how the Puritan saw the divine hand to operate in the context of life's immediacy, in every present moment. This reverence for the present is preserved and intensified by the New Left. Their insistence on action arises indeed from what they consciously ascertain as "an awareness of the unique here and now"[32]—Rubin's "Do it!" So unique is the present that, like the Puritans, the Movement is obsessed with writing its own histories; for an historical account based on the truth to which they bear witness "can come to us only from those who organized and participated in it."[32] In the last analysis, of course, for both the Puritans and the Left this history points toward a vision of the future. For the Left this will be the Third World made manifest, "a new world in which men will treat each other with true respect."[34] By means of such a history the Left quests for a utopia which, judging from the agrarian faction within the Movement,[35] may echo the Puritan desire for an Edenic paradise regained.

Their sense of the present as well as of the nearness of the future—"try to bring this world into being immediately, by acting *now*"—has led the Left to a significant Puritan-like feeling for the future. Anticipating the future was terrifying for the Puritans because it meant the predestined damnation of most of mankind, as Michael Wigglesworth makes all too plain in *The Day of Doom*, in which he depicts the end of time when God's "flaming Eyes" and "ire, more hot than fire" will precipitate the earth's finish:

> The Mountains smoak, the Hills are shook, the Earth
>   is rent and torn,
> As if she should be clean dissolv'd, or from the
>   Center born.
> The Sea doth roar, forsakes the shore, and shrinks
>   away for fear;
> The wild Beasts flee into the Sea, as soon as he
>   draws near.[36]

For the select few, however, this terror will be followed by eternal glory and joy; for them there is finally no horror at all, not even in the loss of those who were dear to them on earth. So, the average Puritan felt an ambivalence, a vacillating sense of hope and despair, when he thought upon the last things.

The New Left is equally ambivalent about the outcome of the future. They too seek a futuristic new world, one of human dignity and joy preserved in universal peace. But this hope, often as forlorn as it was for the Puritan, is overshadowed by a terrible anguish emerging from the recognition that time may run out. For the Left the threat of an apocalyptic finish is as literal as it was for the Puritans, as literal, say, as that bomb in the film *Dr. Strangelove*. There exists in the Movement a pressure exerted by this sense of urgency, and it is this pressure which may well be a major factor behind the motivation of certain factions of the Movement, particularly those which advocate violence; "if our situation leads us to violence," they explain, it "is because the foundation of society is violence."[37] The impression that such groups sometimes give is that their violence will in some way purge society of its ills (for example, the song "Effigy" by the Creedence Clearwater Revival), that perhaps through their anticipatory violence they might stave off the final cataclysm they envision as the alternative to their utopian goals. This dread of the apocalypse is resounded time and again in Puritan-like imagery and with Puritan-like redundance in the new sermons of rock music and the film.[38] The end of the film *Easy Rider* is a good example, but the Jefferson Airplane sing a song entitled "The House at Pooneil Corners" which musically and poetically is especially relevant because in tone and imagery it is not so far removed from Wigglesworth's *The Day of Doom:*

> Everything someday will be gone except silence
> Earth will be quiet again
> Seas from clouds will wash off the ashes of violence
> Left as the memory of men
> There will be no survivor my friend
> Suddenly everyone will look surprised
> Stars spinning wheels in the skies
> Sun is scrambled in their eyes
> While the moon circles like a vulture.[39]

New England Puritanism and the New Left, then, share this feeling that they are working for salvation while the earth is at the very verge of time. Either an older, "fallen" time will pass away or time itself will come to an end. For both this sense of impending doom has led to an emphasis on the present, on the individual (as a private self and as a member of a collective identity) who becomes an agent of historical change. The political-saint must be alert and he must act now in the immediacy of his present experience; his action may be violent or nonviolent, but it must be militant. The New Left sees itself, as did the Puritans, as both the vanguard and the final force for life and truth at the close of history. For them time is short and the future is now.

Notes

1. Daniel J. Boorstin, *The Decline of Radicalism* (New York: Random House, 1969), p. 128.
2. See Michael Walzer, *The Revolution of the Saints* (Cambridge: Harvard Univ. Press, 1965).
3. Alan Simpson discusses this problem in *Puritanism in Old and New England* (Chicago: Univ. of Chicago Press, 1955).
4. Rick Margolies, "On Community Building," *The New Left: A Collection of Essays,* ed. Priscilla Long (Boston: Porter Sargent, 1969), p. 360.
5. Howard Zinn, "Marxism and the New Left," *The New Left,* p. 59.
6. Leszek Kolakowski, "The Concept of the Left," *The New Left Reader,* ed. Carl Oglesby (New York: Grove Press, 1969), pp. 146–147.
7. Nathaniel Ward, *The Simple Cobler of Aggawam in America,* ed. P. M. Zall (Lincoln: Univ. of Nebraska Press, 1969), p. 10.
8. Jerry Rubin, *Do It!* (New York: Simon & Schuster, 1970), p. 38.
9. Kolakowski, *op. cit.,* p. 146.
10. See Perry Miller, *Errand into the Wilderness* (1956: rpt. New York: Harper & Row, 1964), pp. 1–15.
11. Steve Halliwell, "Columbia: An Explanation," *The New Left,* p. 207.
12. See Max Weber, *The Protestant Ethic and the Spirit of Capitalism,* trans. Talcott Parsons (New York: Scribner, 1930).
13. *The Works of Anne Bradstreet,* ed. Jeannine Hensley (Cambridge: Harvard Univ. Press, 1967), p. 273.
14. See Rosabeth M. Kanter, "Communes," *Psychology Today,* 4 (July 1970), 53–57ff.
15. Margolies, *op. cit.,* p. 360.
16. C. George Benello, "Participatory Democracy and the Dilemma of Change," *The New Left,* p. 414.
17. John Winthrop [Speech to the General Court, July 3, 1645], in *The Puritans: A Sourcebook of Their Writings,* ed. Perry Miller and Thomas H. Johnson (1938; rev. ed. New York: Harper & Row, 1963), I, 206–207.
18. Margolies, *op. cit.,* pp. 363, 364.

19. Increase Mather, *The Life and Death of That Reverend Man of God, Mr. Richard Mather* (Cambridge, Mass., 1670), p. 11.
20. C. Wright Mills, "Letter to the New Left," *The New Left Review*, No. 5 (Sept.-Oct. 1960), p. 23.
21. "A Divine and Supernatural Light," *Jonathan Edwards: Representative Selections*, ed. Clarence H. Faust and Thomas H. Johnson (1935; rev. ed. New York: Hill & Wang, 1962), p. 106.
22. Barbara and Alan Haber, "Getting By with a Little Help from Our Friends," *The New Left*, p. 294.
23. Mather, *op. cit.*, p. 6.
24. Margolies, *op. cit.*, p. 361; see also Herbert Marcuse, *An Essay on Liberation* (Boston: Beacon Press, 1969), p. 20.
25. Haber, *op. cit.*, p. 294.
26. *Ibid.*, pp. 302, 308. Cf. Rubin, *op. cit.*, pp. 117–123.
27. *The Poems of Edward Taylor*, ed. Donald E. Stanford (New Haven: Yale Univ. Press, 1960), p. 50.
28. Truman Nelson, *The Right of Revolution* (Boston: Beacon Press, 1968), p. 33.
29. Barbara Deming, "Nonviolence and Radical Social Change," *The New Left*, pp. 70, 71.
30. Zinn, *op. cit.*, p. 67; Hilary Putnam, "From 'Resistance' to Student-Worker Alliance," *The New Left*, p. 334.
31. Margolies, *op. cit.*, p. 367.
32. Zinn, *op. cit.*, p. 59.
33. Régis Debray, "Revolution in the Revolution?" trans. Bobbye Ortiz, *Monthly Review*, 19 (July-August 1967), 16.
34. Deming, *op. cit.*, p. 69.
35. Of late, however, a note of cynicism has arisen in regard to this matter; see, for instance, Ray Mungo, "If Mr. Thoreau Calls, Tell Him I've Left the Country," *Atlantic Monthly*, 225 (May 1970), 72–86.
36. *The Puritans*, II, 590.
37. "The Appeal from the Sorbonne," *The New Left Reader*, p. 269.
38. New Left ideology has for the most part thwarted art, as did the theology of the Puritans. The writing of the Movement is frankly didactic, often given to mere cant; it evidences a baldness in both imagination and technical skill, two things which doubtless must be attributed somewhat to the idea that one should "tell it like it is." Such a notion, like the Puritan reliance on the Bible and desire for a "plain style," denies the very accouterments of art.
39. © RCA (1968).

IV. American Peoples

American Indian Religion and Christianity: Confrontation and Dialogue

Carl F. Starkloff

It is the conviction of Jesuit priest Carl F. Starkloff that the Christian's desire to communicate Christ to mankind must not obscure his appreciation of the cultural differences of those with whom he carries on dialogue. The church's role in relation to the American Indian, for example, should be thought of not in terms of proselytism but in terms of a sharing of cultures. The Christian would do well to let the Indian educate *him* in poetry of religous expression, joy in creation, reverence for all things, and a passionate attachment to the divine. Such qualities are exemplified by the Arapaho tribe of Wyoming—a people who possessed a lofty tribal morality prior to the coming of Christianity. Father Starkloff has spent considerable time among the Arapaho, and their religion is the principal subject of his essay (reprinted from the Spring 1971 issue of the *Journal of Ecumenical Studies**). Author of *The Office of Proclamation in the Theology of Karl Barth*, he has also published several articles on Friedrich Schleiermacher and on religious experience. Assistant Professor of Theology at Rockhurst College, Kansas City, Missouri, Father Starkloff spent two years teaching at St. Stephen's Mission in Wyoming and two years as chaplain at Haskell Indian College in Lawrence, Kansas.

* 1936 N. Broad St., Philadelphia, Pa. 19122.
The proximate preparation for the present article was done with the aid of a grant from the U.S. Office of Education and the Department of Health, Education and Welfare, in association with Rockhurst College. Needless to add, the work would have been impossible without the assistance of members of the Northern Arapaho Tribe, especially Messrs. Ben Friday, Ralph Antelope, Scott Dewey, William Shakespeare, Pius Moss and others too numerous to mention by name. The hospitality of the James Spoonhunter and Lloyd Jenkins families provided me with important occasions for learning.

IN UNDERTAKING AN ARTICLE to discuss the possible rapport or "ecumenism" between Christianity and American Indian religion (more specifically here, Arapaho religion[1]), I am well aware of the limitations involved. Apart from the white man's inevitable tendency to misinterpret Indian actions and statements—a tendency that increases with what one is tempted to call "understanding"—there are also growing manifestations of another obstacle. Indians themselves now often show indifference or hostility towards efforts by whites to meddle in their internal affairs, of which religion constitutes the Holy of Holies. I need not expatiate on the problem of the growing emphasis on separation and distrust that has arisen out of centuries of broken faith in white North America's dealings with Indian peoples. Vine Deloria, in his angry, sarcastic, sometimes unfair but basically accurate book, *Custer Died For Your Sins*,[2] has already covered ground that this writer could not presume to violate. The Sioux Deloria's unequivocal rejection of white society's efforts on behalf of Indians could well be a deterrent to further overtures at dialogue. And yet dialogue we must; the alternative is hatred and suspicion. If this article makes any contribution to such dialogue, it will be by advocating a policy of mutual enrichment and fulfillment between the Indian religious tradition and the Christian, in my own case Roman Catholic, tradition that has so often suppressed it and contributed to the religious vacuum of which Deloria speaks. I would in fact speak more cautiously about "Christian Indians," if this corresponded to the real situation, and would then advocate dialogue along the lines of what is taking place between Christians and other religions of the world. But there are so many actual situations dealing with Indians who are also Christians and wish to remain so, that it seems important to explore the possibilities of one's being a Christian according to traditional tribal religious practices. There are indeed precedents—Ricci in China and de Nobili in India, to name just two. This study, however, could also be applied simply to an investigation of the intrinsic value of Indian religion in itself.

Religion to the Indian people is perhaps the only possession which gives them insulation against the massive culture shock of the last three centuries or more. If the loss of these practices and traditions, for those who still follow them or have returned to them, is implied in "ecumenism," they will reject the overtures out of hand. If ecumenism means that whites can lay profane hands upon the sacred things of Indian belief, in order to "integrate" these into white society, the response will be that "Go back to Europe!" often heard today on reservations. The writer's experience with the Native American Church on the Wind River Reservation is a case in point. Although several influential Arapaho men, friends of mine for a decade, had planned to "put up" a peyote meeting for two of us Catholic priests, this plan was vetoed through the efforts of a committee of the Native American Indian Church,[3] with the argument that what a white man writes, especially if he is a priest, cannot likely tell the truth about any Indian practice or custom. My disappointment over this development, given time to settle, gave way to a grudging admission that such a charge is probably well-founded and accurate, even in the case of one who may be highly sympathetic and supportive. Over the years, I had become friendly with many Arapaho families and other Indian people, and count many of them among my friends (to employ a very risky and clichéd phrase!). Yet, all of these are persons reared at least nominally in a Roman Catholic or other Christian tradition, and consequently I could not lay claim to an understanding of the mentality of the Indian whose native religion is his exclusive "ultimate concern" (and the number of these is growing). Hence my decision to write almost exclusively as an outsider looking in, and even as one willing for now to suspend efforts at integration, in favor of a preliminary exchange of ideas and attitudes. It may be that both sides need to separate and reconnoiter for a time.

There is a guarded remark in Vine Deloria's book, at the end of his invective against Christian missionary efforts, that an Indian Christianity could be of great value to our society. To *allow* this to happen would be the duty of Christian denominations, first, by ceasing to be "denominations" (the overriding scandal in Christian history), and second, by permitting the rise of a national Indian Christian Church. "Such a Church would incorporate all existing missions and programs into one national church to be wholly in the hands of Indian people."[4] The role of the Church, ideally operated by an Indian clergy and assisted by Indian lay boards, would be to implement the redemption and growth of reservation society; the Church would be integrated into the ongoing life of the tribe. This is Deloria's challenge to the churches, calling them back to unity and to a genuine role in the improvement of religious life without destroying native cultures.[5] The present writer is himself skeptical about such a possibility ever being realized. Nevertheless, as a Christian convinced of the vocation of men to unity with diversity (an Indian ideal as well), I have taken up the challenge in at least a small effort at dialogue.

There are further imperatives calling us to seek this intercultural understanding. To begin with, we believe that Christ came, not to destroy, but to fulfill true religion, and that He negates only that "religion" denounced by Barth and his followers—not a religion at all but mere human effort to seize hold of the divine and control it. So that white Christians may learn that this arrogance is totally alien to Indian religion, and thus not try to impose on them foreign cultural concepts and moralisms against "idolatry," this article might serve as a contribution to the education of the white Christian.

The same Karl Barth, who so violently denounced man-made religion, could also write that the Word of God, being free and unfettered, can speak to man not only through the Bible and the Church, but through a concert, a flower, communism, or a dead dog. If this is the case, we can follow with Schleiermacher's assertion that there is a spontaneous religious sentiment in all men, especially in children. We need not re-travel the old route of the battle over the "point of contact" between grace and nature here: belief in creation as a gift and therefore as grace precludes such a struggle. The value of Schleiermacher's notion lies in the importance of appealing to a child's spontaneous ("natural" if you will) religiousness by not thwarting it with theological distinctions before it is ready. Most Indians, young and old, with whom I have spoken, have told me that they see no necessity of conflict between their religious traditions and Christianity— certainly not, we might add, when Christianity is demythologized out of its white cultural *cul de sac*. But in agreeing with this, Indians also insist on the need to educate their children from infancy onward in Indian religious traditions, which appeal to the child's spontaneous reaction to his environment. The education of the Indian child, then, is coterminous with the education of white people to appreciate Indian distinctiveness.

Christianity likewise offers much to the Indian. In proclaiming Christ, it also offers a theology of progress to social justice, implementing his own belief in the Indian destiny to unite mankind through suffering. The modern Christian tradition can help the Indian to articulate and deal with modern problems, as he approaches them with his natural reverence for nature—a reverence that does not lightly accept naive theories of "progress." Pauline theology, especially, now under attack from various separatist groups, can actually demonstrate both an equality before God transcending racial barriers and a respect for the differences of culture within a united community.

It would not be honest to deny that Indian religion, like all religions, needs reform and revitalization. As we shall see later, there is decadence here, no doubt generally caused or occasioned by the invasion of foreign cultures. Most American Indian tribes retain at least vestiges of traditional practices, and many tribes, such as the Sioux, Arapaho, Shoshone in the north and Navajo, Apache, Pueblo in the south, have held onto many rites in their purity. Yet, the general situation of Indian religion is like the situation of Indian culture as a whole: it exists largely in the memory of the elders, not without a vestige of despair about its future. Among Indian youth there is not yet widespread interest in revival. But the various tribes are probably closer to their identities than are white Americans; with encouragement, a renaissance is possible—a renewal that could benefit both Indian and White. Young Indians in some areas are showing renewed interest in returning with college degrees to their reservations to work for their people, and religion figures large in their plans. Hence, the most practical plea for reform of White and Indian alike should no doubt be a mutual search for valid forms of thought, symbol, worship, and community life. The result may be, hopefully, not "Christianity" as we now know it in its fragmented form, but the "assembly of Christ," realized beyond present decadence and confusion on all sides. If this writer shares Deloria's pessimism about any near realization of this cooperation, he still feels under the Pauline injunction to "redeem the time." The redemptive process may turn out to be a combination of inspired activity by white Christians along with that immense admiration of the Indian for all that is sacred, especially for the sacred figure of Jesus the Christ. If the Christian seems to be unwilling to relinquish this in his search for ecumenical dialogue with the Indian, it is because he believes that Christ is transcendent to all tribes and cultures, but demands of none of them that they relinquish their identities.

By way of introducing a format for discussion, we should first take cognizance of the superb posthumous work of Hartley Burr Alexander, *The World's Rim*. This book, which ends with Tertullian's ringing and much disputed "Exclamant vocem naturaliter Christianam" (their cry is by nature Christian),[6] offers us as fine an effort at comparative study of American Indian religion as is available today. The author draws us a poignant picture of the plains Indian standing with arms extended on the "rim of the world, about which walk the winds," covered over by the sky-dome, descending upon the earth at its four cardinal points, praying to the Spirit and spirits who govern all of life.[7] In his ensuing descriptions of important Indian rituals and their rationale, which we shall leave mostly to the reader's own initiative here, Alexander makes strikingly evident what John Bryde has included in his monograph written for the education of Indian children: the Indian is a seeker for integrity, with God, with himself, with his fellow man, and with the world.[8] His search is for the I-Thou in the most extensive and deepest sense. All of Alexander's discussion contributes to this—the Sacred Pipe, the Symbol of the Tree of Life, the Sioux myth of the Abiding Rock whereon stood the Great Elk whose baying summoned the first morning of the world.[9] There are various agricultural myths and rites whose sophistication and poetic content are not exceeded by the classics of Greek and Eastern mythology. One also finds among the Indians, says Alexander, a sense of a "world time" (*kairos* in the New Testament is a similar concept) that transcends chronological time, demonstrating that man's destiny is not profane but sacred, and that, while creation is not God, neither is it so secularized as to lose its redemptive value.[10] As the Kurahu tribe prayed in its contemplation over the life cycle of the earth, "This is very mysterious; we are speaking of something very sacred, although it happens every day."[11] Man will ultimately be granted transcendence even over this cycle, according to most tribes, in a life to come.[12] Thus, to the Indian, nature is sacramental, life is sacramental, and man only shares in these "for an allotted span of petition and proof."[13] There is therefore a deep sense of the mystery of death, dramatized by Indian ritual, for the Indian spirit, like all spirits, protests against death's ultimate victory and love's seeming defeat.[14]

Within the pattern of the Indian sense of self and universe then, we find an integrity that brings all things into one and recapitulates them, to use a Pauline image. In order to discuss the Indian religion, and especially, from personal experience, the Arapaho tradition, in an orderly manner, I have chosen to employ three "categories" used by Joachim Wach. In his *The Comparative Study of Religions*, Wach evaluates religions according to the way in which they respond to man's ultimate concern in *thought*, in *action*, and in *fellowship*.[15] The remainder of this article will be an attempt to relate the religion of the Arapaho people to this pattern.

Response in Thought and Symbol

The great integrity in traditional Indian religion, before it began to suffer from outside attack, renders a categorical analysis difficult. It is possible, however, to follow Wach's simple classifications, allowing for the inevitable overlapping that is found in the totality of a tradition. I have chosen here to discuss the more refined points of the Arapaho belief, both as traditional, and where it could be verified through personal contacts, as it exists today after a century of Christian influence. We shall not spend time, therefore, on the many colorful legends and myths that form part of the folklore. Modern Arapahos do not include these as history, but, as one experienced informant explained, as "fairy tales" that belong to the tribe's oral tradition.

Monotheism

The most carefully defended theological assertion with every Arapaho is that of the Creator of all things—a monotheism reaching back untraceably into antiquity, certainly long before contact with missionaries. This adamant attachment to the uniqueness of God has always been one of the reasons for Arapaho astonishment at the denunciations often levelled at their worship by zealous but uninformed missionaries. However, much as in the Old Testament and all ancient religions, and to some extent in the New Testament, the Arapaho have had many names for Him whom we call "God," as well as many symbols and titles attributed to other supernatural realities. Kroeber gives the name *Hixtabä Nih'a^n ca^n* ("above-White Man") as the Arapaho designation for the God of Christianity.[16] But other titles figure as prominently and are more ancient. We find the expression *Hei-sanäni* ("Our Father"), who, according to Dorsey and Kroeber, may have originally been an apotheosis of Nih'ancan ("White Man"), the legendary epic and anecdotal hero of the tribe. We read, "After this, Nih'a^{n}ca^n lived in the sky and was called our Father."[17]

The title of "Father" is sometimes referred to the Supreme Being, but He is also addressed as "Grandfather,"[18] a title given, as noted above, to "Above White Man" as well. God is of course ultimately the Great Spirit; Indian notions of divinity are anything but materialistic. Here the Arapaho tongue developed a word not unlike the *Wakan Tanka* ("Great Mystery," "Great Holy") of the Sioux and perhaps like the "I am who I am" of Exodus: God is called *Jevanauthau,* generally translated as "The Unknown on High," but also, perhaps by application of other titles, "Father Above." *Jevanauthau,* on the other hand, may also be another pronunciation of *jevat-Nih'a^{n}ca^n,* meaning "White Man-above." Whatever title is used, however, it does not seem to have seriously occurred to most Arapahos, even to those who no longer practice formal religion, that one might ever make an assertion of atheism. Whether this sense of the numinous among Indians even today will ever yield to sophisticated arguments disproving the existence of a Supreme Being is not possible to say, but no culture has ever been free from such a confrontation.

Creation

One dare not proceed into Arapaho religion before he has clarified the question of the unicity and sovereignty of the Supreme Being (a term which, incidentally, does not seem to be an abstraction to the Arapaho), because in myth and symbol many supernatural and preternatural beings emerge, along with apostrophes to the elements under human titles.[19] Thus the narratives are not theologically explicit affirmations of monotheism. However, everything but the One Above comes under the concept of creaturehood, with a strong awareness of the "otherness" of God, who gave men all of creation as a gift. St. Paul's denunciation of those gentiles who confused creature and Creator in Romans 1:25 finds a parallel in the Arapaho conviction that, while nothing created is wholly "profane," neither is any creature divine. A sense of this appreciation of man's creaturehood is voiced in every Arapaho prayer, which is always an integral expression of petition, praise, and thanksgiving.

Appreciation of creaturehood is perhaps the central belief in Arapaho and all of Indian religion. We can find numerous examples of this, with ramifications that spread out into worship and ethical conduct. Thus for example, we read the prayer of Hawkan before the erection of the Offerings Lodge for the 1902 rite, a prayer very much like those recited today:

My father, Man-Above, we are sitting here on the ground in humble spirit and of poor heart, and ask your tender mercy upon us, one and all. Through the merits of your children who taught us this law of the Sacred-Offerings-lodge which we are about to locate, may we do it in such a manner as to obtain your favor and increased good spirit, to the end of the lodge! Give to us all our spirit and abundant mercy, and let us unite in one spirit toward you, who made us and ordered these things! My Grandfather, the Light-of-the-Earth, please look down this day upon your poor and needy people, that whatsoever they may do in their behalf may be pleasing to you! Now, my Mother-Earth, take pity on me, poor creature, and guide me straight! Let me do these things right, in the way your servants used to do![20]

Hartley Burr Alexander asserts that the plains Indians in general believed man to be, not "autocthonous" or born of earth (although the reference to Mother-Earth leaves us with some question as to this), but "heaven fallen," having come from the hand of God.[21] The most detailed and full account of creation available to non-Arapahos, because of the involvement of the story with the secret Pipe tradition, can be found in Dorsey's dissertation *The Arapaho Sun Dance*, already mentioned.[22] In the beginning there appears a primordial man, carrying his precious companion, the Flat Pipe (Säetca^n), walking on an endless expanse of primeval sea. Dorsey and Kroeber indicate that the Flatpipe itself is the Creator,[23] but the imagery does not seem to bear this out, and contemporary Indians profess more a deep veneration for the pipe as a sacred eternal archtype of divine providence. However, there is today a wide variety of ideas as to how to understand the pipe, depending on one's religious affiliation. The man of the story laments that he has no place whereon to lay his pipe, which is his faithful companion. At his loud cry of "Hea" repeated over and over again, various creatures appear to give the man assistance. An account follows of how the man sends different animals down into the water to find the earth. None of the beasts succeeds until the turtle (one of the most highly venerated of beasts among the Arapaho today) dives for a seemingly endless period of time and finally emerges with small clots of red mud adhering to his claws, or as some today say, around his eyes and on his breast. The man then takes the mud and, using his pipe as a drying rack, begins to form layers of mud over the deep until the surface of the earth had been created.[24] Then the animals seem also to take on human form, or to metamorphose from human to beast and back again, and many of them are given special roles in the life of the earth, while the man finishes his task of creation, and he looks upon it and is pleased with its appearance. Another account of the creation of man emphasizes his fallenness and limitation. After Father-Above gives the Arapaho the middle of the earth to live in, and the land around to other humans, we read,

Then man's life was ordained. The one with the turtle moccasins threw a buffalo chip into the water, saying: "As this floats, let the life of man be." But Nih'ancan threw a stone and said: "Let man's life be like this, for if all live, there will be no room for them." And so men die.[25]

The implications of Arapaho symbolism in the doctrine of creation are of course among those celebrated today among whites as a witness to the Indian's natural "ecological" sense. Nature is composed of "good omens," representations of the providence of God; all creation is sacramental. Creatures, of whatever kind, are thus "spirit-filled," as the prayer and thought of the Arapaho show us when carried to the height of his apostrophe to all creatures as having ears to hear him when he speaks in prayer. Alexander's discussion of the Sun Dance as celebration of creation and re-creation[26] will be borne out when we discuss Arapaho worship, especially the remarkable beauty and nobility of the Sun Dance.

Alexander again tells us of a tradition of the Messiah among the Pueblo, and consequently of the historical nature of their religion. The Creator and His assisting spirits dialogue: "Then was Gucumatz filled with joy. 'Thou art welcome, O Heart of the Sky, O Hurakan, O Streak of Lightning, O Thunderbolt!' 'This we have created and shaped will have its end,' they replied."[27] The author comments,

None but a mind seasoned by the centuries and acquainted with thought of human destiny could have formed this judgment; it lifts out of myth and into philosophy, recording not merely the transient gloss of a sensuous imagination playing upon the broken surfaces of nature, but the depth-shadowed thought of a mind long matured in reflection.[28]

This same sense of destiny is witnessed to by Willoya and Brown in their description of the Indian messianic tradition, with its emphasis on purgation and suffering as the creative power that will make the Indian people the ultimate shapers of unity at the end of history.[29] The Arapaho possess this eschatological sense, some of them connecting it with a gradual transformation of the Sacred Pipe itself. It is true, too, according to the as-yet-unpublished paper of William Shakespeare, an Arapaho anthropologist, that his tribe also has a traditional belief in reincarnation.[30] We must further acknowledge that the Sun Dance celebrates fertility and the cycles of the seasons among other phenomena. But this cyclicism, like that of Christian festivals, seems to have more a liturgical value than anything else. The tribe possesses a belief in an ultimate eschatology, a sense of the "last things," which seems already to accept a final destiny for man. Knowledgeable Arapaho today will tell inquirers that the participants in the Sun Dance face the rising sun to dance because it is from the East that the Christ will have His Second

Coming. Indeed, the nomadic life of the Arapaho is itself analogous to the pilgrim spirit of the Old Testament prophetic spirit, which looked to a future and ultimate resting place to be bestowed by Yahweh alone. Thus, the celebration of creation is not an attempt to abet the process of natural cycles, although it respects this too, but more to seek personal re-creation for individual and tribe, and an ultimate New Creation. This takes us into an examination of the Arapaho response to the Divine in action, both through ethical doctrine and practice, and through worship. Between worship and morality we find a remarkable balance and integrity, at least in theory.

Expression in Action

Worship

To separate worship from morality, especially from community, is impossible in the study of Indian religion. While one cannot learn all of Indian tribal morals and ethics from worship ceremonies, it is possible by examining them to arrive at the fundamentals of moral conduct. De facto, most Indian tribal customs and sanctions have been radically altered by the breakdown in culture, whether a Christian would consider this to the good or not. What we are concerned with here are attitudes rather than specific practices, and we shall therefore examine Arapaho worship before we discuss the ethical and communitarian attitudes connected with it. It is in the notion of tribal solidarity that we find the seeds of communitarian life and worship.

The most elaborate and carefully prepared ritual among modern Arapahos, and the one we shall concentrate on here, is the "Sun Dance," now carried out in the Arapaho tribe only by those resident in Wyoming. In former times, until about a decade after the turn of the century, the Sun Dance was a Southern Arapaho rite, performed in Oklahoma. Now any Southern Arapaho wishing to enter the ceremony must journey to Wyoming to do so, and many do make the trip each July, much in the spirit of a great family reunion. But although the dance is now a Wyoming custom, the massive study by George A. Dorsey of the Oklahoma rites of 1902 and 1903 is still invaluable for an understanding of the current practice—an interesting comment in itself on the phenomenon of oral tradition. We find even greater value in this illustrated book today, in light of the fact that the tribe, rightly fearing commercialism and the abuses of tourism, forbids any form of photography or sketching on the Sun Dance grounds, and will confiscate any equipment brought in for that purpose. There is also a shorter account given by Kroeber and Dorsey, and this is helpful.[31] Neither writer, however, since both men are research anthropologists, attempts to speculate on his data. In this article, I shall take a page from Alexander and try to combine data with a comparative religious commentary.

To romanticize the Indian is probably a greater disservice to him than to attack him openly. So I am especially cautious in praising the celebrated attractive elements in Indian tradition. Nonetheless, there is no doubt about the natural Indian gift for poetic expression and inspiring prayer, especially in a "shared prayer" that comes far more spontaneously to him when he is with his own than it does to white Americans who are now struggling to learn it. The following is one of many examples given by Dorsey, the prayer of the old man Hocheni as he begins the preparatory rites of the Rabbit Lodge and eventually the Sun Dance itself:

My Grandfather, Light of the World; Old-Woman-Night, my Grandmother—I stand here before this people, old and young. May whatever they undertake to do in this ceremony, and may their desires and wishes and anxieties in their everyday life, meet with your approval; may the growing corn not fail them and may everything that they put in the ground mature, in order that they may have food and nourishment for their children and friends. May whatever light comes from above, and also the rain, be strengthening to them, that they may live on the earth under your protection. May they make friends with the neighboring tribes, and especially with the white people. May the tribe be free from all wrong, from all crimes, and may they be good people.[32]

This prayer, now over half a century in the past, was responded to with enthusiasm when read by a clergyman at the opening of the Arapaho Community Pow Wow in June of 1970. It still expresses the spirit of Indian worship.

"Sun Dance" is a misnomer for this rite, although the title can be justified in light of the Sioux practice of calling it a "dance facing the sun." In Arapaho, the service is called *hasiha"wu*, or "Ceremony of the Offerings Lodge,"[33] the term "offering" being more inclusive and expressive of all that occurs during the three-day period. The dance is an affair that follows three or four previous days of the aforementioned "Rabbit Lodge," a commemoration of the hunt and the Indian closeness to nature and what it offers him. Around midnight on Thursday, the dancers, all men who have made a vow to carry out the ritual (there were thirty-six in 1970), enter into the previously constructed Sun Dance Lodge—a circular structure some forty feet in diameter, made from cottonwood trees and branches and other foliage. The description and photographs in Dorsey's work show a very close similarity to the lodge of 1970. The dancers have now begun a three-day total abstention from food and drink. They don elaborate paint and costumes, painstakingly prepared by mothers, wives, or grandmothers and applied by a sponsor or "grandfather." The honor of one who completes the ordeal is felt by his entire family, the reward of what has been perhaps a year-long series of preparations.

The dancers move into a circle around the lodgepole, decorated for the present with offerings of sage, sweet grass, colored clothes, and a symbolic buffalo skull.[34] A fire burns a short distance away. This religious dance, unlike the rapid and athletic dancing done by the men at a social pow wow, is stationary and sedate—a mere rhythmic raising and lowering of the body on the balls of the feet to the beat of drum, chants, and rattles. The dancers hold eagle-bone whistles in their mouths and blow on these to the beat of the drum. During all the dancing, one of the two chief dancers—the yearly sponsors of the lodge—waves a carefully constructed sacred wheel[35] in the direction of the pole. All gestures made to the pole—whistling, dancing, waving of the wheel or of eagle feathers—are a prayer of petition for courage and strength from the Tree of Life and ultimately from the Creator.

On the first night, dancing ceases around 2:30 A.M., and the dancers retire to sleep within the lodge on beds of reeds, wrapping themselves in large ceremonial quilts and still wearing their ritual paint of the day. Shortly before sunrise on the following day, and also on Saturday and Sunday, the celebrants are awakened, don their garb once more, and stand alongside their "grandfathers" in a horseshoe formation, facing out of the east entrance, in the direction of the rising sun—the noblest of divine gifts to man. A clergyman then steps into the center of the lodge, faces the pole, and prays aloud for the dancers and their intentions. The drums then begin their solemn beat, the dancers extend their arms toward the sun, and begin once more the vertical swaying of the Sun Dance rite, again "whistling to the sun" as they dance. The medicine wheel is now waved to the sun, which begins to rise over the horizon and slowly bathes lodge and painted dancers with its rays. There were many spectators, both white and Indian at the ceremonies of this year, and all were silent. Speech now would be profane indeed, as all things become relativized to the praise of the Creator who sends daily life to man, who renews the seasons, cleanses men from their sins, and accepts the offerings of men of good will. With such a tradition behind him, the Indian might well be the silent one he is reputed to be. Especially in the realm of mystery, symbols and gestures put all speech to shame as mere chatter. The dance then ceases once the sun is full in the sky, and the participants retire to rest for most of the morning.

Each day of the rite, a ceremonial bathing and repainting of the dancers takes place, following individual bowing to the earth to venerate the altar of sods, reeds, and the buffalo skull, commemorative of the gifts of earth.[36] Dancing generally resumes around 4:00 P.M., to continue until dark, and again resumes along towards midnight. As the ordeal progresses, one can observe fellow tribesmen and women seated within the lodge and standing about, offering encouragement to the dancers, who are engaged in both an offering of the flesh and a test of that stamina for which Indians are known. A deep sense of empathy, symbolic of a tribal solidarity that transcends petty feuds and differences, is now prevalent, expressed by the unabashed remark of one of the women, "My heart bleeds for them." All spectators are somehow drawn into the spirit of this endurance, and will stand for many hours under the scorching Wyoming sun and in the sudden dust or rain storms that blow up there, manifesting their union in trial with the dancers. Many women join in a sympathetic fast for one or more days.

In this particular celebration, it was on Saturday in the afternoon that the Sacred Pipe was carried on foot (as it must be, according to tribal rule) from its resting place several miles away, by the Keeper of The Pipe, and was brought ceremoniously into the lodge. Here, wrapped in the hide of a buffalo, another beast given to man from the foundation of the earth, it was hung from a tripod close to the lodge pole. At this point in the Dance of The Offerings Lodge, all worshippers are invited to "cover the Pipe."[37] This is an individual ceremony much like a visit to the tabernacle in a Roman Catholic church, in which the one wishing to venerate the Pipe covers the entire tripod with a beautifully decorated quilt, often made for the occasion. This quilt is a gift to the Pipe and thus to the Creator, but will later be passed on by some of the women to needy persons of the tribe. The worshipper first spreads the quilt carefully, then lays his or her hands over the offerings with arms outspread, rests his forehead on the top of the tripod, and prays in silence for several minutes.[38] These same practices take place on Sunday as well, until dancing begins around 5:00 P.M., continuing until about 8:00, when dancers may rest for a time if they wish. Formerly there was a ceremony sometime on the final day, in which the ears of children born since the last lodge ceremony, or of those who had not yet been initiated, were pierced, in token of their having been pierced by a lightning bolt and of future protection from arrows.[39] This ceremony was reduced to mere symbolic piercing by 1902, and was not done at all in the 1970 performance. Dancers were formerly tortured by the famous breast-piercing on this final day, but this had ceased before the turn of the century, mainly because it had been considered a preparation for battle.[40]

At about 8:00 on the last night (Sunday), the west end of the lodge is ripped out, leaving a gaping exposure in the direction of the setting sun, which was to set over the mountains by around 8:45. The Sacred Pipe is again reverently carried out through this new exit and taken to a specially erected tepee. The drums begin again, and the dancers now dance to the setting sun, their vows nearly fulfilled.[41] Dancing continues until the Evening Star can be seen above the mountains, and then the offering has been achieved. Bathing and feasting follow in the tepees of Indians camped on the grounds or in homes of friends or relatives. The feast for the participant, who must eat and drink too gingerly to enjoy it, is given by the "grandfather" who has cared for him, painted, clothed, and instructed him, and above all, given him heart to continue.

Ethics

It is in reflecting on the above sketch of the Sun Dance rite that one comes to see the interweaving of the cultic and the ethical in Arapaho religion. The Ceremony of The Offering Lodge is above all a ceremony of re-creation, a Lent of suffering, undertaken because of a vow, to seek a grace, amend a fault, or render thanks, and it ends in a resurrection celebration of emergence from the lodge. Just as the Arapaho dance to pray a requiem for their dead, so too they dance to seek physical and spiritual regeneration. The author, during a discussion with several veterans of the Sun Dance (a man may enter the lodge four times, and three more by special indult), was given to understand that Arapaho symbolism of creation is directed at spiritual and moral rebirth. "Communal penance" is built into this ritual, without, however, a public confession of sins as often takes place during a peyote rite. One participant remarked on his decision to overcome a drinking problem while alone with his thoughts in the Offerings Lodge.

Walter Eichrodt has discussed the prophetic message of the Old Testament as being an attack on both magicalism, which seeks automatic results through ritual, and "moralism," which eliminates all cult in the name of priggish ethical preachments.[42] The Indian possesses the germ of such prophecy deep in his tradition, and it is in one sense unfortunate that the tradition is only an oral one, because numerous prophets have emerged from arduous "vision quests" to lead their people.[43] Magicalism and moralism are both prophetically avoided in Arapaho ritual. Rites are carried out exactly, as the author was told, not out of the fear of an angry God, but because things should be done "just so" out of respect for order. (Ritual, as we know in the case of alcohol among the Jews and peyote among the Indians, seems to prevent the abuse of these elements.) Neither is sacrifice considered a form of what Lutherans would call "works righteousness," at least not when properly performed. When dancers fast, or when they formerly pierced their flesh or gashed it, they were not "bribing" the Deity, but surrendering their flesh to Him, rendering back part of that which was given to them.[44] Alexander compares such rites to the "freeing from the flesh" of Christian tradition.[45]

In all things the Indian tradition seeks unity for man with God, with man himself, with the universe, and with one's fellow man.[46] All symbolism manifests this search for integrity. The sacred numbers and colors used in ritual and decoration are aimed at this search. The number 4 among the Arapaho signifies perfection,[47] and the numbers 5 and 7 develop it. Figures like the rhombus, square, cross, and circle indicate perfect wholeness, as when prayer is made to "The Four Old Men," or the four directions and the four elements of summer, winter, day, and night.[48] Kroeber writes,

Of course, this connection is given in nature by the four quarters determined by the sun, whose manifestations form the greatest visible phenomenon in the world, and there probably is more or less causal relation; but the connection extends to human matters, not in any direct relation with nature.[49]

Even the fertility rite formerly connected with the Sun Dance was itself a search for this integrity with nature and its cycles. Everything that is done in ritual, writes Alexander, is part of a search for that purity of heart that will see visions.[50] Without being conscious of it, Indian religion is naturally "ecological"; harmony with and respect for nature are essential, and this must extend to harmony among men. Alongside the rather flamboyant fairy tales about Nih'ancan, we also find fables about the Badger-Woman, condemning adultery and deception and other antisocial actions.[51]

Let me emphasize that, as in all traditions, abuses can be widely observed. The Indian's harmony with nature is soured at times by a discordant note as one sees the litter and wreckage on the reservation. Indian tradition was not equipped to cope with technology and artificial waste. In human ecology, alcoholism is a grave problem, and family breakdown is not uncommon. A great number of modern Indians themselves seem to have little reverence for ceremonies like the Sun Dance, and the problem of a carnival atmosphere on the premises must be coped with. But solutions to these, we might suggest, will not likely be found by imposing white Christian versions of metanoia on the Indians, but by helping them to rediscover their own culture, religious symbols, and mores, in dialogue with the modern world in which they must live. The melancholy of man's fate, wrote Martin Buber, is that he must objectify and depersonalize his relationship with nature if he is to make progress as a person. But he must also develop a higher I-Thou relationship with nature as well. It may not be too late for pragmatic and objectivist white society to learn something from Indian history about this problem.

Expression in Fellowship

Community is the goal of morality as well as of religion. We have spoken of community with God and nature thus far, and it remains to discuss more in detail how this sense of God—man—nature—fellowship complements and spills over into a human fellowship and solidarity. In some respects, modern society can probably never return to or encourage the close simple tribalism of former days among all Indians in a tribe and among tribes. Yet it can learn much from such solidarity, and Christian "missionaries," whatever their *modus agendi* in the future, will have to be ruthlessly self-denying in their attitudes and their efforts to understand. A brief discussion of the relation between worship and community may aid this understanding.

The reader is urged to consult the works of Alfred Kroeber and other such works of the same anthropological series for details on Arapaho mores before the breakdown from tribal to reservation life.[52] It is enough to say here that individual ethical conduct was tightly sanctioned relative to tribal needs, especially in respect for life, property, and marital integrity. In this treatment, I shall try to illustrate the close relationship that the Arapaho sense of "the Holy" had and still has to solidarity in community. "Secularization" is hardly a meaningful concept to the Arapaho, if that word is taken to mean a code of conduct free of religious motivation and sanction. Whether this connection is strictly a hallmark of primitive culture is for the reader to decide, but anyone reading the works of Eliade will hesitate to push secularization to the degree of ruling out the primitive that is part of essential human nature.

The closeness of man to God, world, fellow man, and to his own self is illustrated in a typical Arapaho prayer quoted by Kroeber—a prayer before eating:

Our Father, hear us, and our grandfather. I mention also all those that shine (the stars), the yellow day, the good wind, the good timber, and the good earth. All the animals, listen to me under the ground. Animals above ground, and water-animals, listen to me. We shall eat your remnants of food. Let them be good. Let there be long breath and life. Let the people increase, the children of all ages, the girls and the boys, and the men of all ages and the women, the old men of all ages and the old women. The food will give us strength whenever the sun runs. Listen to us, father, grand-father. We ask thought, heart, love, happiness. We are going to eat.[53]

Worship enters integrally here, without artificiality or intrusiveness. Solidarity is realized because men and women share in the elements of nature, and the sharing may or may not follow a religious event.[54] Hospitality is given the greatest attention, and sharing is an essential note of Arapaho gatherings. St. Paul would never have to rebuke these assemblies as he did those in Corinth in 1 Corinthians 11—at least not when the Indian feasts are conducted according to tradition.

The author has had a number of occasions over the years to share such hospitality, and to be part of the solemnity preceding it. Seated in a circle on the floor of the home of a "grandfather" as he serves a feast to his Sun Dance "grandson's" family, one is caught by the air of solemnity. The blessing, recited in Arapaho, is long—perhaps ten minutes or more. The Creator is thanked for the grace of the Offerings Lodge, and as the prayer progresses, He is besought for every spiritual and temporal need of those present. Eating goes on then without extensive conversation, though speech is not forbidden either.[55] The Arapaho are not loquacious people, and traditionally do not chatter rapidly. A reticence sometimes mistaken for unfriendliness pervades the atmosphere, charged with special respect if a member of the feast has completed the Sun Dance ordeal. At the end of a meal, with a handshake of thanks, those present carry off a portion of what remains, for any who may be hungry at home; sometimes bags are brought for this purpose. This is quite a practical matter, of course, because Indians even today are not strangers to hunger and deprivation. But along with this, a certain "sacramentality" is in evidence, as the visitor, if he is not an Indian, has to be reminded that he must take some food home to his family or friends. The celebration must be extended into other homes, and none should be in want, if such can be avoided.

Hospitality within the Arapaho tribe, and towards outsiders with whom they desire to be friends, extends to gift-giving of a magnanimous nature. According to Kroeber, "The giving of presents is a very extensive practice among the Arapaho, as among all the plains Indians. . . . Within the tribe, gifts are also very frequent, especially on ceremonial occasions."[56] An Arapaho desires to "give the very best," as I was told, and when he wishes to show friendship, spares nothing of his possessions. This is certainly a "weakness" to modern society, when opportunists and exploiters are on the scene. But to the Arapaho, who is still little touched by the ethics of individualism, the material gesture of the bond of friendship is sacred. And there is a religious foundation to this in the rituals: in addition to the food offered at religious festivals, gifts are given in wide variety and of great value. We have already seen how the Arapaho, never impractical, does not destroy the beautiful quilt offerings made to the Sacred Pipe, but distributes them to the needy. What is offered to God is not rendered profane when it becomes a gift to a human being. Prominent also at the Sun Dance, as at other times, is a "give-away" extending over two days, when families, generally represented by the mother, give away clothing, household items, jewelry, and the like to other persons or families. We can leave liturgists and sacramental theologians to draw their own conclusions about the symbolic values of "gifting" here.

We must realistically acknowledge the negative side of a spontaneous tribal sense, of course. Tribalism can also be a grim experience for the individual, and although Indians are also religious individualists in some sense, they are subjected to intense societal pressures. Such pressure has been witnessed by the author while working among young Indian college students at a boarding school, where the practice of "shaming" by the group can reduce an individual to submission and often to desperation. Perhaps here is where true Christian *agape* is most needed—a love that can assist the spontaneous generosity and solidarity of the tribe to transcend merely natural reactions and become a gesture of love that is greater than mere emotion.[57] Here, of course, example alone will turn the trick, with the working of grace, and it is the lack of the former that explains why Indians often do not in practice draw such lessons from Christian pastoral efforts.

Conclusion

This article has merely scratched the surface of the vast potential for Indian-Christian dialogue as a replacement for imperialism, which in generations to come will be doomed to failure even if attempted. Hopefully I have emphasized the most obvious sources for rapport in thought and symbol, worship and social conduct, and encouraged an opening of attitudes that would make the practice of Indian rites a possibility for Christian Indians. This should not be done uncritically, of course, but there seems to be no reason why such rites as the Sun Dance, Pipe Covering, and Sweat Lodge, as practiced by the Arapaho, should not be considered as possible "para-liturgy," and even as cultural settings for Christian worship for Indians who so choose. Such an opening of interest on all sides could then lead interested persons into further comparative study of symbols, archetypes, myths, and goals of history. This is already being discussed and experimented with in some quarters by Christians on traditional Indian missions. The position of a tribal religious leader, for example, might be fertile soil for the introduction of a new form of diaconate, according to Indian culture and rituals. But the word "ecumenism" is used here designedly;

white-Indian relations indicate a two-way street, and Indian religion offers insights to Christians that might have been long neglected. Recent attempts at liturgical celebrations of Earth Day, and efforts to develop more esthetic and sensually pleasing worship are cases in point. Thus, we should not think merely of "Christianizing" Indian rites, and of imposing a clerical dominance on them. It will be far more authentic if these become rituals practiced by Indians who are Christians, with clergy at most in a guest role, or responding to invitation to include Christian sacramental ministry within certain cultural settings.[58]

I wish to close this work with several important references to the book of H. B. Alexander. What struck this great philosopher-anthropologist was the sweep of thought and symbolism within native American cultures. He observes the traditions. With men like James and Huxley, the American Indian sees through the material world to its Ground:

It is not a material labyrinth in which the soul of man has been incidentally trapped, but it is rather a sense-born phantasm, as Plato held it to be. Nothing is more obvious in Indian thinking than his belief that the Powers are the Realities, and that shapes and functions of things are primarily the exercise of those powers. . . . In the language of our own metaphysics, the Indian is an idealist, not a materialist.[59]

One might not choose to accept this "system" of thought. No Indian would, if he gave it consideration, argue over the defense of idealism, for to him the world is very real, however impermanent. All that genuine Indian religion, when given its true scope, endeavors to remind us of is that we must look beyond the *phenomena* to the *gignomena*, as Alexander writes, to a life that is not merely physical but moral.[60]

Indian myth universally tells of an age of Stone Giants— huge, strong, stupid; like the earthformed men of the Kiché myth their sight was veiled, they had no intelligence, they could not utter the name of their Creator; and this first race was destroyed, or transformed into its kindred rock. Life in a genuine and endowed form issues from another source, and it is instructive that in more than one account the living corn is the substance of man's first flesh, while his intelligence is from the breath of heaven.[61]

I would suggest that, as so often in the past, most lately in the crisis theologians of the post-World War I era, a naive optimism was exploded to turn men back to acceptance of the Real deep within them and transcendently above them, so now in Indian religion men might find a similar experience. What makes for genuine progress is faith. God alone is the only sufficiency of the human mind, says Alexander in writing of the central element of Indian faith.[62] Indian suffering, and the ordeal of Indians over the centuries in the face of every kind of natural and moral catastrophe,[63] makes them a people who will never cleave to a mere "other-worldly" religion. Union with God will be reached only through unity with Earth—as in the past days of hunting and planting, so now in the days of social struggle and scientific progress. But never can man forget the Ultimate. We can hear the *Soli Deo Gloria* even more resoundingly in this powerful and simple Arapaho "Lord's Prayer":

> Father, have pity on me!
> Father, have pity on me!
> I am crying for thirst;
> There is nothing here to satisfy me![64]

Notes

1. The Arapaho are a tribe of Algonquian linguistic stock, who migrated westward from the Minnesota area some three to four hundred years ago. They are closely related to the Gros Ventres and the Northern and Southern Cheyenne. There are approximately 3500 Northern Arapahos sharing the Wind River Reservation in central Wyoming with the Shoshone tribe. This tribe has been more active in conserving the Arapaho religious tradition over the last fifty years. Another portion of the tribe has lived in Oklahoma since the late nineteenth century, and is statistically listed with the

Southern Cheyenne, with a combined population approaching 5000. These statistics can be found along with other valuable information about the social and economic status of American Indians in: *American Indians, Facts and Future: Toward Economic Development for Native American Communities* (New York: Arno Press, 1970), p. 435. This is a publication of the Joint Economic Committee of the U.S. Congress.

2. Vine Deloria, *Custer Died For Your Sins: An Indian Manifesto* (New York: The Macmillan Co., 1969), pp. 101–104 especially.

3. The author had intended a discussion of the Peyote Cult and its place in Indian religion as part of this article, but since there was no opportunity to experience a meeting, this will not be included, even though informants imparted to me their fund of factual knowledge and experience. For a full study of the peyote matter, cf. Weston LaBarre, *The Peyote Cult* (Hamden, Conn.: The Shoe String Press, 1964, enlarged edition), and Molly Stenberg, "The Peyote Cult Among Wyoming Indians," Laramie, 1945. This latter is a master's thesis for the University of Wyoming, and goes into great detail. The author of this work personally shared in a meeting before the founding of the Native American Church in Wyoming. My own evidence from this and other data is that, while peyote is not a traditional part of ancient Indian religion, it would be most unwise for either political or ecclesiastical authorities to try to suppress it. Some evidence indicates that it is a very positive force for unity among tribes.

4. Deloria, p. 123.

5. There is clearly here a hearkening back to an old danger of national churches and their attendant separatism. However, at times such groups seem to be a strong identifying factor and to serve as a transition aid to full and equal entry into the mainstream of a culture.

6. Hartley Burr Alexander, *The World's Rim: Great Mysteries of the North American Indians* (Lincoln: University of Nebraska Press, 1969), p. 232. For additional Indian background, see also Alexander's *North American Mythology* (Cambridge, Mass.: The University Press, 1916).

7. *Ibid.*, pp. 34–35.

8. John F. Bryde, *Acculturational Psychology or Modern Indian Psychology* (United States Department of the Interior, Bureau of Indian Affairs, 1967), pp. 7–8.

9. Alexander, p. 43.

10. *Ibid.*, p. 78.

11. *Ibid.*, p. 111.

12. *Ibid.*, p. 126.

13. *Ibid.*, p. 184.

14. *Ibid.*, p. 222.

15. Cf. Joachim Wach, *The Comparative Study of Religions*, Ed. Joseph M. Kitagawa (New York: Columbia University Press).

16. George A. Dorsey and Alfred Kroeber, *Traditions of The Arapaho* (Chicago: Field Columbian Museum, Anthropological Series, 1903, Vol. V), p. 16.
17. *Ibid.*
18. On this, cf. Mircea Eliade, *Patterns in Comparative Religion*, Trans. Rosemary Sheed (Cleveland and New York: Meridian Books, The World Publishing Co., 1967), pp. 134–135. One Arapaho informant, speaking from six decades of experience, emphatically denied that the Arapaho ever employed the name "Grandfather" for the Creator-God. Its use in English translations of the prayers may either be mis-translations, or else a name given to less personal elements found in nature, such as the directions of the four winds or, as in the case of footnote 19, the sun as giver of light and life.
19. Cf. the various prayers in George A. Dorsey, *The Arapaho Sun Dance: The Ceremony of The Offerings Lodge* (Chicago: Field Columbian Museum, 1903).
20. *Ibid.*, p. 79.
21. Alexander, p. 91.
22. Dorsey, pp. 191–203.
23. Dorsey and Kroeber, *Traditions of The Arapaho*, p. 2.
24. Dorsey, in his volume on the Sun Dance, p. 198, relates this story to the ceremony of the digging of sods for the Sun Dance Lodge altar.
25. Dorsey and Kroeber, p. 17.
26. Alexander, pp. 138–139.
27. *Ibid.*, p. 98.
28. *Ibid.*, pp. 98–99.
29. William Willoya and Vinson Brown, *Warriors of The Rainbow* (Healdsburg, Calif.: The Naturegraph Press Co., 1962), pp. 62–80.
30. William Shakespeare, "The Northern Arapaho," unpublished paper delivered at workshop in Landar, Wyoming, in August, 1969. p. 35.
31. Dorsey and Kroeber, pp. 1–50 esp.
32. Dorsey, p. 36. Generally it is current practice on each of the three mornings of the Sun Dance, to invite a clergyman of the various church groups to open the day's solemnities with a prayer before the lodge pole. 1970 was memorable in Wyoming for the Roman Catholic Church, since it was the first time in memory that a Roman Catholic priest opened a Sun Dance service.
33. Alfred Kroeber, "The Arapaho, Part IV: Religion," *Bulletin of The American Museum of Natural History*, Vol. XVIII, pp. 279–454, New York: May, 1907. p. 280. This entire volume of the Bulletin is devoted to the work of Kroeber on the Arapaho—their general description, art, and religion.
34. Cf. Dorsey, p. 112, for details. Alexander, pp. 150–151, makes much of the Tree of Life symbolism here. Some modern Arapaho of Christian persuasion refer to the central pole and its twelve extended beams as representing Christ and the twelve apostles. This adaptation is not far-fetched,

since Dorsey, in this work (p. 112), says that the pole also stands for Man-Above.

35. Dorsey, pp. 12–13, explains the symbolism of the wheel perhaps being the serpent surrounding the earth at creation. Symbolism differs according to different accounts. On pp. 142–143, Dorsey describes the dance with the wheel, and this has not changed noticeably since 1903.
36. Cf. Dorsey, pp. 118–119, for details.
37. This is not the same ceremony as the elaborate Pipe Ceremony described by John G. Carter, "The Northern Arapaho Flat Pipe and The Ceremony of Covering The Pipe," *Bulletin 119, Bureau of American Ethnology Papers, No. 2*, Smithsonian Institution, 1936, pp. 73–101. This is a four- to seven-hour ritual still practiced in the tribe, and rarely, if at all in these days, open to white people.
38. A comment made by an Arapaho, speaking of another occasion of religious solemnity, was that "Indians have to *touch* everything!" There is indeed no trace of puritanism regarding material things. In the light of contemporary psychology, we can appreciate the soundness of Indian esthetic worship and its "tactile" nature.
39. Cf. Dorsey, pp. 179–182, for details and history.
40. *Ibid.*, p. 179.
41. This is called by the Arapahos "gambling against the sun." Cf. *Ibid.*, pp. 150–151.
42. Walter Eichrodt, *Theology of The Old Testament*, trans. J. A. Baker (Philadelphia: The Westminster Press, 1961), pp. 364–369.
43. On prophecy among Indian peoples, cf. Alexander, pp. 186 ff.; Willoya and Brown, *passim*; Harry W. Paige, *Songs of The Teton Sioux* (Los Angeles: Westernlore Press, 1970), *passim*, and pp. 133–178.
44. Cf. Shakespeare, p. 45.
45. Alexander, p. 148.
46. Cf. Bryde, pp. 7–8 and *passim*, on this.
47. Kroeber, p. 412.
48. Dorsey, p. 113, goes into detail on the symbolism.
49. Kroeber, p. 413.
50. Alexander, pp. 164–167. Dorsey gives a description of the modified rite of 1902, pp. 172–178. This rite is not included at present in the Wyoming version.
51. Dorsey and Kroeber, pp. 190–203.
52. Shakespeare's work is very helpful throughout on this history and its interpretation. The paper can be obtained by contacting the Wind River Indian Agency in Fort Washakie, Wyoming.
53. Kroeber, p. 314.
54. Molly Stenberg gives a description of the feasting ritually connected with the Peyote Rite.
55. Another Arapaho custom gives weight to the Christian notion of the interweaving of liturgy of word and sacrament. When a young person in the tribe wishes to learn from older per-

sons, he traditionally gives a meal for them, and once fellow-ship has been established by this, conversation comes more naturally, and wisdom is imparted from young to old.

56. Dorsey and Kroeber, p. 18.
57. Willoya and Brown, *passim*, discuss this kind of ideological integration of prophetic goals.
58. Leaders of contemporary Indian festivities on the Arapaho Wind River Reservation, as a matter of fact, generally en-courage their charges to bear witness to their good will by a faithful practice of their Christian religion, if they are such. Most Christian pastoral effort concentrates now solely on Indians who are Christians.
59. Alexander, p. 230.
60. *Ibid.*
61. *Ibid.*
62. *Ibid.*, p. 231.
63. Cf. also Joseph Epes Brown, *The Sacred Pipe: Black Elk's Account of The Seven Rites of the Oglala Sioux* (Norman: University of Oklahoma Press, 1963, 1970). This book is a moving recital by Black Elk himself, edited by Brown, of the last effort of the Sioux to preserve their traditions and faith for posterity. With Paige's book (note 43), it is helpful for understanding the status of Indian religion today.
64. Alexander, p. 226.

They Sought a City: The Black Church and Churchmen in the Nineteenth Century

Lawrence N. Jones

"Black church history," writes Lawrence N. Jones, "is a testimony to the hope and strength which the Gospel provided for a powerless people, who had little more with which to seek to change their oppressed condition than the moral power and suasion inherent in the faith." Tracing that history as it unfolded in nineteenth-century America, Dr. Jones concludes that the Black church "was effective mainly because it never was free to separate its interior institutional life from its mission in and on behalf of the world." But the dream of a "beloved community" that was pursued by the Black churchmen of that period is still a dream deferred. A member of the faculty at Union Theological Seminary in New York City since 1965, Dr. Jones was named Professor of Afro-American Church History at the seminary in 1970; his paper, originally delivered as an inaugural address marking that occasion, appeared in the Spring 1971 issue of the *Union Seminary Quarterly Review*.* On July 1, 1971, he took on an additional responsibility—the deanship of the seminary.

IT IS SIGNIFICANT that Union Theological Seminary should have initiated a professorship in Afro-American Church History. By this action it affirms the validity of the subject as an area of intellectual inquiry and seeks to fill a vacuum in a vital dimension of its academic offerings. It is, simultaneously, attesting the importance for the total Christian community of the spiritual pilgrimage of the largest minority in America. In the light of this action it would seem to be important to comment briefly upon the question posed

* 3041 Broadway, New York, N.Y. 10027. Reprinted by permission.

by, and the uses of, Black church history for church historians and for the self-understanding of the Church.

The history of the Christian community among Blacks is one of the neglected areas of scholarship in America. Only one book has been written in the last fifty years dealing with the Black church from an historical perspective.[1] To be sure this history has been alluded to obliquely in some of the general texts, but the major works dealing with American church history have treated the Black churches only casually and only insofar as they were affected by events occurring within the larger, dominant religious establishment. Indeed, one may observe that the Black man has been, until recently as invisible in American theological scholarship as in other areas of American life. From whatever perspective Black church history is viewed, it is a fallow field for scholarship. Fortunately, more and more documents of that history are becoming available and with the careful study and research now being done the future is promising.

But what are the particular uses of Black church history and what is the nature of the questions it poses, to the majority Christian community, and especially to Blacks themselves? The first question that suggests itself is why has this area of the Church's life been so long neglected? The very existence of this new interest in the subject and the recognition of the inadequate manner in which it has been treated creates the necessity for church historians consciously to evaluate the assumptions upon which they have selected the content of the histories they have produced. What and who deserve inclusion or exclusion? From a theological and historical perspective, Black church history raises the particular question of what is integral to the common memory of the whole Church and is therefore important to its self-understanding. Moreover, it provides a perspective from which the incongruous fact that it exists at all can be examined. The presence of a separate Black segment is a commentary on the failure of the evangelizers to embody in themselves the *koinonia* and witness which are the informing tenets of their faith. Thus, Black church history is useful as a mirror to the dominant Christian community of its failures. A minority people to whom the rights and privileges of a community have been denied are peculiarly well-equipped to reveal to that community where it has been unfaithful to the commandments of its Lord. Similarly, this aspect of American church history, faithfully written, shatters the comfortable myths concerning people of color by which the dominant Christian groups have lived, and is an illuminating record of the way religious institutions image forth and embody discriminatory racial attitudes of the culture with which, by definition, it is in tension. Finally, Black church history makes available to the total Christian community the experience of one of its important constituent parts, and whatever of spiritual or theological or religious insight is there becomes the possession of all.

If the study of Black church history is important in its own right for the reasons given, it has decisive importance for Black people in general and for the Black Christian community in particular. In the earlier phases of its history, especially until the end of the Civil War, Black history and Black church history intersected at so many points as to be virtually identical. Thus to understand the history of the religious strivings of Blacks is to gain important insight into their total history.

A study of the religious institutions in the Black community is a means of access to its spiritual roots. This is especially true since its theology is not formal but one which is a response to and engaged in the interior life of the community as it wrestled with God and the meaning of its existence. Black theology has always been in the main contextual and existential. Because it was not filtered through the categories of classical western theology it has an earthy, often crude, but always related-to-the-community quality. In the churches, particularly in the period prior to the Civil War, faith and order, and life and work were so closely intertwined as to be indistinguishable from each other. Because its content is the interplay of the community with its immediate relationship to the life situation, Black church history provides its contemporary descendants a means of appropriating their spiritual heritage and affirms that Black Christians are an integral part of the total fellowship of believers. It provides a common memory, uniquely its own and yet congruent with the memory of the Christian faithful in all times. It is important for a minority people to know that their forebears were not dilatory in the pursuit of the justice denied them, nor in the quest for freedom, and to recognize the important part the Christian faith and the Church played in that struggle. Such history is a source of self-validation and provides a sense of continuity with the past and a perspective from which to view the present.

Moreover, Black church history is a testimony to the hope and strength which the Gospel provided for a powerless people, who had little more with which to seek to change their oppressed condition than the moral power and suasion inherent in the faith. From the standpoint of the self-understanding of Black people, this particular history is of decisive importance because it redefines the perimeters of a gerrymandered history and includes Blacks as integral to the history thus redefined. In this sense, Black church history is a kind of counter-history because it does not fully share conventionally accepted understandings of what constitutes history. As history, it is primarily concerned with an oppressed people, with their religious pilgrimage, and with the quality of life available to them as these have been a concern of particular Christian institutions. Black church history questions whether or not the study of rulers and war, of conquests and kings, of educational, industrial, and scientific development should be the primary focus of historical concern. As an alternative it postulates that the greatness of a society is most adequately to be observed in the quality of existence available to the most disprivileged of its people.

In summary, one may observe that that with which we have to do here is an understanding of history, which if not new, has not been exploited. This understanding challenges some of the accepted canons of the guild of historians and asserts that the feelings, aspirations, and struggles of individuals and people to achieve their full potential and humanity are of equal importance with the conventionally accepted data of history. It raises the question as to whether or not the uncritical, exclusive concentration on whites in American history is not ultimately shortsighted and self-deluding. By its very existence, Black church history is a vigorous assertion that that with which we have to deal in America is a vital pluralism, and a national culture to which all races and creeds have contributed. In this sense it introduces a reality principle into the self-concept of the Christian community and of the nation.

They Sought a City

> O Yes,
> I say it plain,
> America never was America to me,
> And yet I swear this oath—
> America will be![2]

We have been believers . . .
And in the white gods of a new land we have been believers in the mercy of our masters and the beauty of our brothers, believing in the conjure of the humble and the faithful and the pure. Neither the slavers' whip nor the lynchers' rope nor the bayonet could kill our Black belief. In our hunger we beheld the welcome table and in our nakedness the glory of a long white robe. We have been believers in the New Jerusalem.[3]

It is the thesis of this paper that American Blacks, particularly the minority who joined the Christian community, pursued in the 19th century a dream, the twin aspects of which are poetically described in these writings of Langston Hughes and Margaret Walker. On the one hand, their primary faith was anchored in the convictions concerning sovereignty, righteousness, justice, and mercy of God. They looked forward to the New Jerusalem—the city of God. On the other hand they possessed an implicit hope, rooted in the Declaration of Independence and in the Constitution, that one day the ideals enshrined in these historic documents would be actualized and that there would arise an earthly city, a beloved community, in which they would be citizens with all the rights, prerogatives, and responsibilities with which white men were invested. To be sure, at all periods in the history of Blacks in America there have been those who have despaired that the earthly aspect of the dream would ever be realized, because they have despaired of the will or even of the capacity of white Americans to make it a reality. The majority of Blacks were not exposed to, or did not accept, the vision of the New Jerusalem. But the dreams have persisted alongside each other. At different periods in the history of the last two centuries, the intensity of the dream of the New Jerusalem has been in direct proportion to the prospects for achieving the beloved community, though the struggle for the latter had never been entirely abandoned.

From the introduction of slaves into America in 1619 through the years of the Civil War, some measure of the despair of Blacks relative to achieving their dream is observable in the prominence of the heavenly aspect of the dream. There are many reasons for this despair, not the least of which were the repressiveness of the slave system and the deprived status of the Black freedmen. Moreover, though the Constitution and the Declaration of Independence enunciated high-flown ideals concerning "all men," Blacks knew that they were not included in that definition. This awareness was re-enforced by custom, by law, by institutional patterns, by church order, and by judicial decisions. Before the law and in the structuring of government policy, the Black man was a piece of property, though the Constitution did count him to be three-fifths of a man for purposes of determining the legislative representation of the various political units. It is an anomaly, in the constitutional sense, that property thus became one of the bases for determining the allocation of political power. Even the Church acquiesced in the judgment of the larger society in these matters. It rationalized this acquiescence by concentrating upon fitting the "souls of

Blacks" for the heavenly kingdom and upon helping the slaves to adjust to their dehumanized existence on earth. If slaves had no rights which white men had an obligation to respect, the Church appeared to be saying that God had no earthly purposes with which it needed to be concerned so far as the servitude or quality of life available to Blacks was at issue. Nevertheless, it needs to be observed that whatever its misguided conclusions concerning Blacks may have been, the Church was the only established institution in the society which undertook to communicate to Blacks the ultimate beliefs and hopes which both whites and Blacks shared and by so doing tacitly acknowledged that contrary to prevailing racial ideology, Blacks were in fact children of God, human beings, and thus their brothers.

Failure of the white evangelists. The efforts of white evangelists to proselytize among the slaves met with minimal success. When the 19th century dawned, only four or five Blacks in every one hundred in the country were included in church statistics as Christian. By 1860 the number had risen to between twelve and sixteen. Many of these "statistical" Christians were children because the Black adults appear to have been highly resistant to the Gospel. Scholars have adduced a number of reasons for the conspicuous failure of the churches in their attempts to evangelize the slaves,[4] but the central reason for the failure of the mission to the slaves lies mainly in the inability of these Blacks to reconcile the faith of the evangelizers with their conduct. They could not become adherents to a religion or worship a God whose self-acknowledged adherents acted consistently in ways that contradicted their teaching. The fifty thousand Blacks—out of the one million in the country—who had become Christian in 1800 did so in spite of, rather than because of, the evangelists. They were the pioneers in the faith from whom the Black Christian community has grown.

However small their number in a relative sense, they were the first to grasp the dream of the "New Jersualem." In the light of that dream, consistent with the moral imperatives that were explicit in it, and confirmed in their own humanity by its teachings, these Christian Blacks were moved to assume some measure of responsibility for the quality of life available to their fellow Blacks. The overriding and unifying concern of Blacks historically has been for freedom, and the pursuit of its prospects has been persistent, but in the last quarter of the 18th century those prospects were dim indeed. It is not strange, then, that though petitions were sent to state legislatures and to the Congress, the first organized activities of Black Christians had the twin purposes of making available the truths of the Gospel to their benighted brethren, and to carry on ministries of benevolence and self-help. These activities were necessary because they were virtually neglected by the churches insofar as evangelism was concerned, and because the structures of society ignored the physical needs and human rights of the disprivileged freedmen in their midst. The earliest Black church was the Baptist Church at Silver Bluff, S.C., which was organized around 1774.[5] Still others were to follow in the 1790's, but the first self-sustaining groups organized and controlled by Blacks were the benevolent or mutual aid societies, usually found in the cities of the northeastern seaboard.[6] In most instances, these benevolent or mutual aid societies were, in fact, quasi-churches and were only prevented from being identified as such because they could not agree on a denominational affiliation, or else that did not occur as an option. Their charters emphasized the care of widows and orphans, stipends to sick members, provision for the education of orphans, and excluded persons of questionable moral character from membership.[7] For this paper, the significance of the mutual aid societies lies in the fact that they were usually organized by preachers and Christians and that their meetings very much resembled worship services.

Early mutual aid societies. Viewed from one perspective, the Blacks' churches and mutual aid societies were the means by which aggressive Blacks pursued their individual visions of their own possibilities. The first pulpits of the men who subsequently provided leadership in the churches were the mutual aid societies. Moved by a strong evangelical commitment and perceiving themselves to have been called to preach the Gospel, the societies provided an alternative to the pulpits of the religious establishment to which they were denied fully accredited access.

That this was in fact the case is illustrated in the history of the Free African Society in Philadelphia, which was organized by Richard Allen and Absalom Jones. These men formed the Free African Society only after they were frustrated in their attempt to form a religious society which they had desired to do, they report, "from a love of the people of . . . [our] complexion whom . . . [we] beheld with sorrow because of their irreligious and uncivilized state."[8] They failed in this venture because too few free Blacks shared their concern and those who did "differed in their religious sentiments."[9]

As one looks at the rise of these institutions one is struck by the variety of gifts manifested by their initial leadership. Richard Allen is a case in point. Allen was aggressive, an astute businessman, a determined organizer, and a man of unquestioned integrity and zeal. But above all, Allen and many others who led in the founding of these churches and benevolent societies were pre-eminently evangelists, deeply committed to the truth of the gospel and zealous to communicate it to those who had not heard it. For them the "New Jerusalem" beckoned with an allure that made it desirable above all else. Nevertheless, they did not abandon their neighbors, and though their faith had an otherworldly caste, it was radically this-worldly in its day-to-day manifestation of brotherly concern.

Even though Allen was unsuccessful in establishing a church, he nevertheless continued to preach and soon had gathered some forty-two persons around him for prayer and worship. He and Jones, along with William White and Dorus Ginnings, even broached the idea of erecting a house of worship. He was opposed by both influential Blacks and by the clergy of St. George Church, who, according to Allen, "used every degrading and insulting language to us to try to prevent us from going on."[10] They were directly forbidden to continue their prayer services and meetings of exhortation, but they did not accede to these demands for the reason that ". . . we viewed the forlorn state of our colored brethren, and that they were destitute of a place to worship. They were considered a nuisance."[11] Evidently, as a result of Allen's preaching the numbers of Blacks attending the St. George Church became offensive to the whites and conditions were made so intolerable for them that they withdrew. The decision was made to affiliate with the Anglican Church because Bishop White expressed a willingness to ordain a Black to lead them. Allen refused the honor both of being ordained an Anglican priest and of joining the new congregation because he "believed that the plain and simple Gospel of the Methodist was best suited for his people."

The first Black churches. Once again Allen began to gather a group around himself, which must have been disheartening, because he had helped to procure the storefront in which those who withdrew from St. George first worshipped and had committed a substantial amount of his own money in the building of the first sanctuary. Like storefront pastors of a later day, he worked in order to preach and lead a congregation. Nevertheless, he persevered and in July, 1794, in a service in which Bishop Asbury participated, Allen opened the new church and named it Bethel. This was technically not a schismatic movement since Bethel was an official part of the Methodist conference with ministerial oversight and services to be provided by the clergy assigned to the St. George Church from which the Blacks had withdrawn. After protracted debate over who should own the property and over the monetary considerations to be granted to the ministers, and finally after a lawsuit in the Supreme Court of Pennsylvania in which the court affirmed the right of the Bethelites to control their own pulpit and other ecclesiastical affairs, the A.M.E. Church was officially established in 1816 as a separate denomination.[12]

The experience of Allen and his group was similar to that of the congregation which ultimately formed the African Methodist Episcopal Zion Church. They separated from the

John Street Methodist Society in New York because the church offered no possibility for their leaders to be ordained to the itinerant ministry. They, too, tried to maintain their ties to the Methodist Church but ultimately felt they had to withdraw. For twenty years or more, each one of these bodies sought to remain as a separate congregation within white Methodism, but in the end a formal rupture seemed the sole remaining option. The A.M.E.'s were so concerned that the whites might gain control of their affairs that they wrote into their charter a provision that no person not a descendant of the African race could be a member of the church. They inserted this provision to insure control over their property, and to affirm the right of the congregation to discipline its own members and to decide its policies. They hastened to add that they did not intend

. . . willfully or mentally anything bordering upon schism; contrary thereto we rejoice in the prospect of mutual fellowship subsisting between our white brethren and us, and in reciprocally meeting each other in our private means of grace as visiting brethren in bands, classes and love feasts.[13]

The pre-eminent religious reasons for the founding of separate Black institutions was the failure of all but a remnant of the white Christian establishment aggressively to pursue its mission on behalf of Christ among Blacks. Separate institutions were in part a response to the failure of white churchmen to treat their brothers with equity, respect, care, concern, and love.

As Blacks lived out the mission of the Church, it consisted of the task of freeing Black men's souls from sin and their bodies from physical, political, and social bondage, and of setting the conditions of existence so that they could achieve their full humanity. But if most white churches and churchmen did not fully share this understanding of mission, Black churches and churchmen had it unavoidably thrust upon them. Like their brothers outside the Church they were not free, and the single bond that bound all Blacks together, then as now, was their unfreedom. To be sure, the freedman had some prerogatives denied to the slave, but he was seriously proscribed by custom, by law, by judicial decision, and by his previous condition of servitude. Thus, not only did the churches have to deal with the internal problems common to religious institutions, they had to deal with the urgent problem of a nationally endorsed slave system, as well as with the almost universally held assumption that Blacks were inferior to whites.

The first national issue: colonization. The first national issue that confronted Blacks and their religious institutions rested upon this implicit assumption of Black inferiority to whites. This was the question of colonization. It is ironic perhaps that Paul Cuffee, a Black sea captain and a Quaker, had given some impetus to this idea by his successful voyage to Sierre Leone in 1815 with thirty-eight emigrants.[14] The American Society for Colonizing Free People of Color in the United States was organized in Washington, D.C., in December, 1816. This organization, with its president and twelve of its seventeen vice-presidents and all twelve of its managers from the South, and all of the latter slave holders, met with strong negative reactions from Blacks in both the North and the South. They were convinced that the purpose of the colonization effort was the removal of free Blacks, which would have the effect of discouraging further manumission and would leave the slaves more firmly in the grip of the slaveholders than ever before.

The most important meeting in public protest took place in Bethel Church in Philadelphia under the leadership of Richard Allen and James Forten. The resolutions passed by this meeting contained several important propositions delineating the objections of Blacks against the scheme. Many of them are reminiscent of the arguments in the current debates about civil justice and clearly articulate the vision of Blacks relative to their future in America. The preamble is instructive:

Whereas our ancestors (not of choice) were the first successful cultivators of the winds of America, we, their descendants, feel ourselves entitled to participate in the blessings of her luxuriant soil, which their blood and sweat manured; and that any measure or system of measures, having a direct tendency to banish us from her bosom, would not only be cruel, but in direct violation of those principles which have been the boast of this republic.[15]

Furthermore, the members of the assemblage declared their abhorrence of the stigma cast upon free people of color to the effect that "they are a dangerous and useless part of the community." They insisted that they would never voluntarily separate themselves from the slave population. "They are," the resolvers declared, "our brethren by the ties of consanguinity, of suffering and of wrong; and we feel that there is more virtue in suffering privations with them than fancied advantages for a season." Then, affirming their confidence in the justice of God and the "philanthropy of the free states," they expressed their determination to leave their fate in the hand of "Him who suffers not a sparrow to fall without his special providence."

Though the possibility of attaining the beloved community in America continued to be the dream of most Black Americans, there were always in their midst men who despaired of such a dream and felt that the only real solution for Blacks was to remove themselves from the presence of whites. This alternative remained alive during the nineteenth century and is alive today. I have already alluded to Paul Cuffee, but another leading churchman, Daniel Coker, one of the founders of the A.M.E. Church who had the honor of being elected the first bishop of the new church but declined the honor, espoused colonization as the solution to the situation of Blacks and was among the first eighty-eight emigrants sent out by the Colonization Society. Lott Carey, a Virginia clergyman, was among the second group of emigrants.[16] Though a man of some status in Richmond, Virginia, Carey's statement concerning his reason for emigrating might have been the reason most Blacks would have given:

I am an African; and in this country, however meritorious my conduct and respectable my character, I cannot receive the due credit for either. I wish to go to a country where I shall be estimated by my merits and not by my complexion, and I feel bound to labor for my suffering race.[17]

Despite the enthusiasm of men like Coker and Carey, colonization did not win many converts but it re-emerged everytime Black hopes were dashed by events in the nation. Thus, there was a resurgence in the fifties when the passage of the Fugitive Slave Law, the Kansas-Nebraska Act, the Dred Scott decision, the failure of John Brown's raid, and even the election of President Lincoln seemed to indicate that the dream was further than ever from realization.

(It is of interest that even Richard Allen, who was violently opposed to the American Colonization Society, should have been the principal endorser of a resolution of the Convention of People of Colour convened by him in Bethel Church in 1830, which tacitly endorsed the idea of emigration to Upper Canada.)[18]

During this period the colonizationists held three national conventions.

Among themselves they differed as to what would be the best site. Some opted for the Caribbean area, especially for Haiti, whose ruler encouraged their aspirations. Several preferred Lower California and the Far West of the United States. But the most popular place was Africa.[19]

Some Black congregations used the Colonization Society as a channel through which to support the cause of missions, but whatever usefulness the Society may have had was foreclosed for most Blacks because of the implicit racism upon which it rested.

Black Churchmen and the Anti-Slavery Movement

Despite the fact that the support which the colonization scheme garnered from the general public did not augur well for the success of their efforts, Blacks continued to pursue the elusive beloved community and held on more firmly to the hope of the New Jerusalem.[20] The ever-present stumbling block was their bondage in the South and the deprivation of their human rights in the North. In this effort they established alliances with whites who, to some degree, shared their dream. Even so, the efforts in which whites and Blacks worked cooperatively are comparatively few. As might be expected, these "integrated activities" usually involved the various local, state, and national anti-slavery and abolition societies. Here Blacks discovered a remnant in the Christian community, some identified with particular churches and others outside the church, with whom they could unite in the struggle for freedom.

William Lloyd Garrison was the charismatic figure at whose invitation Blacks began to enter the anti-slavery movement in great numbers. Though there had been numerous manumission societies before Garrison sounded his militant call in 1831, Blacks were not significantly involved. Garrison's invitation to the "free colored brethren" to join him came at a crucial time in their collective history, for as one historian has observed: "In 1830 the majority of the 320,000 free Negroes were in the habit of regarding all whites as their enemies."[21] Garrison was to be the exception that challenged the stereotype. When the Garrisonian movement split in 1839, Blacks tended to align themselves along geographical lines, with those in New England, for example, remaining faithful to the old "fire-eater." From the standpoint of this paper it is significant that the eight Blacks who were founders of the American and Foreign Anti-Slavery Society in May, 1840, were all clergymen.[22]

Prior to the split, Garrison had become increasingly caustic in his criticism of white clergymen and churches. With much that he said, Blacks found themselves in ready agreement, but they had considerable misgivings concerning his suggestion that they abandon their efforts to exploit the political process in pursuit of freedom. Moreover, they had misgivings concerning some of his theological ideas, as is indicated by the following quotation from a recent study of the Black abolitionists:

On one occasion they (the Blacks) stated that Garrison's opinions were not necessarily related to the abolitionist movement, and on another they pointed out that they were Garrison's followers so far as abolition was concerned, "but on religious points, we follow Jesus."[23]

Garrison had taken the position that the Bible was not divinely inspired, and he aligned himself with the anti-sabbatarians. This unorthodoxy struck at the bedrock upon which the faith of most Blacks rested. They believed in the Declaration of Independence and the Constitution and they believed that the political process there defined offered the best hope for eradicating slavery. Moreover, religiously Blacks were clearly at one with the dominant religious community in affirming the divine inspiration of the Bible.

In the debate and bitterness which followed the split of the abolition movement, many criticisms which Blacks had previously muted were expressed. White workers in the old society were charged with harboring racial bias. In language familiar in our own day, a Black preacher held up to ridicule a certain kind of abolitionist who hated slavery, "especially that which is one thousand or fifteen hundred miles off, but who hated even more 'a man who wears a colored skin.' "[24] Blacks felt that whites in the abolition movement effectually excluded them from positions of real power, and they charged that concern for the elimination of slavery as an institution was not balanced by a reciprocal concern for the humanity of all Blacks, slave and free alike. This second-class citizenship in the abolition societies was especially galling since presumably these particular whites were their friends. Even here the ugly head of racism was reared.

A similar indictment was leveled against the American Tract Society, the American Bible Society, and the American Sunday School Union. These groups were charged with ignoring the whole issue of slavery in order not to alienate those slaveholders who offered financial support.[25] The American Board of Commissioners for Foreign Missions was the object of analogous criticism.

But if Blacks were critical of the voluntary societies, they saved their most caustic criticism for the Church and for churchmen—to whom they had looked as their natural allies. As a matter of fact, Black and white Christians did share many values and concerns. Both believed that religion was a foundation stone to an ordered society and that the ordered society would to a considerable degree reflect in its laws and customs the commitments of the Christian community. Once again, however, the stone of stumbling in Black-white relations in the churches was implicit and often explicit assumptions of Black inferiority. Samuel Ringgold Ward reports that a learned divine in New Haven, Connecticut, had declared to Reverend S. E. Cornish that "neither wealth, nor education, nor religion could fit the Negro to live upon terms of equality with the white man."[26] Or again:

Another Congregational clergyman in Connecticut told . . . (Ward) that in his opinion, were Christ living in a house capable of holding two families, he would object to a Black family in the adjoining apartments.[27]

It is clear that opinions of this type were not restricted to New Haven, Connecticut, for Blacks early abandoned any hope that Christian churches would be the cutting edge in the effort to abolish slavery or to insure the human rights of Blacks. Nevertheless, they did not abandon their faith in God, nor in individual whites who demonstrated that they did not share the dominant racial ideologies.

It has already been indicated that the majority of Blacks were not won to the banner of Christ, or indeed were ever offered the option. Even some of those who shared the vision of the New Jerusalem couched their acceptance in certain qualifications. Nathaniel Paul, addressing a meeting celebrating the abolition of slavery in New York State in 1827, expressed confidence that slavery would be extirpated and that human rights would be accorded to Black men. Without this faith, he said:

I would disallow any allegiance or obligation I was under to my fellow creatures, or any submission that I owed to the laws of my country; I would deny the superintending power

of the divine providence in the affairs of this life; I would
ridicule the religion of the saviour of the world, and treat as
the worst of men the ministers of an everlasting gospel; I
would consider my Bible as a book of false and delusive
fable and commit it to the flames; nay, I would still go farther; I would at once confess myself an atheist, and deny
the existence of a holy God.[28]

Other black clergy and churchmen found in the Gospel a
mandate for the violent seizure of freedom. Among these the
most notable were David Walker and Henry Highland
Garnet, the latter a Presbyterian clergyman. Garnet coun-
selled his brethren, particularly those in slavery, to revolt as a
matter of Christian obligation. He wrote:

The diabolical injustice by which your liberties are cloven
down, neither God, nor angels, or just men, command you
to suffer for a single moment. Therefore it is your solemn
and imperative duty to use every means, both moral, intellectual, and physical that promise success.

. . . You had far better all die—*die immediately,* than live as
slaves, and entail your wretchedness upon your posterity.
If you would be free in this generation, here is your only
hope. However much you and all of us may desire it, there
is not much hope of Redemption without the shedding of
blood. If you must bleed, let it all come at once—rather
die freemen, than live to be slaves.[29]

But the promise of the dream and its possibilities for realization by other means prevailed. Some Blacks had quite
folksy theological reasons for their confidence. James Red-
path reported a conversation with a slave in Virginia in which
a bondsman, commenting on his reaction to what he heard
from the pulpit, said:

One day I heard [the preacher] say that God had given all
this continent to the white man, and that it was our duty to
submit.
"Do the colored people," I inquired, "believe all that sort
of thing?"

"Oh no sir," he returned, "one man whispered to me as the minister said that. He be damned! God am no sick fool!"[30]

Henry McNeil Turner, later to be a bishop for the A.M.E. church, forbade his congregation to sing the popular hymn, "Wash me, and I shall be whiter than snow," for the common sense reason that "the purpose of washing is to make one clean, not white, and that white is no more a sign of purity than black, and that God is not white."[31]

Actually most Black spokesmen did not join the issue at the level of critical theological reflection, but at the level of intuitive insight into the faith. Henry Ringgold Ward, a clergyman prominent in the antislavery movement, antici-pated the observations of European theologians coming later in the century in making a distinction between religion and Christianity:

Religion . . . should not be substituted for Christianity; for while a religion may be from men, and a religion from such an origin may be capable of hating, Christianity is always from God, and like him, is love . . . the oppression and the maltreatment of the hapless descendant of Africa is not merely an ugly excrescence upon American *religion* . . . no, it is a part and parcel of it, a cardinal principle, a *sine qua non*, a cherished, defended cornerstone of American faith. . . .[32]

Politics and Education

At the conclusion of the Civil War and with the subsequent passage of the 13th, 14th, and 15th amendments to the Con-stitution, Blacks were legally free and the dream of a beloved community in America seemed a possibility. But they soon found that freedom was more an illusion than a fact as state after state re-enacted discriminatory legislation which rein-stated the system which formerly applied to the freedman. By 1896, Blacks had lost any political leverage they had gained and most of their other hopes were in shambles. Simulta-neously there was a differentiation of function in the Black community. As labor unions, news media, business institutions and associations, political parties and alliances came into existence, the weight the churches bore in these areas was both broadened and expressed more locally. Leadership, too, began to be diversified and secular interpretations of the dream began to dominate.

When the hope that political activity might be the means through which their dreams for America could be achieved was dashed, Blacks turned again to education, which they had long viewed as the most promising avenue to their acceptance on a parity with whites and as a means to achieving their full humanity. Like most other Americans of the period, they shared the American creed that temperance, industry, thrift, and stable family wedded to education were the keys to the kingdom.

In the period of slavery, next to a godly life, no grace was more highly prized than the ability to read and write. The benevolent societies frequently had as a part of their purpose the provision of education for the children of the community. For example, the Bethelites in Philadelphia established a First Day School in March of 1796 and six months later inaugurated a night school for adults.[33] In Newport, Rhode Island, the African Union Society, a mutual benefit society, sponsored a free school in 1808 and in 1824 established an independent Black church.[34] In Boston, Prince Hall, founder of the Masonic order among Blacks, and a Methodist minister, organized a school in 1798 which was moved to the African Meeting House in 1805.[35] In city after city the Black free schools were established, often by anti slavery interests and other concerned whites, but more often than not by free Blacks. One indication of the A.M.E. Church's concern is evident in the resolution on education passed at the Nineteenth Session of the Philadelphia Annual Conference in 1834.

Resolved: That as the subject of education is one that highly interests all people, and especially the colored people of this country, it shall be the duty of every minister who has the charge of circuits or stations to use every exertion to estab-

lish schools wherever convenient, and to insist upon parents
sending their children to school; and to preach occasionally
a sermon on the subject of education; and it shall be the
duty of all such ministers to make returns yearly of the number of schools, the amount of scholars, the branches taught,
and the places in which they are located; and that every
minister neglecting so to do, be subject to the censure of
the Conference.[36]

Next to church buildings and related ecclesiastical activities, Blacks invested more of their resources in educational
undertakings than in any other community enterprise in the
nineteenth century. Some impression of the extent to which
education was esteemed is conveyed by the following observation of Booker T. Washington commenting on the freedmen's
drive for education:

Few people who were not right in the midst of the scene can
form any exact idea of the intense desire which the people of
my race showed for education. It was a whole race trying to
go to school. Few were too young, and none too old, to make
the attempt to learn. As fast as any kind of teachers could
be secured, not only were day-schools filled, but night-schools
as well. The great ambition of the older people was to try to
learn to read the Bible before they died. With this end in
view, men and women who were fifty or seventy-five years
old, would be found in the night schools. Sunday-schools
were formed soon after freedom, but the principal book
studied in the Sunday School was the spelling-book. Day-
school, night-school, and Sunday-school were always crowded,
and often many had to be turned away for want of room.[37]

The efforts of the Black churches to provide a means for
educating their members were monumental. By 1900 the Baptists were supporting some 80 schools and 18 academies and
colleges. In addition, the individual associations and conventions reported the publication of some forty-four different
newspapers and journals which were themselves instruments
of education. The A.M.E. Church raised over $1,100,000 for
educational purposes between 1884 and 1900 and supported
22 institutions providing education above the elementary

level. The A.M.E. Church established its first educational institution, Union Seminary, near Columbus, Ohio, in 1844. This institution was later merged into Wilberforce University which the church had purchased from the Methodist Conference in Ohio in 1856. In 1900 the A.M.E. Zion Church was supporting, as a denomination, eight colleges and/or institutes, while the Colored Methodist Episcopal Church had established five schools during their thirty years' history.[38]

These statistics of national bodies do not exhaust the extent of Blacks' commitment to education as the touchstone to the beloved community. In order to treat fully the total involvement of Blacks in the provision of educational opportunities for their children, one would have to survey all the denominations to which they belonged and to investigate their activities at the local level. Many of these activities are not available in the national statistics. Another index to the importance of education to the community is indicated by the fact that at the end of the century, the principal matters in public discussion were education and lynching, and that the nominal national leader was Booker T. Washington. In the debates that swirled around the controversial Washington, the efficacy of education was not in dispute, the style and kind of education was.

"A Dream Deferred"

It is a perilous task to compress the history of a people through a century within the compass of a forty-five minute lecture. Any such attempt is doomed to failure. As I reflect on what I have written, a central fact forces itself upon my consciousness. It is that though the Black Church was effective in the nineteenth century partially because of the circumstances of history, it was effective mainly because it never was free to separate its interior institutional life from its mission in and on behalf of the world. From the perspective of seventy years later, if the Black church has had a diminishing impact it is because it has turned more and more in upon itself, and faced less and less out towards the world. The primary shortcoming of the white Christian community in the 19th century was that it failed to include Blacks, the mote in its eye, as a primary source of its mission.

Thus, during the nineteenth century, the Black churches and churchmen vigorously pursued a dream. But in a paraphrase of Hebrews 11, they did not receive what was promised, yet the majority died in the faith that the dream was possible of achievement. What has happened to their dream is perhaps best attested by the following excerpt from the speech of Martin Luther King at the March on Washington in August, 1963:

I say to you today, my friends, even though we face the difficulties of today and tomorrow, I still have a dream. It is a dream deeply rooted in the American dream. I have a dream that one day this nation will rise up and live out the true meaning of its creed; "We hold these truths to be self-evident, that all men are created equal."
I have a dream that one day every valley shall be exalted, every hill and mountain shall be made low, the rough places will be made plain and the crooked places will be made straight, and the glory of the Lord shall be revealed, and all flesh shall see it together.[39]

And the dream is not yet.

Notes

1. Several volumes treating the history of individual denominations and E. Franklin Frazier's sociological interpretation in *The Negro Church in America* (New York: Schocken Books, 1963) should be mentioned, but no general histories have been produced since C. G. Woodson's *The History of the Negro Church* (Washington, D.C.: The Associated Publishers, 1921). *The Negro Church* by Benjamin E. Mays and Joseph W. Nicholson (New York: Institute of Social and Religious Research, 1933) devotes some eighteen pages to the historical backgrounds of the church but is more an analysis of them in the 1930's.
2. Langston Hughes, "Let America Be America Again," in

Langston Hughes and Arna Bontemps, eds., *The Poetry of the Negro 1746–1949* (New York: Doubleday and Company, Inc., 1949), pp. 106–108.

3. Margaret Walker, "We Have Been Believers," *ibid.*, pp. 180–181.

4. See e.g. Winthrop Jordan, *White over Black* (Chapel Hill, N.C.: University of North Carolina Press, 1968); or Stanley Elkins, *Slavery: A Problem in American Institutional and Intellectual Life* (New York: Grosset and Dunlap, 1963).

5. Walter H. Brooks, "The Priority of the Silver Bluff Church and Its Promoters," *Journal of Negro History*, Vol. III, No. 2 (April, 1922), 172–196.

6. August Meier and Elliott M. Rudwick, *From Plantation to Ghetto* (New York: Hill and Wang, 1966), pp. 74ff., 88–90.

7. "Preamble and Articles of Association of the Free African Society," Benjamin T. Tanner, *Outlines of the History of the A.M.E. Church* (Baltimore, 1867), pp. 140ff.

8. Richard Allen, *The Life, Experience and Gospel Labors of the Rt. Rev. Richard Allen* (Philadelphia, n.d.), pp. 14–15.

9. *Ibid.*

10. *Ibid.*

11. *Ibid.*

12. See Daniel A. Payne, *A History of the African Methodist Episcopal Church 1816–1866* (Nashville: Publishing House of the A.M.E. Sunday School Union, 1891).

13. Tanner, *op. cit.*, p. 146.

14. William J. Simons, *Men of Mark* (Cleveland, 1887), pp. 136–140. See also Benjamin Brawley, *Negro Builders and Heroes* (Chapel Hill: The University of North Carolina Press, 1937), pp. 35–40.

15. Resolution adopted at a Meeting in Philadelphia, January, 1817. Cited in Herbert Aptheker, *A Documentary History of the Negro in the United States* (New York: The Citadel Press, 1951), I, 71–72.

16. William A. Poe, "Lott Carey: Man of Purchased Freedom," *Church History*, 39 (1970), 39ff.

17. Hollis R. Lynch, "Pan-Negro Nationalism in the New World, Before 1862," in August Meier and Elliott Rudwick, eds., *The Making of Black America* (New York: Atheneum, 1969), I, 48.

18. "Address to the Free People of Color," in Herbert Aptheker, *op. cit.*, pp. 106–107.

19. Meier and Rudwick, *op. cit.*, p. 121.

20. See Edwin S. Redkey, *Black Exodus* (New Haven: Yale University Press, 1969), for an overview of Black nationalist and Back-to-Africa movements during this period.

21. Benjamin Quarles, *Black Abolitionists* (New York: Oxford University Press, 1969), p. 40; cf. Carleton Mabee, *Black Freedom* (New York: The Macmillan Co., 1970).

22. Quarles, *op. cit.*, p. 46.

23. *Ibid.*, p. 42.

24. *Ibid.*, p. 47.

25. Samuel R. Ward, *Autobiography of a Fugitive Negro* (New York: Arno Press and *The New York Times*, 1969), pp. 64ff. Ward's criticism is typical of that current in the Black community at the time.
26. *Ibid.*, p. 38.
27. *Ibid.*
28. Nathaniel Paul, "An Address Delivered on the Celebration of the Abolition of Slavery in the State of New York, July 5, 1827," in Dorothy Porter, ed., *Negro Protest Pamphlets* (New York: Arno Press and *The New York Times*, 1969), pp. 16–17.
29. Henry H. Garnet, *An Address to the Slaves of the United States of America* (New York: Arno Press and *The New York Times*, 1969), p. 94.
30. *Anglo-American Magazine*, I (1859), 330. (Reprinted by Arno Press and *The New York Times*, 1968.)
31. Bishop Henry M. Turner in Richard R. Wright, *The Bishops of the A.M.E. Church* (Nashville: A.M.E. Sunday School Union, 1963), p. 332.
32. Samuel R. Ward, *op. cit.*, pp. 42–43.
33. Benjamin T. Tanner, *op. cit.*, p. 157.
34. See Meier and Rudwick, *op. cit.*, pp. 88–90, for a discussion of these affairs.
35. *Ibid.*
36. Payne, *op. cit.*, p. 100.
37. Booker T. Washington quoted in Gunnar Myrdal, *An American Dilemma* (New York: McGraw-Hill Book Company, 1964), II, 883.
38. See W. E. B. DuBois, *The Negro Church*, Atlanta University Report No. 8, 1903 (reprinted by Arno Press and *The New York Times*, 1968), for a compilation of statistics relative to these matters.
39. Martin L. King, "I Have a Dream," in John H. Franklin and Isidore Starr, eds., *The Negro in 20th Century America* (New York: Vintage Press, 1967), p. 146.

Black Experience and the Bible

Robert A. Bennett

What are the parallels between the black experience in America and the Jewish-Christian experience in ancient Palestine? In the opinion of Robert A. Bennett, those experiences are hardly to be equated. Nonetheless, "as the tale of sorrows of a people awaiting deliverance, the black narrative has a message consistent with the biblical witness though not to be found in that witness." And: "As we deal with blackness and black history as potent word and event, we come to see Scripture as relevant not in the discovery of points of contact between the Bible and the black experience, but as it leads us to discern and accept God as speaking to us in the givenness of our situation." An ordained priest in the Episcopal Church, Father Bennett is Assistant Professor of Old Testament at the Episcopal Theological School, Cambridge, Massachusetts. He is currently engaged in completing his doctorate in the Near Eastern Languages and Literatures Department at Harvard University. His essay is taken from the January 1971 issue of *Theology Today*.*

BEFORE EXAMINING the black experience as religious experience, or discerning what is God's word for us in black self-awareness, some note must be taken of the biblical themes of liberation and the creation of community. At the core of the biblical witness is the fact that disparate groups who were nobodies, existing on the fringes of ancient Near Eastern society and who were held in bondage, were liberated from their oppression and became somebodies in a newly formed community. That community, Israel, saw itself essentially as a "people" (Hebrew *'am*; Greek *laos*) or religious congregation bound to its God. But it also recognized itself as

* P.O. Box 29, Princeton, N.J. 08540.

a political expression of that unity in terms of a "nation" (Hebrew *goy*; Greek *ethnos*).[1] Central to the newly formed society was its covenantal relationship with the God Yahweh whom it believed was responsible for this change of events; this relationship was dependent more upon working out the divine intentions for the community than upon ritual worship of the deity. The Old Testament and the New testify to the conflicts as well as to the deepening awareness of what such a priority of responsibility meant. Christian and Jew have found it hard to define and express that community which God's interventions into human history would create, one where human relationships can serve as the paradigm for the God-to-man relationship.

The Bible, as revealed word, therefore, tries to communicate something about the purposeful ordering of society as a sign of God's intentions for his creation.[2] The literature of the Old and New Israel is religious literature because it witnesses to God as the one not only creating but also maintaining and forcefully working out freedom for the oppressed and formation of community for the alien or alienated. Consequently the God and man relationship of peoplehood must be worked out in social and political institutions of nationhood. The quest for justice among men becomes the religious quest. Yet it is not only by the mighty acts of God himself, as at the exodus and conquest and in Jesus' life and resurrection, but also by human response to these divine motions that the model for society is forged. It is not simply divine fiat, but by conflict, struggle, and overt human choice that men are liberated and community is formed.[3] In all this the freedom sought and effected is both political and spiritual; the fellowship created is both social and religious.

I

The black experience in America is not the Jewish-Christian experience in ancient Palestine. But as the tale of sorrows of a people awaiting deliverance, the black narrative has a message consistent with the biblical witness though not to be found in that witness. It is a testimony of its own, distinct from Scripture even as it would proclaim its word to us in biblical images and in the categories of scriptural revelation. In this interplay of the new and old, of the familiar and the unique, the black experience partakes of religious experience as it attempts to speak and thereby mediate to us something of God's intentions for us. Though not of canonical status, the story of the black man in America is a self-validating account of faith which when heard and heeded, helps black and white respond more creatively to the divine word for our present situation.

The hermeneutical task of proclaiming Scripture's meaning for today is based upon the prior descriptive task of determining what the biblical document said in its own day. This methodological sequence seems equally valid for getting at the message which blackness holds for contemporary America, namely, that the texts or documents of the black experience be identified and allowed to speak for themselves within their given situation before dealing with their meaning for contemporary ears. Lest there be any caveat about treating this tradition of a people's faith as if it partook of divine revelation, it must be remembered that the Book of Psalms became part of the divine word because it was such a fine mirror image of the revealed truth. Those hymns of faith were such a powerful response to the revealed truth that they became part of the witness itself. There is no need or intention to elevate these texts to a canonical status; they validate themselves because of the truth they reveal about men and about their faith in God. This literary tradition—oral and written—of prose, poetry, and song extends from the beginning of life on these shores into the present. Two articles by the historian Vincent Harding trace the continuity of fundamental belief through these texts: "The Gift of Blackness," *Katallagete* (Summer, 1967), suggesting that the blues continues the affirmation begun in the spirituals; and "Reflections and Meditations on the Training of Religious Leaders for the New Black Generation," *Theological Education*, 6/3 (Spring, 1970), calling on us to hear the words of the new poets as proclamation. Renewed interest in the slave narratives, the collection and study of sermons and orations, plus the re-issuing of black classics, to say nothing of the push for black studies, all indicate the interest in gathering and hopefully finding the critical tools to let these texts speak for themselves.

The fixing of the tradition in which the black experience has and is today speaking means more than collecting the literature and publishing anthologies. That tradition must also include the historical circumstances surrounding it and the theological interpretation which the community placed upon it. Consequently, there are disciplines such as black history, black theology, black psychology, and black politics, all contributing to making the past and present record of the black experience intelligible and potent for its audience. Interest in black history focuses on the *Sitz im Leben* or social setting of the black experience, which though marked by oppression from without and powerlessness from within, is nevertheless a record of a people's trust in their destiny to be a community and to be free.[4] That account has a pre-history in the black presence in the Bible itself and in the not-forgotten African past. There was a significant black presence in the biblical history from Joseph's sojourn in Africa, to Solomon's transplanting an African court to rule his empire, to innumerable Jewish and Christian colonies in Africa.[5] There have always been ties between the black American and the "old country."[6] Nevertheless even as we note these links with the past, the vital themes are those which focus on the present reality of the black presence in white America, marked by that continuum of oppression between slavery and racism. The setting which black history helps reconstruct is one in which the word to be gotten across is freedom and community here and now.

An important historical as well as theological question is, "Why did the slave ancestors accept the religion of their oppressors?" Here, too, we must note what distinguishes the black experience from the biblical record. Israel had been called out of bondage in order that she might become a people and nation, but the black forefathers were brought into slavery to find the God of justice and freedom. A ready answer eludes us in this puzzle, though several suggestions have been put forward: (a) the slaves accepted the Gospel as a means of survival—Gospel or the sword!—or of advancement in the repressive slave system; (b) our ancestors merely absorbed a veneer of Christianity, keeping much of their African heritage, as in the practice of voodoo; (c) many in fact did not accept the Gospel. The last thesis supposes that it was house slaves who took on "massa's" religion with his hand-me-down clothes, but that more distantly removed field slaves did not. An extension of this hypothesis is that the secular songs and blues developed out of this supposed segment.

Professors Charles Long of Chicago and Lawrence Jones of New York assert that the "middle passage" and slavery did not destroy the African religious heritage, but being a highly developed and sophisticated awareness of creation as divinely ordered it was able to survive in the similar expression of faith found in Christianity.[7] With his deep sense of God as creator, the slave heard in the Bible, particularly in the Old Testament, not a new word but ideas with which he was already more or less familiar. The new faith was not etched on a *tabula rasa*, nor was it merely seized upon as a means of survival. Though this old question is perhaps nearing solution with the study of African religious traditions and their relationship to the biblical word on God as Lord of creation, there is a contemporary taunt hurled at black churchmen which asks how they can accept the religion of the society which continues to oppress the black man and insult his aspirations.

II

A new appreciation of the role of the black church within the black experience may help in responding to the charge that the church as institution—white or black—has hindered more than helped the liberation efforts of black Americans. To begin with, it should be clear that the black experience as religious experience is not synonymous with or at least not exhausted by the story of the black church. Nevertheless the history of this most vital institution is used here as a vehicle for bringing us up to date on the present situation of black America. The story of the black church may be divided into three periods.[8] (a) The antebellum church sustained the community in its hope for freedom in the here and now as well as in the hereafter. The hymns that spoke of life "over Jordan" meant for their hearers the Ohio River or the Canadian border. It was no coincidence that the preachers who preached release were also the leaders of slave revolts and thus became restricted by their masters. (b) The Reconstruction church was an important political force and was the backbone of the community in establishing its necessary institutions. It came about, as W. E. B. DuBois noted, that then and later the church was the only institution that white America let the black man run for himself. (c) The modern church, which dates from the turn of the century, is presently entering a new phase beginning at mid-century with the Civil Rights movement. Up until these most recent decades, the church had to assume a compensatory role in the community in as much as the government and society by "benign neglect" allowed the rise of violent intimidation, segregation, disenfranchisement, and the whole new oppression of the black man. In this period of deep depression, the church became the one place of release from this assault and in this time of trauma it responded with a word of "peace." The contemporary church is learning that once again the vital message must be that of liberation and the building of community.

The most vital message in Scripture for liberation hope is that God acts in the course of human events to bring about his purposes for mankind. As Scripture would not separate what we now call sacred and secular, so the resurrection of black history properly lets the black experience speak its peace as *fana* which cannot be called profane. In its interpretation of events past and present this story of a people under oppression is redeemed from meaninglessness and infused with divine significance. The narrative of the sorrows and of the hopes of black folk in America cannot be equated with the story of the people of God. Its potency lies elsewhere as a story of faithfulness to the message it received even in bondage, namely, that God's intentions were for men to be free, living in a just society. As much out of their African religious heritage as in the Gospel word, the slaves and their descendants learned something of God's intention, even when the color he gave became the occasion of oppression. Black awareness in black history is a fundamental assent to God's justice within creation, but it is also an affirmation of God's lordship within history. In other words, this is no mere recounting or chronicling of events; it is a contemporary expression of salvation history.

This sacred-secular story helps us accept as valid the cries of black revolution about America's consistent and deep-seated racist strain. It provides the perspective to grant that liberation from oppression is indeed the right prescription in such a diagnosis. The American problem thus is seen not as the black presence, but the white refusal to accept that presence, which is also a refusal to deal with its responsibility for that presence. The resurrection of black history helps free black minds of the lie that the problem is a pathology of poverty and lawlessness stemming from cultural privation. If the latter were true, then the social technicians of this society, such as Daniel Moynihan, might have something constructive to say about solving America's racial crisis. But if oppressive policies of a racist society are the cause of the problem, then maybe Stokely Carmichael would be a better advisor on setting right what is wrong. The right reading of events—events interpreted—indicates that white racism and black suppression are the problems to be dealt with in this story of sorrows. Only then can the black participation in the American dream be dealt with substantively.

III

The special significance of black theology is that it is helping to form and articulate the categories for our creative response in acknowledging God's lordship in creation and in history. First of all, it is indebted to the witness of faith already made within the black experience. The church and community that accepted its blackness but rejected its enslavement has already confessed to God's rule in the natural and social orders.

Although it is not in the compass of this study to deal with the emerging discipline of black psychology and making sense out of being black and proud in a racist society, two poems express the questioning and the acceptance of the creator's gift to us of blackness. In the "Harlem Renaissance" of the 1920's, the poet Countee Cullen in his collection, *Color*, lamented the cruel irony of being black in an oppressive white society,

> I doubt not God is good, well-meaning, kind. . . .
> Yet I do marvel at this curious thing:
> To make a poet black, and bid him sing!

There is now, however, a new sense of affirmation whether in the gospel music that talks of "respect" or the poems and political platforms that speak of liberation. At the heart of them both is the acceptance of the "gift of blackness," with color now redeemed of racist perversions as a sign of God's love. A black G.I. dying in Vietnam movingly expressed this acceptance, placing it in the context of his at-one-ness with nature:

> How sweet the darkness
>   The darkness of my tomb
>   How sweet the solitude
>   No one to aim
>   No one to squeeze the trigger
>   No one to give pain

> To this
> Dead nigger.
> Man, I'm back to earth
> They buried me down
> And I'm the same color
> A deep, dark brown. . . .[9]

Black theology, therefore, carries on a traditional role of helping to shape and to articulate those expressions of faith which already exist, and in the black experience, awareness is already an affirmation, a response in faith to God's providential hand in the natural order as well as in the course of human events.

Though not ignoring this theme of God's role as creator, black theology has up to this date directed its attention toward the socio-political phenomenon of "Black Power," as indicated by the titles of two major efforts, James Cone's *Black Power and Black Theology* (Seabury, 1969) and Vincent Harding's "The Religion of Black Power," *The Religious Situation, 1968*, D. Cutler, ed. (Beacon, 1968). This enterprise and this emphasis is not new, however, since it represents the repetition of the liberation theme of the antebellum church and the upbuilding of community institutions as during the Reconstruction era. This theology would articulate the message of black self-awareness, namely, that even in the midst of oppression, black men will be free participants within white America. Despite the church's emphasis on withdrawal from the burdens and insults—but also the promises—of this life during the first half of the century, it was a black Baptist preacher, Martin Luther King, Jr., who helped bring the black community to its renewed thrust for emancipation. The life and witness of King and the new black awareness indicate that the black experience as religious experience reached a new stage. Black theology, therefore, is not merely filling in the gaps left by the suspicious color-blindness of previous theologians; it more importantly is both helping to shape and to articulate the black experience as a religious experience which has a divine message for contemporary America. The effort within black theology to formulate and to communicate what that word is, under the guidance of biblical revelation, is its hermeneutical task. The problem facing black churchmen, therefore, is how to express the cry coming out of black America as an essentially Christian and redemptive word within an oppressive self-righteous society. The divine word spoken in the black experience is one of hope and vindication within this life, but it is also one that judges America's racist society and religious establishment.

IV

Just before his death, Martin Luther King began to deal with that most potent force within the black community, black self-awareness and Black Power. Vincent Harding's article, "The Religion of Black Power," deals sympathetically with Dr. King's cautious appraisal of this phenomenon. Harding himself raises several questions about the militants, particularly their call for "autonomous action" to secure black liberation. He cites the dangers of taking on the mind-set of racist America, and the consequences for the black psyche of attempting to ignore or make invisible the white man. Harding asks if the black quest for guns, mass media, the atom bomb is not a suicidal attempt to fight on America's terms and to become like the enemy in his use of "conscienceless power."[10] And he bids us think how we shall break the psychological dependence upon whiteness so as not to impair the wholeness of our own human perception. It is at points such as these that the message coming out of the black experience stands in real tension with the biblical witness. But first of all, it must be recognized that the biblical tradition stands in tension with itself at many points since it really is something of a palimpsest or tradition made up of many traditions inscribed one upon another. Scholars speak of the prophetic tradition, the priestly tradition, the wisdom tradition, the gospel, and the early church traditions.[11] Each generation and school of faith responds to God's word in its own way while yet in the old or new covenantal relationship. God's power is expressed in the Old Testament as autonomous action, the might of armies, and of natural phenomena, while in the New Testament it is expressed in the weakness and surrender of Jesus. Israel appears earlier as a nation among the nations, but later as a subjugated people highly self-conscious of her identity over against that of her neighbors.

Yet even as these nuances are recognized in Scripture, the Christian witness suggests God's definitive word as given in the life and mission of Jesus and the community he called into being. This being the case, where is Jesus in Black Power? While many would identify Jesus as the revolutionary who liberated the oppressed, he even more clearly is the one who questioned and attacked the socio-religious establishment of his day. And it was most clearly his demonstration of power in weakness which set all the more in contrast and in judgment the corrupt and calcified establishment he was attacking. So it is the New Testament witness which helps Vincent Harding ask his incisive question of militant Black Power—"Shall it seek the autonomous action of the Old Testament tradition or shall it follow that New Testament demonstration of power in weakness in a perhaps more powerful judgment of the conscienceless power of the American way?"

Jesus attacked the established norms of his society so that those oppressed by that society might be free. The black self-awareness in this present situation seeks to free black minds from white myths about blackness.[12] A new form of liberation is taking place where a long nascent community is coming alive in this land, not waiting for its exile to end, longing to be a proud black people. The biblical categories are reversed: men seek to establish community in bondage so they may become free; they reject the alien-exile theme of Israel and the pilgrims who looked for a new land to form their society. The black experience has been one in which a community learned to sing the Lord's songs in a strange land and to pray for the peace of the land where they had been carried. While there is solidarity with Africa and it is seen as the black *Kulturland*, the black American does not see himself as an exiled alien, as did the Israelite in Psalm 137 who couldn't sing the Lord's song in a strange land. Indeed, despite the oppression, he has been a patriot and, taking Jeremiah's advice, he has prayed for the peace of this land. This people does not conceive of itself as being in diaspora. There has been no successful back-to-Africa movement nor anything equivalent to Zionism. The community has no illusions about itself; it is no chosen people; this is no promised land. Its "messiahs" have been few and transitory. It is convinced, however, by its experience on these shores, by its survival under the most oppressive of slave systems, that God does not intend that this people shall die. The black experience is the realization of this as historical fact, and acknowledging God as Lord of creation, it has maintained its hope and communion with the world around it.

This essay has attempted to say that God's word in Scripture comes to us more clearly and forcefully when we understand it as expressing something about the divine purpose for creation and human society not only in the period when it was given form in the witness of Israel, or in Jesus, or in the early Church, but also in the forms of human witness today. The black experience in America is such an expression of faith in God's involvement in life for freeing those who are not free and giving power to those who have none. The biblical story and the account of the black man in America are not the same story. Nevertheless, the same hermeneutical process which confronts us with the message from Scripture also suggests those categories by which we can deal creatively with the word being spoken by the black experience. It is assumed that God's final self-revelation given in Jesus Christ and under the old and new covenant has consequence for the whole course of human history, and that word and event continue as potent in conveying that revelation. As we deal with blackness and black history as potent word and event, we come to see Scripture as relevant not in the discovery of points of contact between the Bible and the black experience, but as it leads us to discern and accept God as speaking to us in the givenness of our situation.

Notes

1. E. A. Speiser, " 'People' and 'Nation' of Israel," *Journal of Biblical Literature*, Vol. 79, No. 2 (June, 1960), pp. 157–163. Cf. J. W. Flight, "Nationality," *Interpreter's Dictionary of the Bible*, Vol. III, pp. 512–515; E. J. Hamlin, "Nations," *ibid.*, pp. 515–523; Leo Spitzer, "Ratio-Race," and "The Gentiles," *Essays in Historical Semantics*, New York: S. F. Vanni, 1948, pp. 147–169; 171–178; Eric Voegelin, "The Growth of the Race Idea," *The Review of Politics*, Vol. 2, No. 3 (July, 1940), pp. 283–317.

2. G. Ernest Wright *et al.*, *The Biblical Doctrine of Man in Society* (Ecumenical Biblical Studies No. 2), London: SCM, 1954.

3. G. Ernest Wright, *The Old Testament Against Its Environment* (Studies in Biblical Theology No. 2), London: SCM, 1950, and *The Old Testament and Theology*, New York: Harper, 1969, Chaps. 2–6.

4. Cf. Arna Bontemps, ed., *Great Slave Narratives* (with editor's essay, "The Slave Narrative: An American Genre," pp. vii–xix), Boston: Beacon, 1969; Melvin Drimmer, ed., *Black History: A Reappraisal*, Garden City: Doubleday, 1968; Thomas Frazier, ed., *Afro-American History: Primary Sources*, New York: Harcourt, Brace, 1970; Dwight Hoover, ed., *Understanding Negro History*, Chicago: Quadrangle, 1968; William L. Katz, ed., *Negro Protest Pamphlets*, New York: Arno Press and *The New York Times*, 1969; August Meier and E. Rudwick, eds., *The Making of Black America*, 2 vols., New York: Atheneum, 1969.

5. Cf. A. Arkell, *A History of the Sudan from Earliest Times to 1821*, 2nd ed., London: London Univ., 1961; *Cambridge Ancient History*, rev. ed., Vols. I–II, Cambridge: Cambridge Univ., 1963; R. Collins, ed., *Problems in African History*, Englewood Cliffs: Prentice-Hall, 1968; A. Gardiner, *Egypt of the Pharaohs*, New York: Oxford Univ., 1968; F. M. Snowden, *Blacks in Antiquity: Ethiopians in the Greco-Roman Empire*, Cambridge: Harvard Univ., 1970; E. Ullendorf, *Ethiopia and the Bible* (Schweich Lecture), New York: Oxford Univ., 1968.

6. Cf. Alexander Crummell, *Africa and America: Addresses and Discourses* (1891), Miami: Mnemosyne (reprint), 1969; W. E. B. DuBois, *Black Folk, Then and Now*, New York: Henry Holt, 1939; Melville Herskovits, *The Myth of the Negro Past*, Boston: Beacon, 1958; St. Clair Drake, "Negro Americans and the African Interest," *The American Negro Reference Book*, J. P. Davis, ed., Englewood Cliffs: Prentice-Hall, 1966, pp. 662–705; and " 'Hide My Face?' On Pan-Africanism and Negritude," *The Making of Black America*, Vol. I, A. Meier and E. Rudwick, eds., New York: Atheneum, 1969, pp. 66–87; H. R. Lynch, "Pan-Negro Nationalism in

the New World Before 1862," *The Making of Black America*,
Vol. I, pp. 42–65.

7. Cf. *African Systems of Thought* (Third International African
Seminar, Salisbury, Dec., 1960), New York: Oxford Univ.,
1965; Henri Frankfort, *Ancient Egyptian Religion*, New
York: Harper, 1948; John S. Mbiti, *African Religions and
Philosophy*, New York: Praeger, 1969; Geoffrey Parrinder,
Religion in Africa, Baltimore: Penguin, 1969; Noel Q. King,
Religions of Africa, New York: Harper, 1970.

8. Cf. E. Franklin Frazier, *The Negro Church in America*,
New York: Schocken, 1963; Benjamin Mays and Joseph
Nicholson, *The Negro's Church*, New York: Institute of So-
cial and Religious Research, 1933; and Carter G. Woodson,
The History of the Negro Church, 2nd ed., Washington, D.C.:
Associated, 1921. Note also: W. E. B. DuBois, *The Souls
of Black Folk* (1903), New York: Fawcet (Crest reprint),
1961; James Cone, "Black Consciousness and the Black
Church," *The Annals*, Vol. 387 (Jan., 1970), pp. 49–55; R.
T. Handy, "Negro Christianity and American Church His-
toriography," *Reinterpretation in American Church History*,
J. C. Brauer, ed., Chicago: Chicago Univ., 1968; and Law-
rence Jones, "Black Theology in the Ante-bellum South,"
unpublished paper delivered at the N.C.B.C. Black Theology
Consultation, Atlanta, April, 1970; Benjamin Mays, *The
Negro's God* (1938), New York: Atheneum, 1968.

9. Poem, "Viet Nam," by Jack DiNola of Trenton, New Jersey,
quoted by John Snow in lectures on "Preaching in an Apocalyptic Age," *Kellogg Lecture for 1970*, Episcopal Theological School, Cambridge, Massachusetts, February, 1970.

10. Vincent Harding, "The Religion of Black Power," *The Religious Situation, 1968*, D. Cutler, ed., Boston: Beacon, 1968,
pp. 3–38.

11. Cf. recent works emphasizing the importance of the history
and variety of interpretation within the biblical material:
Günther Bornkamm, *Jesus of Nazareth*, 3rd ed., New York:
Harper, 1960; Ernst Käsemann, *Jesus Means Freedom*, Phila-
delphia: Fortress, 1969; Klaus Koch, *The Growth of Biblical
Tradition*, New York: Scribners, 1969; Gerhard von Rad,
Old Testament Theology, 2 vols., New York: Harper, 1962,
1963.

12. *The Black Scholar*, Vol. I, No. 5 (March, 1970) is devoted
to the topic of black psychology; *The Black Scholar*, Vol. I,
No. 2 (Dec., 1969) deals with black politics.

What Religious Vision for Youth Today?

Douglas H. Heath

Well attuned to the attitudes, feelings, and needs of young people, Douglas Heath finds today's youth generation to be characterized both by increasing alienation and by efforts to overcome that alienation through self-realization and self-fulfillment. And he sees emerging from that generation a religious vision that is deeply humanistic, emotionally liberating, marked by corporate sharing. Dr. Heath, Professor of Psychology at Haverford College, has had extensive experience working with students as a psychologist, and has done intensive research on student development. His most recent book, *Humanizing Schools: New Directions, New Decisions*, describes in greater detail the trends he outlines in his essay below—an essay which originally appeared in the Spring 1971 issue of *Nexus*,* the alumni magazine of Boston University School of Theology. Dr. Heath is also the author of *Explorations of Maturity: Studies of Mature and Immature College Men* and *Growing Up in College: Liberal Education and Maturity*.

THESE ARE DAYS of deep discontent and despair. Our troubles are many: our interminable Vietnam catastrophe, the suppression of our blacks, the necrophiliac pall with which our technology now shrouds our lives, the intensifications of violence, and the polarization of our society. Then there are the troubles of our youth and their culture of malaise, drugs, defiance, violence, and sexual promiscuity. Each of these troubles hurts us more deeply than we dare to admit, for each is tearing from our consciousness another curtain of illusion and piety. Each is making us more naked

* 745 Commonwealth Ave., Boston, Mass. 02215.

to the truth that our gods are indeed dying. Vietnam tells us our power is impotent; the blacks tell us our form of justice is unjust; the pollution of our technology tells us our knowledge is fallible; the forces of violence and polarization tell us our democratic vision may be but an empty slogan; and our youth tell us our materialistic way of life has robbed us of our humanness and corrupted our spirits.

The sudden emergence of these troubles in the past decade has traumatically accelerated the progressive radicalization of our consciousness—a radicalization that has been evolving much more slowly for the past hundred years. That God had died for Nietzsche then has become true for increasing numbers of persons since. The secularization of our thought, the de-mythologizing of our beliefs, and the rejection of the mythic world have meant that the invisible threads of meanings and purposes, myths and truths, that wove our grandparents, parents, and us into the fabric of our society have become unraveled. We and our society have lost that sense of cosmic patterning, of purpose, that unconsciously provided the fit, the match, of our individual purposes and values with those of our fellow-man. As we became more secular we turned more eagerly to our gods of power, knowledge, democracy, and affluence. The crisis of the sixties is that these substitute gods have begun to die too. We are beginning to confront the terrifying inner darkness of emptiness, the blackness of the inner void, now that no god "out there" is creditable any longer.

Many of us adults have yet to be really disturbed by the death of our gods. Some of us, probably a majority, defensively protect ourselves from confronting our own inner emptiness by denying and suppressing those troubles that could radicalize our consciousness. We blind ourselves to the moral questions of our Vietnam policy, isolate and ignore our blacks in our center cities, or mount a holy crusade against our provocative youth. Others of us are protected from confronting the death of our gods by our professional roles that anchor us firmly to the established society. Our routines, institutionalized commitments, and familial and social responsibilities provide secure rituals we live out without questioning their meaning. But our most powerful defense against the troubles of today is a consciousness that was formed forty and fifty years ago in a radically different era. Our memories of the past do shape how we perceive and interpret this world of today. Our consciousness was shaped before we knew the possibility that the human species could destroy itself as a species. We were taught before television had massaged and molded our consciousness for thousands of hours. We grew up before sexuality in all of its forms was publicly displayed on paperback covers, in *Life*, and in the movies. Margaret Mead is right. The real world is different from the world most of us *believe* we live in. But for an increasing number of us, our values and memories shaped in the past are no longer protecting us from the shocks of the present. Our current troubles are too acute for us to be able to deny them any longer. So more of us are now aware that our truths and values, our gods, no longer meaningfully integrate us and us with our society. Increasingly, more adults are in crisis—a deeply religious crisis. *The* questions for us today are: "For what are we to live in this world? In what are we to believe? What integrative meaning and ecstatic vision can there be for our lives in this society?"

Where are we to look for clues about what may be a religious vision for contemporary man? Social commentators like Paul Goodman, who claim we are in the midst of as profound and powerful a religious revolution as Luther initiated in 1517, identify the impetus to that new reformation to be the radical searchings of our youth.[2] Academicians like Theodore Roszak describe the emerging counterculture of youth in similar, almost apocalyptic terms.[3] Theologians like Sam Keen suggest we are witnessing the birth of a new religious vision of man in the revolt of youth.[4] It is too easy to project our poignant wishes for a spiritual rebirth, for a new god, into the frenetic searchings of our youth. It is too easy for us middle-aged and jaded adults to adulate the passion of youth and sanctify its excesses as expressions of a new religious spirit. It is too easy to identify a Woodstock and its sacraments of drugs, folk rock, nudity, and free love as a deeply spiritual experience that justifies such values and behavior. And it is certainly premature to assume that such allegedly religious experiences are healthy, mature, or even integrative for our youth.

However, it is not unreasonable to look to the lives of our more sensitive youth to understand if a new religious vision is emerging. Why? Religious visions are transmitted and given conscious form through the lives of human beings. Such visions provide meanings and purposes that bind, bring together, integrate, make more whole that which is estranged in our lives. The lives of our youth are more vulnerable to the alienating effects of our society than are our lives. They are closer to the psychological frontiers of change. They are struggling more than we are to find a more integrative way of life in a society that is losing its sense of coherence and mythic patterns. Their search is not as encrusted by routines and roles or by memories of past realities. Their lives reflect more transparently the psychological currents alive in this world. Our youth are the harbingers of our future.

My thesis is that increasingly more of our youth are suffering very deep cleavages that are alienating them from their animal vitality, their corporateness, and their mythic traditions. They are experiencing deep inner divisions that many adults also feel, but not as sharply. By understanding how our youth are becoming more deeply alienated, as well as their efforts to heal themselves, we can glimpse the form a new religious vision of man *must* take if it is to be meaningfully integrative and provide that sense of wholeness and oneness that is close to the heart of religious experience.

I do not intend to imply that the deepening alienation I describe characterizes the majority of today's youth. The trends I note emerge from experience with and studies of middle-class affluent youth.[5] If the trends continue, they may well describe a majority of youth within a few years. The changing values of our more sensitive and bright youth, particularly when nurtured by the restlessly searching and questioning environment of a Berkeley, Antioch, or Harvard, frequently do prefigure incipient cultural changes that, in time, begin to affect a wider sector of youth. The anti-Vietnam sentiment, long hair, and drug culture that have spread so rapidly among adolescents are cases in point.

Several decades ago Erich Fromm identified the emergence of man's reflective reason as a primary cause of his estrangement from his own instinctual or animal nature and from nature itself.[6] Since then our technological society has accelerated that estrangement in all of us, and particularly in our youth. The post-Sputnikian societal demand for academic excellence and the schools' premium on verbal abstract ability, the television-induced expansion of our youths' consciousness and knowledgeability, the internalization of the scientific ethos of rational objectivity, and our assimilation of Freudian insights about how man defends himself against his passions and anxieties have produced a generation exquisitely aware and sensitive to every injustice and problem of our society as well as to their own inner impulses and demons. The leading strength of our youth is their increased capacity to symbolize their experience.

Yet this more advanced level of consciousness has also made more youths hyperconscious particularly of themselves. The consequence has been a progressive inhibition of their own primitive sources of passion and vitality. They are becoming disembodied, walking heads. They speak of themselves as up tight, hung up, cool.[7] They find themselves to be primarily observers of their own lives and only critics of a society that provides little opportunity for them to lose themselves in action or indeed even in physical work. They value control and critical reason and fear being emotionally vulnerable in their relationships. They fear being in a submissive or dependent position. They don't know how to let themselves just be spontaneously emotional, like children again. Increasingly, more youth do not feel themselves to be alive, vital, earthy persons. Boredom, apathy, and an inner feeling of emptiness result. They feel cut off from themselves. Rollo May talks of the schizoid consequences of our technology.

Our youth experience that loss of feeling and depersonalization much more pervasively than we adults are aware.[8]

At a deeper level, contemporary youth have lost touch with the irrational, the sources of madness and emotional power that made Zorba the Greek, for example, a superbly passionate but whole human being. Not only have we lost contact with the poetic and mythic within, but we have also cut ourselves off from the primitive power of nature. All of us, and particularly our youth, have severed our psychological tie to the rhythms of nature, of other animals, of our earth. We seek to manage the weather, tame or kill off other animals, and shape the earth to our desires. A crusty Vermont farmer consulting me about why his son was doing poorly in college gave his own diagnosis. His son, he said, lived too much in the world of abstractions and symbols; he had lost contact with the earth, and hence the healing power of his natural heritage.

Carl Jung was making the same point when he said:

In development, we lose the primitive wholeness of the child, and in the development of rationality we lose our vitality and more primitive side. . . . The more the critical reason dominates, the more impoverished life becomes; but the more of the unconscious, and the more of myth we are capable of making conscious, the more of life we integrate.[9]

Could not the flight by so many of our youth into drugs be an attempt to blow their minds, to destroy their ever-present consciousness and rationality, to experience the primitive wholeness of their suppressed emotionality, and secure a vision of how beautiful life can be when they dare to abandon themselves to their more irrational selves? Could not the episodic outbursts of violence and destructiveness in our schools and the fury of youthful resentment be massive cathartic releases of a more primitive wildness and vitality too severely repressed in our schools and society? Could not even the hippie eating organic foods, growing long hair, eschewing fashion and pretense, and accepting his own bodily odors, sweat, and dirt be trying to recover a primitive naturalness, to accept his own animal sensuousness, and to live his body more fully? Could not the attraction of the sensitivity movement suggest our youth now need to be taught how to be more inwardly accessible to their own feelings, to learn how to be vulnerable to their own childish feelings, to learn how to experience awe, wonder, adoration, and even reverence for the irrational—the mystery of our being and our universe that religions have always affirmed and celebrated?

The emotional, even compulsive, excesses of some of our youth indicate the depth of the chasm between their intellects and their primitive emotionality. It is not human to grow partially; when we are stretched too far out of shape, we snap back, like a rubber band. Drugs and confrontations may be primitive, even seemingly destructive, but desperate attempts to regain that sense of organic wholeness our rational and self-conscious age has denied to us.

If a religious vision of future man is to be integrative for our youth it will value organismic honesty, the "rightness" and "goodness" of bodily sensuousness and impulses, and encourage the irrational mystical and ecstatic experiences to which a whole person is able to abandon himself in awe and reverence. An emerging truth for this generation is that the body does not lie; it tells the truth. Religious worship services will become more active, affirmative, emotional experiences in which communal dance, drama, bodily rhythm and movements, chanting, music, and meditation will become the preferred means to more deeply experienced openings to and the forms through which to express the power of the immanent within.

When Christ said, "Suffer the little children to come unto me, and forbid them not; for of such is the kingdom of God," could he have meant, among other things, that a child was more accessible to his inner promptings, to the God within; that he was not paralyzed by a self-consciousness that robbed him of a sense of wholeness and spontaneity?

A second manifestation of the deepening alienation of man is the destruction of his sense of corporateness. Man is more than just a unique individualist who does his own thing. He is born dependent on others; he has bodily needs to be touched and caressed by others and to touch and caress others; and he becomes human through the love of others; he needs to love others. Within the past several decades, we have developed a society that has divided and separated us from each other. No longer do we have large families whose members live and work and sleep and play and worship with each other; no longer do we have stable neighborhoods in which our neighbors care about us or we about them; no longer do we have small schools in which children can be known all the way around by their teachers, and who, therefore, experience that feeling of being known as whole persons; no longer do our youth take time to learn how to be dependent upon and cooperative with other youths in a television-dominated society that usurps thousands of hours of their time and in a competitive school system that encourages them to outdo and cut down others.[10]

Increasingly, more of our youth feel that, because they are unique, no one, not even their parents, can understand them. Because they fear being hurt and cut down, they fear initiating relations with others; they must struggle to communicate. Loneliness and isolation are becoming more prevalent. More youngsters express a distrust of long-term, enduring relationships like marriage. In fact, more youth believe they must learn how to move into and out of close relationships very quickly, for they do not anticipate that such relationships will endure.

At a deeper level, more of our youth have lost the experience of belonging to a community, of identifying with a transcendent corporate purpose, and sharing a communion of value with others. What happens to our sense of humanness when we never experience being a part of human history, when we remain aloof observers of others? Don't we become arrogant in our self-sufficiency, closing ourselves to the opportunity to share ourselves with others? In contrast, a student who felt a deepening identification with others during college said, of his relation to society:

I think that perhaps the whole idea of what you work for and what you gain from society is really not all your own, that you are only part of a long continuing process and what you have accomplished is, in part, a result of your own endeavor but also, in part, a result of the people who have gone before you. So that any claims that society may make on what you have done or accomplished, I think, are valid claims.

Could not the effort to create a commune in which openness, trust, acceptance, sharing, and love are the organizing values be an effort to recover man's need for a sense of corporateness? Could not even a riot or confrontation, as destructive as it may be of the fragile educational community, be another expression of a need for human solidarity? Why do participants report in riot after riot that they "felt very, very together," like brothers and sisters, in the midst of such violence? Could not the increase in premarital sexual relations and cohabitation on the college campuses be primarily a means by which to reclaim a sense of intimacy, even of belongingness, more than just to gratify erotic desires? It is remarkable how de-passionized many such relationships really are. Actually, our youth and we ourselves may need to learn how to develop more richly erotic relations with each other, for passion is being washed out of many of us in this society. The erotic does bind us together.

As more and more of our youth feel cast adrift in our society, alone and homeless, we will witness more and more diverse, even bizarre, efforts to reach out to others to reclaim a sense of familial and tribalistic corporateness. The Israeli kibbutz, the commune in the Rockies, the group marriage will appeal to the primordial need to be one with other human beings.

The religious vision our youth are struggling to form will be more deeply acceptant of a person's need for other persons, will value his reaching out to touch another and to be touched by him, will encourage physical expressions of solidarity and love, will value corporate sharing more than indi-

vidual achievement and competition. Religious worship services will discover ways to use the power of the presence of
others to release and affirm expressions of love and community; more meaningful ways of experiencing communion together will be developed; corporate meditative sharing and
mutuality experiences will become more prominent.

Paul's injunction in his letter to the Romans (13:8-10)
may be the ethic for our youth in the future:

Owe no man anything, but to love one another; for he that
loveth his neighbor hath fulfilled the law. . . . Love worketh
no ill to his neighbor; therefore love is the fulfillment of
the law.

Our youth assert that no custom, no convention, no law
should bind and constrict their love. Who and how and when
they love are not relevant to the law. If they love, their love is
the law. Religion will become less obsessed and punitive, for
example, about sexuality in all of its forms. The religious
leaders of the future will know how to help us love more
genuinely and wholly.

The third and last form of the estrangement of contemporary man is his increasingly skeptical repudiation of those
mythic traditions and meanings that organized the identities
of earlier generations. Man is, I believe, a meaning, searching, and creating animal who needs to locate himself with
respect to his past and his future. But what happens to a
youth who now believes his past to be irrelevant and his
future improbable? The rapidity of change makes yesterday
quite remote. The probability of a nuclear holocaust in the
lifetime of our youths deadens their hope for the future. The
dissolution of consensually accepted values and the secularization of our beliefs have been marked in the past decades. Not only traditional organizing "truths" like a belief in
the existence of God or of a heaven or hell, but also related
religious values and practices increasingly are being rejected
by more and more youths.[11] A national survey of college
youth noted 77.5 percent claimed that the churches do not

appeal to today's youth.[12] Young people are just not interpreting their experience as frequently in traditional religious categories.

Nor do our traditional economic myths and values appeal to increasing numbers of estranged youths. The Puritan ethic is no longer as highly valued among both Christian and Jewish youth.[13] Such things as achievement, the entrepreneurial attitude, initiative, postponement of pleasure for some future reward, thrift, orderliness, and hard work that shaped us are not central to the lives of our youth. The pursuit of affluence and its materialism holds singularly little appeal for many of today's youth.

Perhaps because of the demise of the Puritan ethic and the growing revulsion of the effects of our hard-won scientific knowledge, increasingly more youth do not value the pursuit of knowledge. The quality of academic work in many of the better colleges and universities has diminished in the past few years, as students find that academic man's accentuated rationalism is too narrow a vision of the life they need to live.

Nor is the god of power likely to be a central organizing value for many. True, youth cry for power; yet upon receiving it they find that it corrupts. Increasingly, youth don't wish to be in dominant, controlling hierarchial political offices on the campus. There is a deep cynicism among our more sensitive youth about the use of power in any established institution. Their inclinations are for structureless or anarchic institutions.

As strongly liberal in their social values and concerns for justice as are many of our youth, I remain uncertain that their commitment is to more than a slogan and ideology. For far too many fail to implement such beliefs in sustained, patient, organized, cooperative social action. The social idealism of many of our youth has been severely blunted by our societal failures to respond to the agony of the blacks, the cries of the poor, the hurts of millions of suffering persons here and abroad. Too many are becoming predisposed to give up on the "system."

At a deeper level, more of our youth no longer can believe or have faith in any absolutistic principle or ethic. They know there is no certainty, no truths out there, to be apprehended or discovered. Life is relativistic, contingent, absurd, and, for increasing numbers, inherently meaningless. The present moment becomes primary. To live in the imminent present, to collapse time to this moment, to live above history and outside of eternity is to risk never encountering one's humanity. Not to identify with what one has been, like one's ancestors, traditions, and homeland, or with what one could be, like one's grandchildren, hopes realized, and the Kingdom, surely must truncate one's perspective, aggravate one's arrogance, and diminish one's understanding of the potential of the human procession and thereby one's self. Not to believe and have faith can produce despair and hopelessness. Many of our youth are deeply despairing. They will have to learn how continually to create their own contingent meanings in which to have faith. That will demand great maturity of our youth in the future.

Could not the increased interest in academic courses on religion, the excitement of the visit of the Maharishi, the attraction of Zen, and the popularity of Alan Watts suggest a deep religio-philosophical hungering in our youth for some ordering principles and meaning for these days? Could not the attractions of pot and acid, the fascination of Jungian archetypal patterns, and interest in the meditative religions represent a deepening inward search for what is eternally immanent? Could not the flirtation with the Tarot cards, I Ching, astrology, witchcraft, alchemy, and other sources of divination suggest the depth of the need for a magical sign that some truth is to be revealed? Does not the colorful psychedelic movement with its flowers, beads and baubles, symbols and posters, pins and outlandish attire reveal not only an attempt to break free of our cultural hang-ups and suppressive customs but also a search for a life style more integrative of the personally subjective, aesthetic, and even the irrational?

But our youth are too pragmatically rational and critical to identify their future belief with some institutionalized or "out there" concept or tradition. Deeply distrustful of authority and its pronouncements, they are turning to themselves and their own self-fulfillment as the core value for their identities in their future. Self-realization, self-actualization, freedom to be one's self, do your own thing, the human potential movement, and Neill's *Summerhill* are the emerging symbols of this new identity. No longer trustful of external authorities and their symbols, they search within for their own authority.

What does this trend portend for their religious beliefs in the future? The religious vision of tomorrow will not be otherworldly. Nor will its terms be reified into personifications as traditional Christian concepts as God and the Devil have been in the past. Certainly, the emerging symbols of this new religion will be organized around the idea of potentia—hence the popularity of existentialist thought, Fromm, and *Gestalt* therapy. In contrast to some traditional theology, their religious hopes will in principle be realizable. There will be no unbridgeable gulf between their god and themselves. The immanence rather than the transcendence of their god-symbol will become dominant. Their religious beliefs will be deeply humanistic. They will be against any anti-life concepts and beliefs. They will be more acceptant than we have been of man's frailties, irrationalities, and bodily impulses. I can't see them sympathetic with much of Pauline theology as I understand it. I even doubt that their Sermon on the Mount will urge them to cast out thoughts of adultery or refrain from profanity! Their beliefs will emphasize expressiveness and fullness rather than restraint and asceticism. A commitment to self-fulfillment will sanction explorations of many forms of what we now label to be deviant behavior. Pastoral counselors will have to modify their concept of what is healthy and unhealthy behavior. And society will discover that the religion of the future will not be either its handmaiden or an apology for its injustices. For the emerging religious vision will *in fact* value man more than it will his accommodation to Caesar.

I doubt that the religious vision of future man will be so encumbered with the esoteric abstractions of theology. Not even traditional concepts of God, Christ, or the Trinity will be central to the future. People's prayers will become free of the abstruse and complicated verbiage that now intrudes into so much of our worship language. If they pray at all in the future, their prayers will be very simple and spontaneous. Their religiousness will be much more deeply experiential and may resemble the spirit of the early Christians. They will seek emotional liberation in unashamed bodily expression, corporate reaffirmation, and experiential meaning to their lives. I doubt that form and institutionalization or even a professional ministry will be their concern in the foreseeable future. They will certainly not allow themselves to be preached to by somebody else. Certainly, to carry a church mortgage will not appeal to many. The church of the young will not be like most churches of today. Their religious services may resemble transitory and minimally organized encounter groups or folk rock festivals or saturnalia in which they will seek to liberate, intensify, and reaffirm the primitive wholeness of which Jung spoke.

Such is the religious vision I believe youth today are seeking to create. The themes of this vision are not new. Man has sought his god in all imaginable forms and in all different ways throughout his history. If religion is to serve as an integrative force in the future, as it has in the past, then its vision must provide the symbols and forms by which to help today's youth heal and reconcile their deepening inner divisions. Will youth be able to give life to this vision or will the vision remain stillborn? What dangers will our youth encounter that could abort this spiritual reformation, of which Goodman, Roszak, and Keen talk?

Certainly, the desperateness of our youths' need for meaning and integration may drive some to repudiate part of their own potentia, particularly their own rationality or its societal symbols and forms as manifested in our schools and scientific technology, which they identify as the cause of their estrangement. The abandonment of their Apollonian heritage in frantic pursuit of their Dionysian archetype risks only substituting one form of estrangement for another: that is, replacing their severely inhibiting hyperrationality by a driven, impulsive hedonism. The cult of drugs may accentuate the value of irrational mysticism but negate the value of the rational intellect. The flight of some of our most intellectually acute and sensitive youth into rural communes may lead to the sacrifice of their own leading talents and potentials. A *healthy* pursuit of one's suppressed primitive, irrational self will not snuff out the civilizing powers of the rational mind. A healthy religious quest seeks to reconcile and integrate opposites, not suppress or destroy them.

Another danger is that the loneliness and lostness of some of our youth may predispose them to submit to any power or hero that promises corporateness or belongingness. To become a member of Charles Manson's commune, to become possessed by the spell of a folk rock hero, to abandon one's self to a violent confrontation or street gang or a demonic political leader or even to a knight in shining armor on a white horse is to risk the destruction of one's individuality and autonomy. The intensity of the alienation of youth from others accentuates the need to overcome such isolation by fusing one's self with a larger group or movement. Estrangement is overcome, temporarily, by the abdication of responsibility for the self. But such abdication eventually leads to the destruction of the self. A healthy religious vision integrates the need to be a member of a corporate witness with the enhancement of one's self.

The third potential danger that confronts our youth is that the value of self-actualization may be used to justify narcissism. When a youth repudiates the authority of his tradition and defends his acts in terms of his own self-actualization, then he risks becoming his own god. A popular folk rock singer, Janis Ian, has indeed said of her generation:

We have no need of a God;
Each of us is his own.

What does it mean to be one's own god? That we respect, love, and worship ourselves? Now, it is true, as Fromm has insisted, to be able to love another does require that we be able first to accept, respect, and love ourselves. The danger in being our own god, in being committed to the fulfillment of our own potentia, our own self, is that we risk remaining only a narcissist unable to say with the psalmist, "I will praise *thee*; for I am fearfully and wonderfully made." Narcissism is estrangement from others. A narcissist is unable to praise or love another. And as Freud says, a man "must begin to love in order that [he] . . . may not fall ill, and must fall ill if, in consequence of frustration, [he] . . . cannot love."[14]

Therefore, *the* imperative for our youth, if they are not to remain narcissists and so become ill, is to learn how to praise and to love others. Unless self-actualization comes to mean to this generation the release and cultivation of the power to love another, it may never experience the wholeness that heals its deepening alienation. Jesus said two thousand years ago, ". . . he that loseth his life for my sake shall find it." In the language of our youth, to become a more whole person, to fulfill the emerging religious vision, one must lose himself, that is, love another. We don't love another for the purpose of finding ourselves. We find ourselves only as the unsought consequence of loving another. Our youth are right when they make love their central value. If they fail to learn how to love, they will remain estranged, become ill, and their religious vision will be unrealized.

Notes

1. An address delivered at the Conference on the Ministry, February 22, 1971. Revised versions of the Fifth Annual John Sutherland Bonnell lecture, The Fifth Avenue Presbyterian Church, New York City, November 15, 1970, in press in the *Journal of Religion and Mental Health*.
2. P. Goodman, "The New Reformation." *New York Times Magazine*, September 14, 1969.

3. T. Roszak, *The Making of a Counter Culture*. New York: Doubleday & Co., Inc., 1969.
4. Lecture, Second Research Conference, Academy of Religion and Mental Health, September, 1970.
5. D. H. Heath, *Humanizing Schools: New Directions, New Decisions*. New York: Hayden Book Co., 1971.
6. E. Fromm, *Man For Himself*. New York: J. J. Little & Ives Co., 1947.
7. D. H. Heath, "The Cool Ones." *Journal of Religion and Health*, 1968, 7, 111f.
8. R. May, *Love and Will*. New York: W. W. Norton & Co., Inc., 1969.
9. C. G. Jung, *Memories, Dreams and Reflections.* Ed. by A. Jaffe. New York: Pantheon Books, 1961, 302.
10. D. H. Heath, "Student Alienation and the School." *The School Review*, Chicago: University of Chicago, August 1970, Vol. 78, No. 4, 515–528.
11. D. H. Heath, "Secularization and Maturity of Religious Beliefs." *Journal of Religion and Health*, 1969, 8, 335–358; D. Hoge, "College Students' Religion: A Study of Trends in Attitudes and Behavior." Unpublished Ph.D. thesis, 1969.
12. D. C. Beggs and H. A. Copeland, Report of Survey. *The Evening Bulletin*, Philadelphia, November 20, 1970.
13. Survey of College Freshmen Conducted by American Council on Education for the American Jewish Committee. *The Evening Bulletin*, Philadelphia, December 12, 1970.
14. S. Freud, "On Narcissism: An Introduction." *Collected Papers*, Vol. IV. London: The Hogarth Press Ltd., 1949, 42.

Beyond Eve and Mary

Margaret N. Maxey

In the view of Margaret N. Maxey, protest on behalf of women's liberation is not enough: "Protest can vocalize the effects
but cannot thereby eliminate the origins of injustice or exploitation." What is needed, she argues, is a recognition on
the part of women that past identity models have held them
captive, together with the construction by women of "more
promising and plausible models for interpreting not only
themselves, but their present and ultimate meaning." And
this task is one for which theology has an empowering role
to fulfill. Dr. Maxey is Assistant Professor of Theological
Ethics at the University of Detroit—where, she says, she
is endeavoring to "raise the consciousness" of a Jesuit
theological faculty. She is also a Roman Catholic nun; her
order is the Sacred Heart of Jesus, a congregation dedicated
exclusively to education. Her "incautious essay" originally
appeared in the Spring 1971 issue of *Dialog**—an issue
focusing on the women's liberation movement.

DETAINED BY AN INCAUTIOUS TITLE, a reader
should expect an incautious essay into a doubly forbidding
realm: a Theology of (and for) Women. I am fully aware
that in introducing this expression I may appear far less en-
lightened than some of my colleagues or seem ignorant of
their strictures.[1] As a matter of fact, those strictures are
precisely what this essay is about. But not only that.

As if all were not about Eve, a "Women's Liberation"
theme at once freights an inquiry with overtones of com-
plicity in, or undertones of compliance to, a movement pro-
pelled by a psychology of protest. But protest is not the

* 5100 W. 82nd St., Minneapolis, Minn. 55431.

cutting edge for the kind of liberation I have in mind. Protest can vocalize the effects but cannot thereby eliminate the origins of injustice or exploitation. Moreover, recent opinion polls among the women who are presumably being "liberated" indicate that their attitude quotients cover the entire spectrum from Right to Left. Evidently a "silent majority" of women are rejecting the strategies and rhetoric coined by their self-styled Liberators of the New Left. Yet just as evidently, contemporary women are instinctively (if silently) rejecting an androcentric cultural and religious heritage which continues to assume that Man sets the standards and is in fact the norm for being human, and that Woman is man's indispensable complement and companion—a divine but gratuitous afterthought. The women who refuse to compete for masculine roles in Church and Society are thereby refusing to emulate man as their norm. From my reading of the evidence, I have concluded that women are instinctively searching for a different and peculiar kind of liberation. This is why I would assign to theology a peculiar task.

I

Clearly, woman's identity is in trouble today. She feels compelled to carve out anew or to relocate her identity by competing for those economic, socio-political, sexual roles with which Western culture and history have presumably awarded men their "superior" status. Her logic is not to be faulted. Her *models* are. When women look back over cultural and religious history for facts to document their demand for "liberation," their arguments are not inconsistent. Their presuppositions are.

This essay wishes to take seriously the dictum, "He [she] who is ignorant of history is condemned to repeat it." Its seriousness emerges from a sobering realization: we ourselves shape history by the kind of questions we address to it thinking, mistakenly, that we somehow recover a *neutral* or *objective* past. Contemporary women (and men) cannot change the history which has produced them and their problems. But women (and men) do control their interpretations of history —the modeling character they confer on it. More and more women are reviewing their past and protesting their present condition of exploitation. It would be unfortunate if the "solutions" women project were to be truncated and narrowed by a past from which they only seek "liberation." The need for a critical instrument—for a "theology" of and for "women"—inserts itself precisely at this point. An instrumental theology would have the task of liberating women from past models by displacing them with new models.

A particular notion of "theology" is just as much at issue here as a notion about "woman." The credentials qualifying a person to assume that her notion about woman is valid do not yet qualify as valid supports for her notion about theology. And so I must look for support from accepted theologians—who happen to have been men, who also happen to have been celibates, yet who did not therefore disqualify themselves from speaking as experts about, to, and for unknown and unknowable women. The case I am trying to make for a "theology of woman" would define theology as an instrument for criticizing and constructing models for self-interpretation—in this case, of women. It would appear that theologians in the past have already made my case.

Take Augustine of Hippo. The misogynistic deliverances of a Jerome[2] or a Tertullian[3] or a John Damascene[4] or an Ambrose[5] are generally disallowed by the theological purist. The basis for disallowing statements of these early Fathers is that they reflect, in each case, some controlling idiosyncrasy in personal biography, or a polemic occasioned by a cultural climate of opinion. With Augustine, however, the margin for disallowance is embarrassingly diminished, not only because the weight of his "theological authority" in Western Christian tradition has been considerable, but because his theological doctrines still find resonances in Christian consciousness. It is from Augustine the Christian *theologian*—not Augustine the repentant father of an illegitimate son, or unfaithful lover of a mistress—that Christians have inherited a theology of human sexuality, of marriage, of virginity, and summarily of

Woman. As a consequence, Christian women have had to locate themselves somewhere between Eve and Mary.

Whatever the wellsprings of Augustine's theology, it has given to Woman a theological significance and explanatory function distinct from Man. My point is not to *discount* the psychological conflicts which at one time shaped Augustine's theological speculations. To the contrary, my concern is to insist upon their theological indispensability. The point I wish to press is not the obvious one that some emotional or intellectual bias can always be held to account partially for why a thinker has the theological (or any other) perspective he has. The point is that a *psychology* is inevitably ingredient to any theological accountability for the human condition.

The initial question is why Augustine should have developed his doctrine of "original sin" by linking the *Fall* of man and woman to their *sexuality*. The consensus of recent scholarship seems to point to one primary explanatory factor.[6] This factor is the primacy that a dualistic faculty psychology has awarded to *rational control*, both as a means for differentiating man from other species of animal, and as a means for differentiating Man from Woman.[7] The evidence for this factor in Augustine's theological development is impressive.[8]

Against the pessimistic dualism of the Manicheans who condemned coitus and marriage as intrinsically evil, and against the optimistic naturalism of the Pelagians who declared the natural goodness of man and his endowments despite the Fall, Augustine had to develop a theology of sexuality which avoided both extremes. Moreover, Augustine had to account for man's original transgression without compromising two other extremes. On the one hand, Augustine had to affirm that man was a perfectly created being, lest some imperfection or weakness in man be ascribed to a divine deficiency in power or in goodness. On the other hand, man's original condition had to allow for the origination of sin from man's own activity, as a distortion of the goodness of God's primal gift. The keystone in the arch bridging both sets of extremes was to be Augustine's theory of concupiscence.[9]

Originally neutral in meaning "desire," *concupiscentia* in

Augustine's theory assumed the explanatory function of "lust," the insatiable and inordinate drive for self-satisfaction operating in every human impulse, but most powerfully and typically in genital sexuality. In Augustine's exegesis of the Genesis account of the Fall of Man, we discover his account of the cause and subsequent manifestation of "original sin." Eve and Adam, by their respective disobedience and rebellious act against God's express command, were themselves infected by their disobedience. It recoiled upon their natural powers, impairing the control of their bodies, organs, and especially their genitals.[10]

The fact that Adam and Eve covered their nakedness (according to Genesis) was a confirmation for the theory Augustine proposed. He argued that the original shame of Adam and Eve continues to be reenacted in man's sense of shame and guilt when he recovers his rational powers, after they have been engulfed by uncontrollable and unseemly sexual pleasure. The greater strength of sexual impulses has not only clouded the mind, but disabled the will, making it incapable of inciting or controlling either tumescence or impotence.[11]

Whereas God intended and implanted sexual desires to assure the continuance of mankind, man has corrupted sexual desire by his concupiscence (lust), causing every concrete act of coitus he performs to be intrinsically evil (irrational), sinful (disobedient), and shameful (guilt-ridden). Virtually, if not explicitly, Augustine is responsible for having formulated a theological equivalence between original sin, concupiscence or desire, and sexual passion.[12]

Augustine acknowledged that the intention to procreate would excuse a husband and wife from the sinfulness inherent to their marriage act. Nevertheless, coitus remained the channel by which parents transmit concupiscence and its accompanying guilt to their children. Without exception, "Everyone who is born of sexual intercourse is in fact sinful flesh."[13]

It makes little difference whether we trace Augustine's doctrine of the Fall and concept of sin to his own psychological history or to a then-current Christian asceticism and its ideal of perfection. The theological fact remains that a dualistic *psychology* has been ingredient and presupposed to the theological doctrine which has produced an Augustinian model of Woman. To Augustine's theological man, woman as a theological datum is the visible incarnation of sexual desire and lust, the carrier of evil and guilt, the occasion of man's original Fall and subsequent transmission of sin. For Augustine, it is only proper that, "since through a female death had occurred to us, through a female also life should be born to us."[14] As mother of all the living, Eve had brought dishonor upon all women. Through Mary, however, women can be honored if they imitate and reflect her Virginal Motherhood.

Augustinian man was exhorted to obey the divine command to love woman in the same way that he was to love an enemy. That is to say, Man must regard Woman not as an opposing adversary, but simply as a similar human being. Or in other words, man must regard woman not as a *sexed* being, but simply as a *sinful* human being to be redeemed. Augustine writes:

. . . it is characteristic of a good Christian to love in a woman the creature of God whom he desires to be transformed and renewed, but to hate corruptible and mortal intimacy and sexual intercourse—that is—to love the human being in her, but to hate what belongs to her as a wife.[15]

A recent commentator on Augustine has noted that, for this theologian at least, "sex was no more intrinsic to human nature than hatred to one's adversary."[16] Augustine's evaluation of sexuality, and thus of woman's relation to man, has long given theological support to the insistence that "being sexed" is inconsequential and nonessential—if not detrimental—to "being a person."

Parenthetically, I find a disturbing redivivus of Augustinian Man in the assertions of those who hastily dismiss a "theology of woman" in favor of a homogenized "theological anthropology." One argument for this dismissal has suggested that ". . . a 'theology of woman' . . . is misbegotten in that it places sexual differentiation above personhood." As a corrective, we are urged "to develop a theological anthropology which will study the dynamics of human personality and social relationship from a radically evolutionary point of view."[17] It is quite possible that we can agree upon the objections to a "theology of woman" without, however, agreeing that the correctives proposed are sufficient or able to meet those objections.

Given woman's present stage of self-interpretation, it will not do simply to substitute one form of theological dogmatizing for another. It cannot be the theological task to debunk "natural" or "essential" sexual differences summarily, and then proceed to substitute socially-conditioned "persons-in-relation," presumably displacing distinct "sexes" or "essences in isolation."[18] Such an enterprise is, I submit, methodologically wrong-headed and theologically shortsighted.

Theology must at present perform a *liberating task*, not impose still another set of dogmas, however different. If theology is to acquit itself of its most urgent task, it must begin to recognize not only the modeling and remodeling functions it has performed in the past, but also the source of its models. This recognition would require, among other reconstructions, a Theology of Woman which would first locate past models dominating woman's self-interpretation; then it would locate and criticize the source of those models; finally, it would reconstruct or propose new models for woman's (and man's) self-understanding.

In our brief examination of Augustine, we have, in fact, illustrated this mode of inquiry. Augustine's model of Woman has been traced to his equation of original sin with concupiscence and sexual passion, an equation which depends on a dualistic psychology which awards primacy to rational control as the index of man's superiority over women and over animals. Augustine's model of Woman is clearly inseparable from his model of human sexuality, with its ideal of virginity. The result is that Woman is to be located between Eve and Mary.

Is it accurate to insist that what we have inherited from

Augustine are *models* for self-interpretation and for evaluating human behavior? We may evaluate this insistence by assessing our response to a number of questions. How extensively does our culture still retain the notion that sexuality is somehow tainted with sin or evil? Do men and women still equate being moral or Christian with suppressing sexual desires? Do we contrast Christian love (*agape*) with sexual love (*eros*), or relegate an ideal sexuality to the nonself, to an a-personal or infrahuman domain? We might also evaluate the modeling character of an Augustinian inheritance by asking if our ideal in liberating women is to render them *equal* to men as *human beings*—that is to say, insignificantly distinct from men on the basis of *sexual* differences, and thus, distinct from men only as individual persons are distinguishable. Do we exhort and expect men and women to be simply equivalent as "creatures of God" and distinguishable only as individual persons? Those who refuse to collapse the differences between men and women by reducing them to "individuality differences" are in effect, if not in conscious intent, refusing to perpetuate the theological models of Augustinian Man and Augustinian Woman.

II

The thesis I am attempting to argue is that we shall never liberate women (or men), Christian or otherwise, until we have induced *theology* to liberate women. First and foremost, theology must liberate women from an Augustinian model by refusing to reduce woman's theological significance to some a-sexual, homogeneous, or relational "human" being. Human sexual differences are neither theologically evil nor theologically nonessential. The alternative to homogeneity is to construct a new theological model of woman—a model introducing correctives from an updated depth-psychology that will counteract not only Augustine's *concupiscentia*, but also Freud's *libido*. The theological model I propose to construct would rely primarily (though not exclusively) on the depth-psychology of Jung and his interpreters.[19] It would supply a *model* for interpretation, not a touchstone of orthodoxy.

According to the thesis I am arguing, the theological task of "liberating" women would get underway primarily by rejecting and counteracting an Augustinian inheritance; it would then construct a corrective formed as a more promising alternative. This task would at once be compounded, however, for theologians have authorized more than an Augustinian model for woman's self-interpretation.

III

Consider the case of Thomas Aquinas. What a Neoplatonic psychological dualism had provided for Augustine, an Aristotelian biological naturalism provided for Aquinas, but with an important difference. Preoccupied with the problem of grace and the human will, Augustine had addressed himself to the problem of sin in Fallen Man; only indirectly did he address himself to Woman as acquiring significance from that theological problem. But Aquinas, preoccupied by the problem of grace and human nature, addressed himself directly to the problem of Woman as having been produced by the Author of Nature. The problem of woman's divinely intended *place in nature*, rather than her contingent *role in sin*, dictated the terms in which Thomas accounted theologically for the distinction between women and men.

From the self-evidence of woman's nature—her predestined maternity and inferior powers of reason—Aquinas deduced the general intention of the Universal Author of Nature:

It was necessary for woman to be made . . . as a helpmate for man—not indeed as a help in some other work, as some maintain, for in fact, in any other work a man can be more efficiently helped by another man than by a woman—but as a help in the work of generation.[20]

Woman's maternal function indicated to Thomas that the natural order had appointed to woman a social location in the family. In that location, it would be contrary to "good order" (unnatural) ". . . if some were not governed by others wiser than themselves. So by a kind of subjection, woman is naturally subject to man, because in man the power of reason predominates."[21] Woman's inferior powers of reason and limited contribution to man's work could not result from nature's general tendency, nor could it be ascribed to its Author's universal intent. Therefore, it was evidently due to accidental factors which could in the end work Nature's will and weal.

Adopting Aristotle's *homunculus* theory (the male sperm precontains a "little man"), Aquinas accounted for and justified woman's existence in these terms:

Woman is misbegotten and defective, for the active force in the male seed tends to the production of a perfect likeness in the masculine sex; while the production of woman comes from a defect in the active force or from some material indisposition, or even from some external influence, as such as that of a south wind which is moist.[22]

Woman's defective condition, however, is not to be considered totally detrimental to humankind. Woman fulfills a limited task, that of contributing to the greater efficiency of nature's general tendency. Thomas avers that, ". . . as regards human nature in general, woman is not misbegotten but is *included* in nature's intention as directed to the work of generation."[23] Hence, Thomas is led to interpret woman's biological defectiveness and rational inferiority as a divinely willed asset: woman contributes to the common good by generating members of the human species.

Although he acknowledges the Genesis account—where God's intention in creating woman appears to be that man have companionship or an "other" to enrich self-knowledge —Aquinas persists in his biologism by insisting that the divine purpose for human sexuality, thus for woman, is human reproduction. In the first place, it is by the divine order that sexual organs are given to man, for they are intended for procreation. As such, sexual endowments are for a social or common good, not for individual purposes.

Generation is the only natural act that is ordered to the common good, for eating and the emission of waste-matters pertain to the individual good, but generation to the preservation of the species.[24]

In the second place, the divine order requires that man respect the purpose for which woman has been allotted to man.

A woman is taken into man's society for the needs of generation [reproduction]; with the disappearance of woman's fecundity and beauty, she would no longer be able to associate with another man.[25]

Consequently, since woman has been reproductive, Thomas concludes that man ought in justice and out of duty to remain with his wife after she grows old.

Despite his skillful departure from an Augustinian condemnation of sexual pleasure as intrinsically evil, Thomas could not depart from a rationalist perfectionism which both justified and preserved the purely *biological* purpose of sexual functions. Thomas insisted, on the one hand, that the purpose of certain natural powers was unquestionably good. On the other hand, he had to agree with Augustine that sexual pleasures were more oppressive to the reason than pleasures of the palate; and since sexual pleasures are more impetuous,

. . . they are in greater need of chastisement and restraint. . . . Hence, Augustine says, "I consider that nothing so casts down the manly mind from its heights as the fondling of women, and those bodily contacts which belong to the married state."[26]

Moreover, Thomas declared that ". . . in the sex act, man becomes like the animals because the pleasure of the act and the fervor of concupiscence cannot be moderated by reason."[27] Again, he insisted that "the man who is too ardent a lover of his wife acts counter to the good of marriage," and therefore he might be termed "an adulterer."[28] In these affirmations, however, Thomas is much less a psychologist than a biologist. In his perspective, the *purpose of Nature's*

Creator is adulterated or frustrated when men substitute the good of *individual* pleasure for the *common* good of continuing the species.

Clearly, Thomas Aquinas has not bequeathed to theological posterity and religious piety a model of Woman who is either a carrier of evil, sin, and guilt, or a carrier of salvation, purity, and holiness. Thomistic Woman is not located between Eve and Mary. Perhaps more damagingly, Thomas has reduced woman's theological significance to a biologically determined and divinely intended *natural function*: the reproduction of human creatures. The naturalism that has dominated and truncated Thomas' model of Woman is to be traced to his biologism. Thomas' biology devalues the (divinely intended) potential in sexual endowments, thereby devaluing the model of Woman which presupposes his biologized sexuality.

The naturalism and biologism on which Thomas grounded his theological model of Woman have long since been superseded. Recent research in biology and genetics, as well as psycho-sexual research, have marshalled evidence that woman and man are sexed for other than reproductive purposes. In general, sexuality involves an apportioning between two individuals of potentials for pooling the mutation-experiences of two lines of hereditary descent.[29] In particular, sexuality in highly complex organisms intrudes itself upon the cycle of reproduction to assure greater individuality and to enhance the autonomy of sexed individuals.

Human sexuality provides human persons with an unparalleled mode of disclosures between one "self" and another, enriching and enhancing their powers of self-knowing. We must not limit inferences from recent research merely to affirmations which concern the greater uniqueness or individuality of the human child, in contrast to infrahuman offspring. If human sexuality does not exist primarily or essentially for purposes of reproduction, then the sexuality of men and women must be explored along parameters which will discover not only the conditions appropriate to modes of disclosure for self-knowing, but also the criteria appropriate for enhancing and protecting self-disclosures. The outcome of such an exploration would certainly provide theology with data on which to construct new theological models of Woman and Man.

More importantly perhaps, new theological models might cut through the Gordian knot which moral theologians (at least, in the Roman tradition) have been busily tying with arguments against "artificial" contraception, against "unnatural" abortion, or against "immoral" methods of population control.[30] From their arguments, it would appear that traditional moral theologians are held captive by the same biologism and naturalism that once captivated Thomas Aquinas and Aristotle before him. But theologians will not be able to relinquish their arguments unless and until they have recognized that their logic is controlled by an assumed *model* —in this case, a biological model of sexuality underlying a model of Woman. Failing that recognition, a Thomistic theological model of Woman and sexuality seems destined to prevail, especially in controversies about contraception, abortion, and means of genetic control.

IV

Let us consider one more instance of theological modeling. I suggest that we look at the controversy between opponents and advocates of continuing a mandatory priestly celibacy, as the "discipline" has become institutionalized in Roman Catholic tradition. The arguments advanced clearly contain an implicit theological model of Woman.

Advocates of mandatory celibacy (when they venture beyond authoritarian *fiat* to some reasoned justification) presume that an unquestionable and divinely advocated *celibacy of Jesus* provides everyone concerned with two requisites: (1) a convincing *social legitimation* for a celibate priesthood; and (2) a sufficient *personal motivation* for choosing between personal values which, in fact, stand opposed as equally personal and equally valuable (e.g., authentically human love of others, "requiring the sacrifice" of normal human expressions of authentic love). The Christology which official advocates of mandatory clerical celibacy have assumed without question has recently become more than ever questionable *theologically*.[31] Our first concern here is with the sociological consequences of such a Christology, as it affects ecclesiastical practice in the twentieth century.

What sociological implication and inference should we draw—both for the institutional Church and its hierarchical priesthood—from the data amassed by recently conducted opinion polls?[32] In increasing numbers, ordained clergy and "lay" persons alike evidently favor and even demand that priestly celibacy become a matter of choice separated from the choice to serve God in a particular form of commitment within the institutional Church. A church endeavoring to *serve* the needs and "best interests" of its committed members would conceivably recognize an expression of majority opinion as a remarkable "sign of the times." A *Servant Church* would count it an unmistakable mandate from God to pay heed to the experiences and values expressed by those whom it attempts to serve. A Servant Church would listen to the expressions of need for compassion, for understanding, for awareness of changed conditions in which the values and goals of contemporary men and women must now be expressed.

Instead, Christians have recently been instructed by the highest authority-figure in the Roman Catholic church, acknowledging that the "authority" of the hierarchy is indeed divinely instituted to serve "the faithful." Yet "[the faithful] are the object, not the origin, of the authority which is established for their service, and is not at their service."[33] Why has the issue of mandatory celibacy been met with intransigent refusals by highest authority even to reconsider or officially to reevaluate the necessity of continuing such an ecclesiastical discipline?[34] Many who have confronted this question regard the issue to be, in fact, a drama enacting a long-rehearsed conflict between *two sources of Authority*.[35] Some contend that Authority derives from a sovereign ruler who is humanly selected (by a College of Cardinals), yet whose social location has been theologically legitimated as the "Vicar of Christ." Others contend that Authority derives from a sovereign people, or (in the case before us) from a priestly people who must express the authority of their experience. It would appear that our era, especially in the issue of mandatory clerical celibacy, is witnessing not only a theological, but a sociological conflict.

Significantly, if not obviously, the conflict reveals a dimly recognized theological rejection of a sociological axiom. Considered sociologically, not even an ecclesiastical institution can continue if it ceases to be supported with and by "plausibility structures." That is to say, it must continue to be affirmed and confirmed by human persons who find that institution and its structures meaningful, who find in it a continuing *expression of* and *response to* their deepest needs for ultimate meaning. I am suggesting that this sociological axiom is covertly (or unconsciously) rejected because of a theological axiom. According to this axiom, a "divine institution," by a self-legitimating claim to its "divine origin," need not be socially plausible or receive human confirmation from a consenting majority or a sovereign people.

Assuming this axiom, the advocates of an allegedly non-human (divine) origin for the discipline of priestly celibacy set forth their claim as self-evident or self-legitimating, as *exempt* from having to be socially and personally plausible. Those persons who are allegedly served by a celibate priesthood and who question its serviceability do not know what is in their best interests. It is assumed that "authority knows best." Dissenters who seek reevaluation of mandatory celibacy are suspected (sometimes accused) of being undisciplined, pleasure-seeking, *disobedient* creatures of God. Consequently, the self-legitimated status of mandatory celibacy continues to be imposed by an "authority" beyond the range of human reason, logical argument, and social plausibility.

The issue, however, has an increasingly precarious immunity from human questioning. A common conjecture is that "authority" can continue to impose the discipline only as long as men are persuaded that (1) a monarchical concept of a Divine Being, (2) a hierarchical concept of power descending through a Vicarious Authority, and (3) a disparagement of sexuality and of women in an androcentric Creation, are unquestionable Christian verities. The third factor returns us to our second concern, namely, whether or not an ecclesiastical institution and an ecclesiastical discipline rest on a theological model of Woman.

Undoubtedly, some model of Woman is operative when men are exhorted to forego marriage, sexual intercourse, the "society of women," in order to pursue their personal purity and to preserve an institutional image of holiness and chastity. Theological authority can trace an uninterrupted line of descent from the fourth century to the twentieth. In *Duties of the Clergy*, Ambrose, bishop of Milan, asserted that married priests were "foul in heart and body"; consequently, "the ministerial office must be kept pure and unspotted, and must not be defiled by coitus."[36] In the twentieth century, Pope John XXIII confided to Etienne Gilson that it would be quite simple for him to sign a decree permitting priests to marry; but then the Church would no longer be worthy to be considered "holy and chaste." Officially, Pope John declared that celibacy was unquestionably "one of the purest and noblest glories of [the Church's] priesthood."[37]

Several who have studied the historical development of sacerdotal celibacy suggest that we should distinguish between the "actual purpose" and the "ostensible purpose" of polemics insisting that priests be celibates.[38] Ostensibly, the preservation of a celibate clergy has a religious purpose, namely, to guarantee that "purity of heart" and single-minded devotion to a sacred ministry which would be compromised or "divided" if the clergy had wives to love and care for. Actually, the preservation of a celibate clergy has socio-political and economic purposes, namely, to guarantee solidarity and political effectiveness within a body of men intending to be unimpaired by emotional ties, an elite who will not be subverted by their own vested interests or secular pursuits from an unquestioning obedience to the will of authorities who have ecclesiastical power over the sources of Salvation.[39]

If we grant this distinction, we would have to admit that a model of Woman subserves only the *ostensible* purpose of preserving sacerdotal celibacy. This model has proved instrumental (useful) in perpetuating both the social image of the institutional Church, and the personal image of priestly celibates whose motivation for sacrifice must be justified. According to this model, actual women are considered an institutional liability and a personal impediment to the ministrations of an androcentric, power-oriented, hierarchically-controlled "divine institution."

A masculine version of personal asceticism and disciplined control of others has fashioned a socially useful model of Woman dictated by institutional and ecclesiastical requirements. This model does not locate women primarily between Eve and Mary; nor does it locate women by their place in Nature and natural maternal functions. Women are assigned a third "utility" (*utile*)[40] in and through a model locating them institutionally. Women are supposed to be *recipients* rather than *mediators* or *ministers* for a sexually defined institutional "holiness and chastity." Once again, but with social consequences, Woman acquires theological (and sociological) significance because of her *sexuality*, now considered as an institutional liability.

The theological model of Woman resulting from and required by social institutionalizations of Christianity is losing its plausibility for several powerful reasons. Unprecedented methods of scientific control over genital sexuality have precipitated a "sexual liberation" which is already revolutionizing every behavioral pattern and mode of human interdependence. Not only is human sexuality being liberated from a morality based exclusively on the equation of sexual intercourse with human reproduction; there is also a liberation of marital fidelity and "total commitment" from an individualistic morality based on genital and psychological exclusivity.

A theological model of Woman as a *divisive* force—*opposed* to man's institutional commitment and impersonal service to others—must be linked with an increasingly questionable ideal for monogamous marriage. Traditional definitions and exhortations assume that the a-social character of intimate sexual relationships and the dis-social character of marriage naturally require married persons to be absorbed in mutual concerns and interests, thereby forming a self-sufficient and enduring social unit. On this view, men could selflessly commit themselves to an institutional "She," to "Holy Mother Church," but men could not commit themselves *both* to an institution and to a concrete woman. According to accepted (masculine) standards for a ministry extraordinarily "ordained" to accomplish a privileged work of redeeming the faithful, the requirements for marriage and for an ordained ministry involve distinct, mutually exclusive types of total commitment. An assumed model of Woman underlying this distinction is called into question by changing conceptions of marital fidelity and commitment.

Furthermore, the unsuitability of women themselves for ordination can no longer appeal to genetics for support of social prejudices. The emotional quality of objections to ordaining women was recently epitomized in the question of one horrified reactor: *"Pregnant priests?"* Anatomy, of course, destines women to be pregnant just as inescapably as it destines men to be celibate. Nevertheless, anatomy and celibacy have been major reasons for excluding women both from having positions with political decision-making power in Christian churches, and from having mutual bonds with those who do. The denial of ordination to women is but a consistent conclusion from the premise that woman's *sexuality* nullifies her access to any institutionalized religious power to fulfill functions ordained for the service and concern of others. Sexual liberation is overtaking such a premise.

The sociological and ecclesiastical concerns which have required theologians (in the Roman tradition) to construct an implicit social model of Woman might be counteracted partially by a critical reexamination of two assumptions. One would require a reassessment of the apparent antithesis between "total commitment" to an institutional Church and its ministry, and "total commitment" to a monogamous marriage and its domestic responsibilities.

The other would require celibates and ecclesiastical authorities to scrutinize both their presuppositions regarding the "work of redemption" by a divinely "ordained ministry," and their image of "institutional holiness." This scrutiny could induce a reevaluation of both mandatory priestly celibacy and the rejection of women's ordination under the harsh light of their concrete social plausibility for actual women and men in today's world. It is altogether possible that a new theological-social model of Woman would discover women to be an institutional asset, and that the ministry of women would relieve men of that assumed burden of "total commitment" which for centuries has divided men from women under an outmoded theological model.

Lest my insistence upon past theological modeling in the case of Woman should become tedious, I shall in conclusion only underscore the *liberating optimism* to which my thesis extends credibility. If, in fact, contemporary women are enabled to interpret themselves as originating from—but not determined by—past theological modeling of woman's role in Sin, woman's place in Nature, woman's status in an institutional Church, then at the least these models are vulnerable to displacement by new theological models. Liberation in an ultimate sense—its theological sense—can thus acquire a profound and pervasive meaning whose social consequences for women (and men) should be immense. Once we recognize that the process of liberation is an *authorizing process*—one of displacing the "authority" of past dominant models-for-self-understanding and behavior by constructing more meaningful or authoritative models—then theology might once again perform its central humanizing task. Theology might liberate women (and men) by authorizing models for self-expression through more plausible life-styles and social institutions.

My thesis contains a hypothesis: if women are brought to realize that past *models* hold them captive, then perhaps they will recognize that the task of "liberation" will remain but half accomplished until new models are constructed to displace the old. I submit that *theology* must empower women to criticize and reconstruct more promising and plausible models for interpreting not only themselves, but their present and ultimate meaning. A Theology of Woman would endeavor to accomplish this liberating task.

Notes

1. In her competent study, *The Church and the Second Sex* (New York: Harper & Row, 1968), Professor Mary Daly concludes her discussion of "Theological Roots of the Problem" by asserting "it is necessary to opt for a clear-cut rejection of that approach which is suggested by the expression, 'theology of woman.' This approach contains a built-in assumption that 'woman' is in fact a distinct species which can be understood apart from the other sex. It is founded on the unproved supposition that there is an innate psychosexual complementarity. Invariably, attempts to develop a 'theology of woman' fall on their various faces because they naively assume that the sex images of a patriarchal culture infallibly correspond to 'nature' and to God's will." (p. 147) It seems unfortunate that Professor Daly does not recognize that the expression need not indicate an uncritical acceptance of the "naive assumptions" which she attributes to those who adopt the expression for other purposes.

2. Besides praising marriage grudgingly because it brings forth virgins, Jerome can also be credited with asking: "If we abstain from coitus we honor our wives; if we do not abstain—well, what is the opposite of honor but insult?" (*Adv. Jov.* I.7) Concerning woman, he writes: "As long as woman is for birth and children, she is different from man as body is from soul. But when she wishes to serve Christ more than the world, then she will cease to be a woman and will be called Man [*vir*]." (*Comm. in epist. ad Ephes.*, III. 5 [PL 26, 567])

3. Characteristically, Tertullian addresses the "guilty sex" by asking woman: "Do you not know that each of you is also an Eve? . . . You are the devil's gateway, you are the unsealer of that forbidden tree, you are the first deserter of the divine law, you are the one who persuaded him whom the devil was too weak to attack. How easily you destroyed man, the image of God! Because of the death which you brought upon us, even the Son of God had to die. . . ." (*De cult, feminarum*, I. 1)

4. John Damascene is reported to have described woman as "a wicked she-ass, a hideous tapeworm . . . the advanced post of hell." (Cf. "A History of Catholic Thinking on Contraception" by Daniel Sullivan in *What Modern Catholics Think About Birth Control* [New York: Signet Book, 1964], pp. 28–73)

5. Ambrose measures Woman against the standard of Man in these terms: "She who does not believe is a woman and should be designated by the name of her sex, whereas she who believes progresses to perfect manhood, to the measure of the adulthood of Christ. She then dispenses with the name of her sex. . . ." (*Expos. evang. sec. Lucam*, X, 161)

6. See D. S. Bailey's discussion of Augustine in *The Man-Woman Relation in Christian Thought* (London: Longmans, Green and Co., 1959), pp. 50ff. Also, Daniel Sullivan, *op. cit.*, pp. 36ff.

7. The view that woman is "the irrational half" of mankind is expressed by St. Methodius, among others, in support of his assertion that woman is "carnal and sensuous." Ambrose, Pope St. Gregory, and Cyril of Alexandria are of one mind, writes Callahan (*op. cit.*, p. 32) in discoursing on "woman's slow understanding, her unstable and naive mind, her natural mental weakness, and her need of an authoritative husband."

8. Augustine has himself insisted that it was rational and spiritual *certitude* he had been seeking in vain through Manichaeism, skepticism, and Neoplatonism. When he seemed at last to have found certitude in the Christian faith, the condition for its attainment was radical—*sexual continence*, the renunciation of sexual pleasure or "sensuality" via disciplined asceticism. At the heart of Augustine's conversion to Christian faith was a decision *for* rational certitude and a contemplative life, but only by way of a decision *against* sexual pleasure, even in legitimate marriage. Augustine was obviously a man of his time in his esteem for a reasoned and disciplined "contemplation of divine things" attainable through a single-minded "way of perfection."

9. For a fuller discussion of this point, see Bailey, *op. cit.*, pp. 52–58.

10. Augustine, *De civitate Dei*, XIII. 13 and XIV. 16–17.

11. *De nupt. et concup.* I. 6.

12. See the discussion of Norman P. Williams in *The Ideas of the Fall and of Original Sin* (London, 1927), esp. pp. 366–67.

13. *De myst. et cont.* I. 13.

14. *De agone Chr.* XXII. 24.

15. *De serm. Dom. in mont.* I. 15. 41.

16. William E. Phipps, *Was Jesus Married? The Distortion of Sexuality in the Christian Tradition* (New York: Harper & Row, 1970), p. 173.

17. Daly, *op. cit.*, p. 147.

18. *Loc. cit.*

19. For example: C. G. Jung, "Women in Europe," *Contributions to Analytical Psychology* (New York: Harcourt Brace, 1928); R. S. J. Hostie, *Religion and the Psychology of Jung* (New York: Sheed and Ward, 1957); Erich Neumann, *Amor and Psyche* (New York: Bollingen Series LIV, Pantheon Books, 1965); E. C. Whitmont, *Basic Concepts of Analytical Psychology* (New York: C. G. Jung Foundation, 1967).

20. Thomas Aquinas, *Summa Theologiae,* I. 92. 1.
21. *S. Th.* I. 92. 1, ad 2^m.
22. *S. Th.* I. 92. 1.
23. *S. Th.* I. 92, 1. ad 2^m.
24. *Summa Contra Gentes* III. 2. 123.
25. *S.C.G.* III. 2. 123.
26. *S. Th.* II-II. 151. 3. Thomas later writes: "Sexual intercourse casts down the mind, not from virtue but from the height, that is, the perfection of virtue." (II-II. 153. 2)
    Again: "For those people who devote their attention to the contemplation of divine things and of every kind of truth, it is especially harmful to have been addicted to sexual pleasures." (S.C.G. III. 2. 136)
27. *S. Th.* I. 98. 2.
28. *S. Th.* II-II. 154. 8.
29. Cf. Julian Huxley's "Evolution and Genetics" in *What Is Science?* edited by James R. Newman (New York: Washington Square Press, 1961), "Sex itself is illuminated by our genetic knowledge. In origin it has nothing to do with sexual differentiation, the difference between males and females of a species; its basic and universal function is to provide the species with greater genetic variability." (p. 285)
30. I can only suggest briefly how interpretations of human sexuality might overcome excessively biologistic and naturalistic theological justifications and condemnations of contraception, as well as arguments against abortion of a foetus in early stages of development. Moral theologians have insisted that a person, and what constitutes a person, is already present in the embryo within a woman's uterus. Their arguments usually appeal to analogies from lower organisms. Against these analogies, the data from genetics and psycho-sexual research suggests different criteria and alternative models. The sheer presence of *structures* or *conditions* for personal and psycho-sexual development neither guarantee the inevitability nor preprogram the mode or quality of that development. Recent research does not provide ethicists or moral theologians with a "new naturalism," but with an awareness of specifically human modes of novel disclosures. The conditions for being human persons are not biologically predetermined, nor can decisions about preserving human embryos be settled with biological criteria, excluding the social and temporal conditions which will prevail after birth.
31. I refer here and commend to the reader the work of Phipps cited above, n. 16; see esp. pp. 177ff.
32. For example, Joseph H. Fichter, *America's Forgotten Priests* (New York: 1968).
33. The account and quotation were reported by the UPI, appearing under a dateline of 28 January 1971 in the City Edition of *The Detroit News.*
34. Pope Paul VI, in an *address* on 1 February 1970, said:

"[Celibacy] is a capital law in our Latin church. It cannot be abandoned or subjected to argument."

35. In December of 1920, Pope Benedict XV addressed a group of Czechoslovakian priests who were pressing for the right to marry: "The Latin church owes its flourishing vitality . . . to the celibacy of the clergy. . . . Never will the Holy See in any way even lighten or mitigate the obligation of this holy and salutary law of clerical celibacy, not to speak of abolishing it. We also deny . . . that the innovations of a 'democratic' character for whose introduction into ecclesiastical discipline some are agitating, can ever be approved by the Holy See." *Address*, 16 December 1920. (Cited by Phipps, *op. cit.*, p. 192)

36. *De offic.* I. 50.

37. Phipps reports this account of a conversation with Etienne Gilson (*op. cit.*, p. 192). Pope John's *address* was dated 26 January 1960. Gilson's "Souvenir du Père" appeared in *La France Catholique*, 862, dated 7 July 1963.

38. Cf. Bailey, *op. cit.*, pp. 150–52.

39. *Loc cit.*; cf. Fichter, *op. cit.*, p. 210; Phipps, *op. cit.*, pp. 179, and 193–94; also Joseph Blenkinsopp, *Celibacy, Ministry, Church* (New York: 1968), pp. 61–62.

40. Woman's "utility" (*utile*) has long been a linguistic staple in theological discourse on sexual relations and the purpose of marriage (Cf. Bailey, *op. cit.*, pp. 234–35). Theologians have in the past defined two "uses" of woman: one maternal, the other remedial. Woman is "useful" to man in generating his progeny; and she is "useful" in providing a release or remedy for man's imperious sexual impulses. The third "use" I am suggesting is woman's *institutional utility*. We need little clairvoyance to see that a theological model of Woman enables ecclesiastical authorities to measure (1) the nobility of the sacrifice which women make possible to celibates who are pursuing their personal purity; and (2) the "divine origin" of an institution which preserves its image of holiness and chastity by rejecting the ministrations of women both officially and in practice.

Theology and the Liberation of Man

Rubem A. Alves

Brazilian scholar Rubem A. Alves is perhaps best known for his book *A Theology of Human Hope*, in which he concludes that theology which is firmly rooted in the radical historicity and messianic humanism of the Old and New Testament languages does offer the linguistic tools requisite for the creation and maintenance of a truly human society in the world. In the essay that follows he relates his search for a new language of faith to the problem of development. In technologism and radical utopianism he sees two basic languages which seek to promote development. Rejecting the first, he finds in the second a close affinity with the ultimate concern of biblical language as well as a radical opposition to the spirit of traditional theological language. Dr. Alves' essay is a slightly emended version of a paper which he prepared for the Consultation on Theology and Development sponsored by the Committee on Society, Development and Peace (SODEPAX) in Cartigny, Switzerland, in November of 1969; the earlier version appears in the book *In Search of a Theology of Development.** Dr. Alves is head of the Department of Philosophy at the State School of Philosophy, Rio Claro, São Paulo, Brazil. During 1971 he was Visiting Professor of Christian Ethics at Union Theological Seminary, New York City.

I. Language and Theology

WHAT ARE THE NEEDS which move us and what hopes do we have when we speak about creating a theology of development or a theology for the liberation of man?

* Available from the Publications Department, The Ecumenical Centre, 150 route de Ferney, 1211 Geneva 20, Switzerland, at $1.50 per copy.

The need: We live in a world which is both shockingly different and radically new in its quality. Accordingly, its problems are not only different but qualitatively new. Such problems cannot be solved along the lines prescribed by our inherited recipes. Recipes are formulas which indicate what is to be done and how. All languages are recipes. Together with all the old prescriptions, traditional theological languages are in crisis because they are not able to handle the ingredients which our present world contains.

The hope: That a new language of faith can be created which may become an effective tool for the transformation of the earth into a place of recovery.

Not only that. We hope that the new language can be learned and actually spoken by Christian communities because it is only when this happens that a language becomes powerful to inform men's understanding of the world and their activity in it.

From this hope we derive the following methodological presupposition: a theology of development cannot be born out of the illusion (or as Wittgenstein would have said, "bewitchment") that words, by virtue of their intrinsic "truth," are powerful. Words do not have an *ex opere operato* power. The power of words is totally derived from the power of those communities which sustain and utter them. There is a sense in which it can be said that the reality of words is a function of power. This correlation is vividly illustrated in the following dialogue between Alice and Humpty-Dumpty:

"When *I* use a word," Humpty-Dumpty said in a rather scornful tone, "it means just what I choose it to mean—neither more nor less."
"The question is," said Alice, "whether you can *make* words mean so many different things."
"The question is," said Humpty-Dumpty, "which is to be the master—that's all."[1]

The task, then, is to create a theological language which can actually be spoken by real communities.

But how is this to be done? Of one thing we are sure: to

create and learn a new language is a process which implies much more than simply adding new themes to the old prevailing structures. Linguistics, the sociology of knowledge, and psychoanalysis all agree that the conscious articulation of language is built upon unconscious structures. New themes added to old structures is the same as new wine in old wine skins. New themes are always reduced to the logic and limits of the structure into which they are added. Man learns a new language only when he undergoes a structural change. Is not this the sense of the word *metanoia*?

When we attempt to change a language we are actually involved in social change because language is the "memory" of a social group. In the words of Gerhard Ebeling, language contains the "spirit" of a community. Robert Merton makes an observation on the issue of social change which will help us immensely in our effort toward linguistic change. He says that "to seek social change, without due recognition of the manifest and latent functions performed by social organization undergoing change, is to indulge in social ritual rather than in social engineering."[2] This means that we cannot hope to create and teach a new language if we do not pay attention to the function of a language for a certain community.

Berger and Luckmann observe that the tendency of all communities is to stick to the prevailing linguistic recipes to the extent that, from their point of view, they remain functional. "The validity of my knowledge of everyday life is taken for granted by myself and others until further notice, that is, until a problem arises that cannot be solved in terms of it. As long as my knowledge works satisfactorily, I am generally ready to suspend doubts about it."[3] For our purposes, this means that it is primarily for those who become aware of the dysfunctional character of traditional theological languages that a new language can be created and taught.

Language is an instrument created by man in order to solve the problem of alienation between himself and the world. Through language he imparts a human meaning to the world. He keeps the world under the control of man-made values and hopes. Rosenstock-Huessy remarks that "man is a name-giving animal."[4] This means that the name-less things which surround man lose their strangeness when they are called by a man-given name. Name-giving is the act whereby man imparts human meanings to the world. Human language, therefore, contains both the existential and the objective. Man and the world are united in it. This means that language is an instrument of mediation.

Suppose now that one of those poles undergoes change— man or the world, the existential or the objective. The language which mediated between them is then no longer adequate. It no longer performs the function of relation. Today we live in a linguistic crisis because both man's self-understanding and the situation of the world have undergone radical changes. A new language, in order to be functional, has to be able to relate the new existential exigencies of the communities which have undergone radical revisions in their self-understanding to relate their new values and hopes to the new problems of the present day world.

In order to be actually accepted and spoken by a community a new language has to articulate in conscious form the already existing existential conditions of the community. Mumford states that a new language becomes effective only when "it develops by means of clearer images, the ideas already present in a more or less latent form in the praxis and spirit of the people."[5] Mannheim makes the same point when he analyzes the formation of the utopian mentality. He indicates that utopias which are elaborated by individuals become active forces in society only when they express the dissatisfactions and hopes already active in social groups: "Only when the utopian conception of the individual seizes upon currents already present in society and gives expression to them, . . . only then can the existing order be challenged by the striving for another order of existence."[6]

In other words, language becomes power when it serves to express the unconscious striving, protest, and hope of concrete communities, or, in the words of Paul, when it articulates the "groaning of the creation" which, to be sure, is the groaning of the Spirit!

When we say that language is created by man in order to solve the problem of his relationship with the world we are touching on the fundamental difference between man and animals. Animals have their relationships with the world biologically programmed. Their organism is a biological "memory"; they are programmed by it. Man, on the contrary, has a defective or incomplete biological programmation. His biological memory, in many aspects, is open. Therefore, he is not determined, but free; his relationship with the world is not solved or closed. The world is a permanent problem which man has to interpret and solve over and over again, in many different ways. The incompleteness of his biological "memory" and "programmation" forces him to create or invent the program of his relationships with the world. From this need human consciousness and language are born. They did not fall from above. Their roots are down in the world of men and the need to solve the problem of human survival.

If this is the origin of consciousness and ideas, what about "truth"? Man gives the name truth to those ideas which have functioned satisfactorily for the solution of his concrete problems of survival. Truth is practical. Its seat is not an abstract a priori realm of ideas. This, however, is what Plato and much of Western philosophy and theology (both of which have properly been called a footnote to Plato!) had assumed. Truth lives where man lives, in his concrete relationships with the world.[7]

Obviously, when we talk about the concrete problems of survival we do not have in mind only its organic, biological, and economic aspects. The fact that man is not programmed biologically means that for him the idea of survival becomes closely related to values and meanings. His biological interests are enveloped by the cultural ones. "Before other 'interests' can claim satisfaction," says Werner Stark, "one basic 'interest' must be satisfied—namely, the necessity to live in an understandable universe; without it no concrete thought is possible at all, not even selfish thought."[8]

Man's values (biological, cultural, etc.) are the center around which a community constructs its language. If we want to know the secret of a language we have to look for its value center which constitutes the ultimate concern of the community, the issue on which its survival depends.

This center expresses the "spirit" of a community. This is why in order to understand the mentality of a group we have to look for its hopes, aspirations, and purposes.[9]

Moreover, this existential center is what determines the world created by the community and in which the community lives. "It is the . . . nature of the dominant wish," says Mannheim, "which determines the sequence, order, and evaluation of single experiences. This wish is the organizing principle which even molds the way in which we experience time."[10]

This ultimate concern is, therefore, the key for the understanding of the structure of the mentality of a group and the world-vision in which it lives.

If we take the needs of survival (biological, cultural, etc.) as the ultimate concern around which a community organizes itself and its world, through its language, then religious language is the outermost circle and represents the logic of the programmation worked out by the inner circles. Religion is the widest possible generalization and legitimation of the solutoin of the problem expressed by the ultimate concern of a community.

The origins of a symbolic universe have their roots in the constitution of man. If man in society is a world-constructor, this is made possible by his constitutionally given world-openness, which already implies the conflict between order and chaos. . . . In the process of externalization, he projects his own meanings into reality. Symbolic universes, which proclaim that *all* reality is humanly meaningful and call upon the *entire* cosmos to signify the validity of human existence, constitute the farthest reaches of this projection.[11]

Here we come to the origins of theological language. As language it is created by man or, more precisely, by a community, because man speaks only as a member of a community. We will see that what gives theology its specific character is not that it has a divine or revealed origin, but rather the concrete, historical horizon which determines its structure and content. There is a legitimate way of saying that "theology is anthropology: since as language it is human creation." Feuerbach was wrong not because of this statement but because he took the anthropological in a purely psychological sense, thus transforming theology into a reversed way of speaking about man's essence. But he forgot that even man's psychological structure is social and historical. This is the substance of Marx's critique of Feuerbach. When we understand man as social and historical it becomes clear that he is always responding to something outside of himself. Man is relation—struggle with, reaction to, moving towards. To the extent to which language is man's creation it is anthropology, but to the extent to which it articulates a response to something outside man it has a dimension of transcendence.

Theology traditionally refused to recognize its human origins. It assumed that its subject matter was a language which had been given "by a power independent of us. So that it could be a kind of scientific investigation into what the word *really* means."[12] This idea was subsumed under the head of revelation. The pragmatic origins of language and the contents of truth were ignored. Language and truth consequently became abstract, self-subsistent, and divorced from activity (praxis). Efficacy was not intrinsic to truth. It was taken for granted, along the lines of Platonic tradition, that truth had its own sphere and that efficacy was "doing the truth" which was learned a priori.

When we recognize the origins of theological language as having been born in history in order to articulate the ultimate concern of a community we put it back where all human languages belong, thereby creating new possibilities of dialogue otherwise impossible.

II. Theological Language: Truth as Power which Makes Men Free

The shift from abstract truth to truth as praxis represents a movement from Greek to Hebrew ways of thinking. The Greek mind combined a deep concern for a-historical truth and theory, as existing in themselves, with contempt for *techne* (praxis). Truth is discovered by speculation and pure thought. For the Hebrew mind, on the contrary, truth is derived from praxis. Truth is the name given by an historical community to those historical acts which were, are, and will be, effective for the liberation of man. Truth is action.[13]

For biblical language, facts come before words, praxis before theory. Language is a footnote to historical events.

Here is the mistake of the existential hermeneutics. It forgets that the existential always takes place in response to concrete events which happen outside of man. The critique used against Feuerbach is valid here.

In order to understand the "spirit" of biblical language we have to discover the center around which it was built. This center is the same event which gave birth to the people of Israel: the Exodus. The Exodus is not one event among others but rather the center which is the principle of organization of the whole biblical language.

Even Jesus Christ lacks meaning outside the context of this linguistic a priori. The universe of discourse about Jesus takes place within a linguistic structure which antecedes it and which gives it meaning. Much of our Christology has been extremely ignorant of this fact, to the extent that the "logia" about Christ, usually derived from Christological dogmas, becomes the hermeneutical a priori for the reading of the whole Bible.

The Exodus is the primary fact. Its immediate meaning for those who participated in it was liberation from bondage, liberation for the future, liberation for life. Its practical center, its content as ultimate concern, is therefore the liberation of man.

To speak of God is a derived way of speaking about these events. The events, it is obvious, were not created by man. Biblical language indicates this in referring to them as God's acts; that is, as facts which are bearers of freedom, facts which are future creating, which express the intention and power of a will which is not man's will. Man, therefore, is not the primary subject in history. The symbols which are used to keep the memory of these events, however, are created by the community.

The community of Israel understood that the liberating events were not simply something of the past. The meaning which it derives from the Exodus is projected over the whole cosmos, space, and time. The God of the Exodus, consequently, is a living God. He is the power which fills the whole of reality with the promise of liberation revealed in the Exodus. This fact determined the unique way whereby biblical language looks at the past: it is prophecy in reverse; it is the bearer of promise; it points toward the future.

Instead of being an abstract idea, therefore, God is to be verified by the fulfillment of the promise of human liberation from bondage and freedom for life. This is the meaning of the recurring references to the "faithfulness" of God: that the future brings the verification of the promises made in the past. Faith, in a certain sense, is confidence in the verifiability of what is promised.

Theological discourse, therefore, is not that of ontology but of praxis. It articulates an ongoing activity which mediates a new future to man.

Since knowledge of God is derived from events which changed the objective structures of society, biblical language speaks about God only in relation to events which create a new future for man.

Therefore, transcendence takes shape in history. It has to do with the power which makes the present pregnant with a new future. It does not direct man's hope to his liberation from history but rather to the liberation of history and man's liberation in history.

Transcendence in history is a radical negation of the transcendence of Greek philosophy, which perpetuates a dualistic world of oppositions: matter versus spirit; the natural versus the supernatural; the existential versus the structural; etc.

God is the power which in order to liberate man submits the structures of the world to the project of freedom and creativity. The reconciliation of man with the world, the overcoming of alienation, can be gained only through the dialectic between freedom which aims at the future and the structure which, either by inertia or open rebellion, wants to preserve the present conditions of oppression. Transcendence takes shape not as dualism but as dialectic.

Nature and the objective structures of the world become human as they are submitted to the dialectic of freedom which gives them a human meaning. The priority of freedom over nature in the Old Testament is derived from the fact that the Exodus is primarily an experience with the power of liberation. Accordingly, nature without freedom is considered a form of domestication and abomination, because it means vitality with future, that is, animal vitality. This is why there is such a strong polemic throughout the whole Old Testament against the religions of nature.

This fact should lead us to revise the concept of natural law, which is still so central in certain theological and ethical formulations as, for example, in the papal encyclical *Humanae Vitae*. We should recognize that it is derived from Greek philosophy and not from the Hebrew heritage. The concept of natural law can have a paralyzing effect on the liberation of man.

A question could be raised about the authority of the Bible. If its language is one language among others, if it was created by men, can we still speak about revelation? Can we speak about authority in the Bible? The first thing that needs to be said is that revelation, too, is a word created by men. When does man apply this word to some experience, event, or situation? Obviously he uses it to indicate that experience, event, or situation which solved his fundamental problem of survival. For the Bible it is the Exodus and all those events which are incorporated into its structure.

The other thing which is to be said is that authority is not displayed in theory but in practice. The correlate to authority is obedience, the willingness to live as if—in other words, to take the risk. This is not a situation specific of the life of faith. Thomas Kuhn, as he discusses the process by which science moves from one paradigm to another, indicates that in the crucial events the scientist has no certainties behind him. He has to take risks. But until this happens he has to move ahead in his experience "as if" it were true. "As in political revolutions," Kuhn says, "so in paradigm choice— there is no standard higher than the assent of the relevant community."[14] We might paraphrase Kuhn and say that "there is no authority higher than the faith or willingness to take risk of the relevant community."

What is faith if not readiness to rise, without certainty in its pocket, in a total openness to the future, in the hope that the future will bring the verification—or fulfillment—of the promises? This is the "spirit" which moves the language of faith, and which determines a life which is a permanent experiment—always open—life which lives not by its truths but by faith, hope, and love.

III. The New Situation in the World

Above we said that "a new language, in order to be functional, has to be able to relate the new existential exigencies of the communities which have undergone radical revisions in their self-understanding, to relate their new values and hopes to the new problems of the world." We have tried to outline the "spirit" of the language of faith. We now have to see if there is any homogeneity between the spirit of the language of faith and the spirits of the new communities which are defining themselves vis-à-vis the problems of development.

A theology of development will have to clarify the ideas already present in a more or less latent form in the spirit of communities. Our outline of the spirit of biblical language serves as the critical element for us to "discern the Spirit." Our task is to discover where and how the Spirit is speaking today "with sighs too deep for words," and to help human communities transform the wordless groaning into articulate and conscious speech. This is the new language we are looking for.

The appearance of new problems which cannot be solved in terms of the old languages requires more than simple adjustments, reforms, or improvements in these conceptual structures. Conceptual structures do not grow the way organisms do. This is true even for science:

Scientific discovery is often carelessly looked upon as the creation of some new knowledge which can be added to the great body of old knowledge. This is true of the strictly trivial discoveries. It is not true of the fundamental discoveries. . . . These always entail the destruction of or disintegration of the old knowledge *before* the new can be created.[15]

The destruction or disintegration of the old knowledge creates a vacuum. Due to the novelty of the problem the prevailing linguistic structures do not contain the theoretical tools to analyze it. This means that to the extent that we try to look at new problems through the glasses of the old optica, we make it impossible to see the novelty which they contain. New theoretical tools are required. But until they are created there is a period of uncertainty, of groping in the dark, or trial-and-error procedures, in the attempt to interpret the new disturbing problem.

The new problem which requires new tools for its understanding is here provisionally called development. We use the word with great reservation and only with the function of pointing to a constellation of new phenomena, without giving it any descriptive or analytical function.

This is so because in this phase of theoretical vacuum we

can only say that something new is occurring, without being able to say yet what its nature is.

The primary task is to interpret the problem, to say what it is. Interpretation is a dialectical activity because man gradually corrects his first hypothesis through his contacts with the problem. He elaborates a hypothesis, probes it, and corrects it, or elaborates a new one, probes it again, and so on.

When the problem at stake is related to man and his values the process is dialectical in a twofold way. First, because of the dialectics of knowledge, just mentioned. And second, because of the fact that the person or community engaged in interpretation is led to change its own value attitude toward the problem. There is no "value-free" approach.

In order to understand the objective problem of development we have to understand the process of its interpretation and the different attitudes toward it which in their turn have become the center around which communities took shape.

The first aspect of the problem to be noticed by consciousness was that the world is divided into nations which are rich and nations which are poor; nations which are developed and nations which are underdeveloped.

It was noticed, at the same time, that the whole world was in a process of "rapid social change."

Rapid social change was believed to be the process whereby the division between rich and poor nations was to be overcome. It was thought that the same structure which contained the contradiction between rich and poor contained the dynamic which would solve it.

Moreover, it was believed that the rapid social changes created by industrialization would have two effects: First, they would free man from the mental attitudes which had kept him as a simple object of history, so that he would become the subject and creator of history. Second, they would break those religions, traditions, and ideologies which kept countries, as such, under the spell of immobility.[16]

Underdevelopment was then interpreted as on-the-way-towards-development, as a stage which chronologically antecedes development.

Since the rapid social changes were caused by industrialization, and industrialization came from the rich nations, those nations were considered both as leading the triumphant procession of development and as the cause and hope of the development of the underdeveloped. They were thus seen as part of the solution of the problem.

This hypothesis faced a serious difficulty, namely, the growing gap between the rich and the poor nations.

A new hypothesis was advanced: development and underdevelopment, far from being successive phases of the same developmental process, are rather interdependent poles of the same structure in which underdevelopment is both caused by and the cause of development, and development is the cause of and depends on underdevelopment.

The industrialization and modernization of the underdeveloped countries came to be seen as a process which would inevitably lead to greater economic and political dependence and to the aggravation of their internal contradictions.

It became obvious that no solution was structurally given. In order to overcome the contradictions man had to become the subject of his history. For the nations of the Third World nationalism became the symbol of the conviction that the center of decisions had to be located inside the geographic and political limits of the nation if the problem of underdevelopment was to be solved.

In this sense, two basic languages seek to solve the problem of development.

The first language can be called technologism. It assumes that *techne* is the logos, that is, the principle of intelligibility of social order. Its main presuppositions are the following:

Underdevelopment is an economic problem.

Economic problems and solutions have to do with quantitative relations and not with qualitative or value questions.

Therefore, economic analyses and solutions are to be worked out on a highly technical level, that is, by a technological elite.

The participation of the people, to the extent that it combines technical incompetence and emotional attitudes, is a dysfunctional factor.

Therefore, the economic solution requires that the people be prevented from participating in the process in an active or critical way.

This is what explains the wave of dictatorships in many of the countries of the Third World.

The participation of the people can be prevented in two different ways and at two different levels: (1) by making their participation impossible through an "interim" dictatorship which has as its sole purpose to save the people from their own irrationality. Such dictatorship would be the only means whereby reason (*techne*) would triumph over the irrational. (2) Or by the elimination of the people's volitive dimension in such a way that they would be unable to operate except within the logic of the system. It is possible to make the oppressed love the oppressors, as George Orwell shows in his story of Winston Smith: "He had won the victory over himself. He loved Big Brother."[17]

These two techniques for preventing the participation of the people are in harmony with the anthropology which is presupposed: that man is a being of consumption whose primary needs are passive and receptive. Consequently, the elimination of man's critical participation cannot be considered as violence (because this is not an anthropological need), nor can the creation of patterns of exclusively passive participation be considered an improvement of man (because this is his sole need).

This language establishes the following relationship between man and structures: Man is a function of structures. He is to fit into the structures created by the elite because only they are bearers of the logos (*techne*) of the social order (which is basically economic, and therefore quantitative). This model does not see any relationship, therefore, between quality and quantity, or between the existential and the structural. It preserves an irreducible dualism.

The other language inverts this logic. It knows that man

does not live without bread but it knows also that he does not live by bread alone. Any society which creates the conditions for the hypertrophy of the stomach and requires the atrophy of the will is intrinsically violent and repressive, regardless of its economic measures.

The anthropological presupposition of this second language is that man is a world creator, that he needs to live in a world which makes sense to him—a world filled with human values, a world which is friendly. This is why he makes culture and builds his world—in order to humanize it, so that it will no longer be strange and threatening. He creates order with the purpose of overcoming alienation. Theologically speaking, he does this in order to be reconciled with the world.

But this is possible only through man's activity. This means four things:

The conquest of alienation is a process whereby man externalizes himself through his activity, thereby creating structures in his own image and likeness. It is not enough for man to eat bread. Bread must be eaten as a "sacrament," as a symbol of a meaningful world.

The process of humanization begins when man becomes aware of the contradictions between himself and his world. Theologically this is the contradiction between freedom and bondage, history and nature, love and law, creativity and conformity to the world (cf. Romans 12:1-2). Under this situation man experiences the world as violent and repressive, and his reconciliation with it is seen as a task to be carried out through power. The process of humanization is thus one of a political character in the broadest sense of the word—as conscious and free activity for the creation of a new tomorrow.

This process is not only a means to an end. Man is human when he creates. Therefore, it is in the process that man finds his true humanity.

Man is a process. He is an unfinished experiment.

The focus of the problem was radically changed from economy to creativity. The new language which articulates this understanding created a wide universe of communication which includes large groups in the affluent nations—students and members of the Black community, for instance. If the liberation of man were simply an economic problem members of the affluent nations and communities would be left out. If these groups feel, however, that the functional exigencies of the technological utopia are destroying their creativity and making their critical participation impossible, then they are indicating that man is human only when he is free to create his own society and future. If with the world of affluence, of functional excellence, and of technological ominipotence "history comes to an end," as Mario Savio said, then a different society must be created.

When we say that for this language alienation is overcome only in the act of creation, the act which unites the existential and the objective, man and the structures, the subjective and the world, then it is obvious that any sort of dualism is rejected. This language makes the dialectic between freedom and structures the dynamic principle of its logic.

This language may be called radical utopianism.[18] I call it radical in order to differentiate it from utopian technologism. Technologism, as a utopia, aims at the overcoming of all utopias through the creation of a society in which operational and functional modes of thought and action will definitely supersede those which involve negation, imagination, creativity, freedom, and dysfunctionality. It is "the end of history."[19]

The radical utopia, on the contrary, aims at no utopia but at a society which remains permanently open and unfinished. It is a radical utopia because its future is not a day or a place but a permanent horizon, a point of reference which both invites and informs that the task is permanently unfinished.

This discussion has revealed how void the word development is of meaning. What do we mean when we use this word? Where do we stand?

The new situation of the world is thus mediated by the interpretation and commitment of certain groups and communities.

IV. Discerning the Spirits

Our primary task is to discern the spirits: to separate the spirit which tempts men with the promise of all things, provided that they renounce their freedom (Matthew 4:8-9), from the Spirit of God who groans with and through human communities and whose groaning can be discerned in the "memory" of His liberating activity in the past. "Where the Spirit of God is, there is freedom."

Radical utopianism, to the extent that it sees that man does not live by bread alone, that man's vocation is freedom, that only through man's free activity will he receive the gift of the earth and his reconciliation with it, and to the extent that it remains open for the future, is structurally homogeneous with the "spirit" of faith.

Radical utopianism represents a radically new ultimate concern. Although it has remarkable similarities with the ultimate concern of biblical language, it is radically opposed to the ultimate concern of traditional theological languages.

Obviously, this means that there is a radical opposition between the spirit of biblical language and the spirit of traditional theological languages.

Traditional ecclesiastical languages have their ultimate concern in eternity, God, and salvation of the soul. Their relation to the world, to life, and to history, when it is not negative, is purely tangential. Or they put the world and life in an inferior rank: the supernatural over the natural; the religious over the secular; the spiritual over the material; the eternal over the temporal.

For this traditional language man's ultimate concern is in the beyond. Man's destiny is outside the world. This language therefore perpetuates a radical dualism between freedom (will) and the objective structures: the will is primarily centered in the beyond and only secondarily in the here and now. As indicated above, biblical language does not know of any dualism, since its God is transcendent in the midst of life, power, and history, and this makes men free in and for the world.

Dualism makes traditional theological languages akin to the language of technologism.

To the degree to which these traditional languages dislocate the ultimate concern from its real locus to a virtual one, they are a form of "bewitchment" (Wittgenstein) of language, since they reify and ontologize symbols which were derived from history and are to be subordinated to their practical efficiency.

This being the case, traditional languages become "substitute-gratifications." They are derived from man's fear of, and inability to deal with, real problems. Man therefore takes refuge in a verbal world now invested with ontological density.[20]

This explains the resistance to change by those who are under the "bewitchment" of the traditional languages.

Part of the task of reconstruction in theology and of liberation of men is to break this bewitchment.

It is not enough to purify or reform the traditional languages. If their basic structure is preserved their alienating function is also preserved. Many of the attempts to change these structures have simply been efforts to add new chapters to the old structures (Matthew 9:16). "Those who criticize only the parts of a structure bind themselves, by this same criticism, to the structure as a whole" (Mannheim).

If we make of a theology of development simply a new chapter to be added to the old structure, without radically changing its ultimate concern along the lines indicated by biblical language, the result will be a language in which the concern for life, time, and the earth will always be penultimate and derived from the ultimate (timelessness, salvation, the beyond, etc.). If the previous analysis of the biblical language is correct, regardless of how much such a language of development preserves of biblical words and symbols, it is a structure alien to the structure of biblical language, and, therefore, alien to faith.

I believe that Bonhoeffer was both the prophet and the

theologian who indicated the direction to be followed. "It is not with the next world that we are concerned," he said, "but with this world. . . . What is above the world is, in the Gospel, intended to exist *for* this world."[21]

Today's theological crisis is due to the contradiction which exists between the "spirit" of traditional theological languages and the "new spirit" created by the activity of the Spirit of God in and among Christian and secular groups. The task of theology is to transform the "groaning" into conscious and articulate language.

A language defines the "spirit" of the community which speaks it. The implications of the above reflections for ecclesiology are radical and they mean at least the following:

Much of what we call "church," if analyzed from the perspective of the "spirit" which its language articulates, is not the community of faith.

And much of what we consider not as church will have to be considered by this analysis as a social creation and expression of the Spirit of God.

The structural analysis of the biblical language and of the consciousness of the community of faith implicit in it consequently opens new avenues for our understanding of ecclesiology and of the basis for ecumenical unity.

Notes

1. Lewis Carroll, *Through the Looking Glass* (Chicago: The Goldsmith Publishing Co., n.d.), p. 182.
2. Robert Merton, *On Theoretical Sociology* (New York: The Free Press, 1967), p. 135.
3. Peter L. Berger and Thomas Luckmann, *The Social Construction of Reality* (Garden City, N.Y.: Doubleday Anchor Books, 1967), p. 44.
4. Eugen Rosentock-Huessy, *Out of Revolution* (Brunswick, Maine: Four Wells, 1938), p. 693.
5. Lewis Mumford, *The Condition of Man* (Portuguese edition), p. 358.
6. Karl Mannheim, *Ideology and Utopia* (London: Routledge & Kegan Paul, Ltd., 1960), p. 187.

7. Cf. John Dewey, *Reconstruction in Philosophy* (Boston: Beacon Press, 1962), Chap. IV; Berger and Luckmann, *op. cit.*; Jean Piaget, *Biologie et Connaissance* (Paris: Gallimard, 1967); and Ernst Cassirer, *Essay on Man* (New Haven: Yale University Press, 1944).

8. Werner Stark, *The Sociology of Knowledge* (London: Routledge & Kegan Paul, 1967), p. 50.

9. Mannheim, p. 188.

10. *Ibid.*

11. Berger and Luckmann, *op. cit.*, p. 104.

12. Ludwig Wittgenstein, *The Blue and Brown Books* (New York: Harper Torchbooks, 1958), pp. 27–28.

13. Cf. G. Ernest Wright, *God Who Acts* (London: SCM Press, 1952). Cf. also Jürgen Moltmann, *Theology of Hope* (New York: Harper & Row, 1967), who shows that the biblical God is not an intellectual principle for the explanation of the world but rather a transforming exigency.

14. Thomas S. Kuhn, *The Structure of Scientific Revolutions* (2d ed. enlarged; *International Encyclopedia of Unified Science*, Vol. II, No. 2; Chicago: University of Chicago Press, 1970), p. 94.

15. John Dewey, *op. cit.*, p. xvi, quoting C. D. Darlington. For a detailed discussion of the issue see Thomas S. Kuhn, *op. cit.*

16. Cf. Arend Th. van Leeuwen, *Christianity in World History*, trans. H. H. Hoskins (London: Edinburgh House Press, 1964).

17. George Orwell, *Nineteen Eighty-Four* (New York: Harcourt, Brace and Co., 1949), p. 300 (the last two sentences of the novel).

18. For the meaning of utopia see Mannheim's "The Utopian Mentality," in *Ideology and Utopia*.

19. Henry Lefebvre, "Reflexoes sobre o Estruturalismo e a Historia," in *O Método Estruturalista*, ed. Carlos Henrique Escobar (Rio de Janeiro: Zahar), p. 80.

20. For a discussion of the problem see Norman O. Brown, *Life Against Death* (New York: Vintage Books, 1959), esp. pp. 150–51.

21. Dietrich Bonhoeffer, *Letters and Papers from Prison*, ed. Eberhard Bethge; trans. Reginald H. Fuller (New York: The Macmillan Co., 1953), p. 168.

V. Theological Syntheses and Prospects

Communication and Community

Paul S. Minear

"A true conversation . . . fully engages both partners at deeper levels of selfhood, where no single question and answer will suffice. Such conversation marks the voluntary opening of an invisible door that ends an inner isolation between persons. Their meeting and their conversation create for both a new situation out of which unpredictable developments may emerge." Having thus defined the nature of genuine dialogue, Paul S. Minear proceeds to analyze nine types of conversations "according to the factors which make for frustration or fulfillment." Throughout his analysis, he is concerned with how language relates to community—in particular, how God's word creates community. For many years Professor of Biblical Theology at Yale University Divinity School, Dr. Minear recently took the post of Vice-Vicar of the Ecumenical Institute for Advanced Theological Study in Jerusalem. The author of many books and articles, his most recent work is a study of the Book of Revelation titled *I Saw a New Earth*. His essay is reprinted from the July 1970 issue of *Theology Today*.*

IT IS THE ANXIOUS FATE of the Bible to win, without much competition, a double award as the best-selling and the least-understood book. Circulation figures appear to increase in direct proportion to pronouncements on the book's unintelligibility and irrelevance. The more study, the less consensus on the meaning.

> Both read the Bible day and night,
> But thou read'st black where I read white.

Willian Blake's couplet can be demonstrated *ad infinitum*

* P.O. Box 29, Princeton, N.J. 08540.

wherever the Bible is read. It is for this reason that the Bible escapes sustained attack from those who should oppose its use. Why attack a book that is so ambiguous in meaning and so capable of supporting both sides of every issue? To be sure, there are those who still find in the Scriptures a single, clear, and compelling verdict which supports only one side of every issue, but their number dwindles rapidly. The more typical response to reading the Bible is bewilderment, confusion, frustration, and perhaps more often the dulling discovery that even the desire to comprehend the text has evaporated.

Although we shall seek to deal primarily with causes of this aborted communication with the Bible, let us proceed by classifying the various types of conversation in which all of us engage, hoping thereby to clarify the different kinds of obstacles to effective discourse. Martin Buber called attention to four kinds of speaking. First is the monologue, that continuing restless muttering, whether audible or not, by which the self talks to itself about whatever forces its way to the screen of consciousness. Although this form of speech invites greater attention than it usually receives, we shall decline that invitation. The second form is a monologue disguised as dialogue. We have suffered this type of punishment from others all too often, so it might vent our phlegm to study it. Even so, we must set our sights on other targets. Buber's third form is called a technical dialogue because it deals with technical matters and is carried on for technical purposes. Information is exchanged from one person to another, and then the deal is closed. For example, I find that my watch has stopped. I ask a passerby, "What time is it?" He says, "Eight-forty-three." I set my watch, wind it, and go my way. The purpose of the dialogue is fulfilled. Probably a vast majority of the dialogues by which human society carries on its business falls within this type: airplane schedules, news broadcasts, mathematics, books, monthly bills. Yet for all their importance in daily affairs, these dialogues proceed on the superficial levels of self-engagement.

A true conversation, Buber's fourth kind, fully engages

both partners at deeper levels of selfhood, where no single question and answer will suffice. Such conversation marks the voluntary opening of an invisible door that ends an inner isolation between persons. Their meeting and their conversation create for both a new situation out of which unpredictable developments may emerge. A genuine dialogue produces a new orientation for both participants. Two centers gravitate together, so that by standing at the same point each comes to see what the other sees. Along with the movement of the two centers, there occurs a coalescence of horizons and ceilings. In speech, a common past is both discovered and created. The futures of the two persons converge as they talk together, at least for the time-and-the-persons being. True dialogue involves the total existence of the participants along with the continuing stories by which they bring their pasts and futures into the conscious present. Any genuine dialogue is worth studying, for in it life-stories are being told and retold as a way of celebrating the death of an older world (before this particular meeting) and the birth of a new (in which these two are, as it were, charter members). Our interest centers on dialogue of this fourth kind, and our concern now is to analyze various conversations according to the factors which make for frustration or fulfillment.

I

Type 1. *Direct conversation, with both parties present, when the desires of both are realized and there is therefore perfect communication.* In verbal form this may characterize the speech of a man and his wife who have lived together for many years. In non-verbal form it may characterize the co-ordination of a chamber music ensemble whose members have played together for many years. This form is not as rare, however, as these examples may suggest. Wherever two persons enjoy a genuine friendship, there a genuine dialogue can and does take place. I take it as obvious that this degree of rapport represents the implicit goal of all genuine dialogue but that it is all too seldom attained. The experience of frustration in reaching this goal offers a constant stimulus for locating and removing obstacles to communication, that is, for arriving at hermeneutical adjustment. Yet where communication moves on the desired level of selfhood, where it leads to adequate two-way traffic in thoughts, feelings, and wills, there are no problems which require hermeneutical attention. It would actually be gross violation of human community to intrude an analytical eye or ear into that conversation.

Type 2. *Direct conversation with both parties present, when there is an apparent breach of understanding between them.* Because both speakers are present, they will normally become aware of the imperfect communication and will instinctively seek to locate and to remove the obstacles. If the dialogue has been such as to engage vital concerns, the hermeneutical problem will be taken seriously by both. Denied the desired mutuality, they will spontaneously retrace the chain of speaking and listening in the hope of finding the snapped link. Any link may have been faulty: the choice of words and symbols, intonation and accompanying gestures, the burden of the silences, the *non sequiturs* of thought, the alertness of the listener. So words will be repeated, intentions and thoughts will be rephrased, greater empathy will be sought. One will say, "I don't get you"; and the other will try another route for getting through. The first reaction to ineffective rapport may well be impatience and petulance, with the tendency for each to fix the blame on the other. But when elemental courtesy and desire for understanding are present, each will soon look into his own speaking and listening for clues to the breach and for ways to repair it.

When they so listen, it is frequently discovered that what one partner had first rejected in the speech of the other becomes the essential clue to understanding him. Its nuisance value serves a positive function in communication, since the basic goal of the conversation is understanding, not agreement. The assumption that both partners should arrive at an agreement is altogether deceptive and quite incompatible with the goals of genuine dialogue. Only those whose stance is different can profit from conversation. Almost all hermeneutical problems appear *in nuce* at this level and they can almost all be solved at this level, where each participant can become his own most effective trouble-shooter. An example of this type would be the kind of discussion which Paul had with the congregation at Corinth when he was present with them, as described in I Corinthians 2:1-5; 16:1-7.

Type 3. *Conversations which are indirect because the two partners are separated and they must therefore rely on impersonal means of communication.* The new factor of geographical separation is relatively unimportant if the dialogue is conducted for technical reasons only. A telephone operator or radio announcer may tell me the time more dependably than a friend. The factor of separation gains importance in proportion to the depth of personal engagement, the level of selfhood. Hearts may grow fonder with absence, but they also may grow more impatient, and such impatience is aggravated by inadequate means of exchange. A telegram is better than vague rumors, a personal messenger better than a telegram, a personal letter still better, and a telephone conversation superior to any of the others.

What makes one medium preferable to another? It is not usually the distance of separation as measured in miles. It is rather the fact that different media place varying restrictions on the length and character of the message. The interval between one "speech" and the reply becomes a source of frustration. Inability to share the situation from which the words come provokes even greater chances of misunderstanding. For one type of message, the use of impersonal but accurate means of communication may serve adequately; but for another type, where the goal is personal rapport, less accuracy and more personality may be imperative.

What happens when the line breaks down? Greater efforts on both sides will be called forth. Both will speak or write more carefully, choosing words less easily mistaken. They will try to cut down on the interval between one speech and the next. They will refer more fully to the previous situation and to occasions before the break took place. Each will listen more alertly, visualizing the gestures, sensing the emotions, imagining the situation in the other's stead. Efforts at empathy will be more sustained; each will become more ready to absolve the other for sins due to external conditions. No matter how great the difficulties posed by the physical separation of the partners, conversation can succeed. Two people can overcome those problems and be brought together even more closely by them. Absence does indeed make a difference, but the difference need not destroy effective conversation. I have friends whom I rarely see whose letters I comprehend much more quickly and fully than I do the remarks of others with whom I talk almost every day. Even so, we should not forget these lessons when we move into regions where hazards are higher. An example of the type of conversation we have been discussing may be found in I Corinthians, and especially in 5:3-5.

Type 4. *Conversations which are indirect in a double sense: Speaker and listener are absent from each other and the speaker does not have this particular listener in mind, although the listener rightly includes himself among those addressed.* As examples we may cite a radio or television program, a newspaper or magazine article, a recording, a book. In such a case the external, impersonal character of the means of communication is accentuated by the lack of mutual knowledge among the participants. The speaker knows that his listeners do not know him personally, and he does not know them. Yet both wish to carry on the conversation even under these handicaps. This type of conversation presents many new possibilities for miscarriage. The two are separated not by a single impersonal medium but by a long series of impersonal media, any one of which may prove defective. Of course the mechanical or external obstacles to communication (for example, radio static or typographical errors) may be identified quickly and remedied, but it is more difficult to adjust the speaking itself to the needs of a particular listener. Where intimate and crucial issues are involved, the lack of personal knowledge is more inhibiting than mere radio static or typographical errors.

Rarely do modern media give the opportunity for strangers to become friends. Friendship requires not only the possibility of immediate rejoinder on the part of a listener (a letter to the editor, perhaps), but frequent chats outside the spotlight of public attention. Few firm friendships are formed among the members of television panels. The tacit address of most voices—whether on the air or in print—is "to whom it may concern." Very few people like to be addressed thus, since there is no opportunity for further discussion among those whom it does concern. The mass media go to extraordinary lengths to deal with the lack of personal rapport. The speakers who are most effective are those who can break through the wall of impersonality. But in seeking a breakthrough, they become aware of an unwritten law: The larger the audience, the less the impact on any one listener and the shallower the level on which he is affected. To gain a larger audience, the TV personality must reduce the effort required by each listener; and this results in more superficial conversation.

Dialogue that moves toward a more intimate and ultimate involvement requires something more. Both speaker and listener must be concerned with more serious issues and must be willing to put forth the greater effort needed for grappling with them. They must be willing to confess their mutual vulnerability and their apparent inadequacies. Their ties to a common society must be stressed if their awareness of being strangers is to be transcended. They must appeal to the images and symbols of this common society. The closer the web of attachments to this inclusive community, the more quickly the chief obstacle to communication can be overcome. The sense of belonging to the same community will carry with it the recognition of a common past and a common future. It is quite possible to realize a family solidarity with total strangers if one sees convincing signs of their sharing the same memories and hopes. The communication gap, which is so frequently cited as the reason for all sorts of social unrest, is in good part due to the fact that the conversational partners remain in the profounder sense unknown to one another. Each experiences a lack of that trust, affection, openness, and solidarity which are essential to any discussion of the things which really matter. For this reason, the goal of all Type 4 conversations should be a movement in the direction first of Type 3 and then of Type 2. In terms of biblical hermeneutics, an example of this type would be the situation of many Christians in Rome on hearing the Epistle to the Romans when it first arrived.

II

Type 5. *Indirect conversation between two persons who are known to each other, who are separated not by the absence of the speaker but by his death, the listener having nevertheless received a direct communication from him.* This happens more frequently than is commonly supposed. In the past six months I have received a letter after the death of the sender, and I have sent mail to a person of whose death I was unaware. Some instruments of communication are intended to deliver their message after the death of the writer, as in the case of personal diaries and wills; others are not, such as speeches of a man re-broadcast after his death.

The continuation of the conversation will obviously be contingent upon the wishes of the survivor. He can readily write *finis* to the whole fabric of relationships, tacitly expressing this verdict both on the power of death and on the importance to him of his "sometime" friend. Or he can recognize the continued presence of that dialogic partner by giving even greater priority to his wishes and by recalling with enhanced affection the gist of remembered conversations.

Each person should be able to describe how the death of particular people has given added meaning and intensity to dialogue, rather than terminating it. To some, of course, all such dialogue perforce becomes a monologue, since only one of the persons exerts control over the conversation. The departed lose their chance to shatter the egocentrism of the survivors. Yet, the dialogue can now more easily be reduced to essentials and can move at deeper levels of memory and hope. It can become less limited to specific times and places since for one partner death has ended the tyranny of maps and calendars. In fact, the remembrance of the dead, as Kierkegaard saw it, becomes a supreme test of whether a person can transcend self-interest in a love which "seeks not its own." To love the departed is an action which cannot be repaid in the coin sought by a self-centered person. The communion of saints may thus provide the context within which the most effective conversations are shared. The event of death is not as great a hermeneutical disaster as many suppose. Language presupposes community; the greater the solidarity before death, the more possible an effective conversation after death.

Type 6. *A conversation that is indirect because both the speaker and his first audience are dead. Readers now living were not included intentionally in that conversation, yet they find sufficient grounds for participation.* Reading any document more than eighty years old illustrates this type of discourse. In basic principle, the goal of the dialogue remains constant: a personal sharing in the two-way discourse between an ancient speaker and his original audience. But it is obvious that all the potential difficulties of other types of conversation reappear here, and so many difficulties are added that this type seems to represent a different order entirely. In fact, observers often deny that it is possible for later persons to break into an earlier dialogue by way of written texts alone. Everything that has happened since the original conversation separates the reader from the written document. This distance, of course, is not to be measured only by centuries or by cultures. Plato's message may be more intelligible to us than that of some modern philosophers, and African drums may be more in tune with today's temper than nineteenth century American hymns. Of greater moment are the answers to such questions as these: Was the original interchange one that involved its participants deeply? Is there any continuity between the ancient and the modern communities within which the discussion proceeds? At best difficulties are so great that the reader's efforts to surmount them must be strenuous and sustained. No one else can provide for him all the adaptations in perspective, in language, in sentiment, which he will need for understanding. Put bluntly, it requires hard work on his part.

Even with the best of intentions, readers will require professional help, even though they dare not rely wholly on that help. Sooner or later, such help usually involves consulting those historians who have specialized in the epoch under consideration. Such historians provide information concerning what life was like at that particular place and time. They may even try to recapture the immediate mood and motives of the ancient conflicts and to communicate a sense of what it was like to have participated in those conflicts, without knowing what their outcome would be. Some may go still further and seek to create the conditions for a dialogue between the modern reader and the inherited text. In the terms made familiar by R. Bultmann, the historian may confront the reader with his own historicity and thus enable him to recognize that he and the ancient writer do, after all, share the same existential situation.

It is the convention and the custom today to ignore or to belittle the relevance of voices from the past. How easily one can leave the book on the shelf, or, if he reads, immunize himself in advance! Modernity generates its own ghetto-mentality. We don't want the privacy of an ultra-modern apartment (where we hurry to become post-Barth, post-war, post-Christian) to be broken down by invasions from the past. However chaotic contemporary urban life may be, it is at least familiar, and we hesitate to venture far beyond familiar horizons in order to chat with ancient writers. Provincialism manufactures a full supply of alibis against conversation with outsiders and agitators, whether of this or of former centuries. Alibis gain a specious plausibility because of the difficulties we have mentioned—to learn the dead languages, to reconstruct the dead environment, to witness dead men in debate with dead men over issues which are dead. Perhaps never in recent centuries has there been so little vital encounter with earlier generations as today.

The truly amazing thing is not so much the problematic

quotient as the degree of success that has been and can be achieved. An old book, dusty and ill-used, can and does come alive. However large the generation gap, many readers do bridge it. When one considers the obstacles, the fact that any conversation from the past is being continued today becomes a mystery and a miracle. The time-span which separates also unites; cultures which seemed so alien betray intrinsic kinships; languages which seemed dead come alive. Hearts wrestle with the same ultimate questions and in so doing disclose a solidarity with ancient writers and ancient communities, a solidarity made all the more impressive by the temporal and cultural distance.

Type 7. *Conversation in which a specific community addresses a community which responds to that address.* Our habits of thought in the realm of speech are individualistic in the extreme. Only an individual has organs of speech and organs of hearing. What he says can best be analyzed in terms of his individual intentions, and what is said in response depends mainly on individual feelings and thoughts. But what do we have in mind when we think of a corporate voice? Where is to be found a body so tightly knit, so well coordinated, that one member can voice its will without being challenged by other members?

The problems are real. Yet it is clear that society would have no other fate than anarchy if it were totally impossible for groups within it to act as units. We may shout the slogans of participatory democracy, with its principle that every person should share in every decision which affects him personally, but carried to the extreme, that principle would dissolve every communal tie. Unless some functions are assigned to specific members, unless they are granted requisite authority and responsibility without the necessity of consulting every member involved, the ordered life of mankind would disintegrate. Even a group of rebels can operate only by accepting spokesmen of its own to speak for it. A community cannot survive as a community except as a speaking and listening unit.

Actually it is the very activity of speaking and listening

that determines the identity and shape of a community. A group is composed of those who accept a particular voice as its own; it is created by the authoritative word spoken by that voice. It declares its existence by speaking through its representatives and by responding to the word that they address to it. Its solidarity in speaking and responding is so axiomatic that it is usually unconscious of what is actually happening. Within any group a continuous internal dialogue is going on, along with many external dialogues with "outside" communities. Whether or not an individual participates will depend upon the extent to which he has made his own those concerns which are common to the whole group. The strength of his own solidarity will be tested by his spontaneous identification with those "conversations" which are essential to the life and work of the community. A repudiation of the group's spokesmen will betray, on either his part or theirs, a repudiation of their reading of the text of the community's existence. Social life consists of an endless trial-and-error process in which what the community is saying is tested as true or false to the inner realities of the community's memories and hopes, its living tradition. It is deceptively simple to view any community in terms of its institutional framework at a particular time and to judge that framework as archaic. It is not the institutional element which is at stake, but rather the traditions, both oral and written. Are they accurate verbalizations of the continuing corporate experience?

Rebels in every decade may depose those representatives through whom a particular tradition finds expression. When the spirit of rebellion becomes endemic, it becomes extremely difficult for a contemporary generation to conduct fruitful discourse with any preceding generation. Contemporaries fear arbitrary control by ancestors and suspect any appeal to the latter as a devious way of diminishing freedom. The generation gap is a way of asserting the indifference of a contemporary community to the voice of its predecessors. The problem of bridging that chasm is much more complex than in the case of the individual parent and his child. It is also more crucial, because a community dies unless it continues its distinctive tradition—that is, unless its conversation with its own forebears remains central to its sense of mission and destiny. Deafness and dumbness isolate communities even more disastrously than they do individuals. Speech that can end such isolation is as necessary as it is difficult. No speech will be able to accomplish that miracle unless it evokes and expresses those realities which bind the present community to its predecessors, those realities which constitute the deepest level of common experience in the community. Perhaps the most alarming phenomenon on the horizon of the Christian community today is the rarity of such speech. It is this rarity that alone can explain why there is so much pother about hermeneutics today.

One may illustrate the conversation of Type 7 by pointing to the present-day church's use of the canon of Scripture. Although some elements in the New Testament writings were composed by individuals, other elements are best treated as communal products—hymns, confessions, liturgical and catechetical materials. But whatever the origin, the canonization of Scripture indicates that all of the writings have become a message from the ancient church. All represent a corporate judgment of the essentials of God's word to men. And therefore all these writings are addressed not simply to successive individual readers but rather to subsequent generations of the church. When the lector reads a "lesson" each Sunday morning to the congregation, he is relaying a message from the historic Christian community to its modern descendant. A corporate address assumes a corporate response.

III

Type 8. *A conversation between men or communities in which it is tacitly or explicitly asserted that a message from God to his people is involved and a response to him is expected from them.* It is indeed difficult to describe what is entailed in this conversation, because it is never wholly separated from the other types so as to form a distinct species, nor is it reducible to the others. One cannot limit it to a single form of discourse, nor exclude it from any. To treat it too casually is to risk profanation of the holy, but to treat it as "wholly-other" is to deny the biblical witness to the ways in which God sends forth his word. In the delivery of this message, there is no novel vocabulary, no new range of auditory impressions, no predetermined methods for human responses. There are no convenient tests for validating a discourse as actually conveying a word from God or one sent to him. The encounter takes protean forms which cannot be diagrammed in advance. There can be no recording of this message. It is always open to doubt whether the conversation is not after all a matter of hallucination.

It takes little time or thought to realize that all the difficulties experienced in other types of conversation are raised to the nth degree in this case. Moreover, it is easy in this case to solve these difficulties by simply denying the existence of the speaker. Especially does this seem the best option when he calls for dangerous decisions. Those who hesitate to deny the possibility of such discourse have at hand a thousand ways of closing their ears to it. The impulse to do so is all the stronger because of the fact that conversation with God so rarely deals with the trivia of man's life. In such conversation God usually opens up abysses within the self, caverns of hope and dread, of emptiness and guilt which the self would prefer to keep sealed. Yet, when the self succeeds in quarantining that region, it dies. It lives on the possibility and actuality of that conversation, however fragmentary and contorted it may be. Moreover, something happens to all the other forms of conversation with men when the participants rule out in advance the possibility that God, that omnipresent third party, may be speaking to them through that medium.

Among the things that happen is the closing off to routes to community. By speaking to the deepest levels of human existence, God's word creates a community among those who respond, a community that is most durable precisely because of the depths at which it emerges into existence. The term religion points to the places where conversation with God (through the media afforded by all other conversations) is proceeding to create a community that knows itself in touch with primordial and eschatological realities at the very point of its creation. That form of hermeneutics which deals with God's participation in speech will therefore never be reducible to a science. It is the prophet rather than the scientist who can disclose to a community the substance of this conversation which is so vital to its existence. Such disclosure requires the detection of the community's escape mechanisms more than the elaboration of hermeneutical methods. It also requires the appeal to tradition, to the community's memory of those events, documents, activities in which God has chosen to order his discourse with many successive generations in the pilgrimage of his people. That tradition must be interpreted, of course, and so the historian has a modest role to play as a hermeneutist. But the chief difficulty remains the same: In the exchange of messages from men to men, how should one respond to the divine message which may be concealed and yet conveyed within those messages?

Because most of us are conditioned by living in a culture where God is not real, we suppose that it is more difficult to talk with God than with men. We assume that understanding is relatively easy if we are conversing with friends, but that it is quite another matter to hear God speaking. From some standpoints that is certainly true. Moreover, we should never suppose that we can hear God better by ignoring or distorting the messages of men. On the other hand, it may, on occasion, be easier to hear God speak than to understand man's speech. He is a living God whose word is as near as lips and heart— that is, much nearer than human companions. Men encounter him from day to day, even though recognition is often lacking. He may choose to speak through anonymous spokesmen or through strangers. When he does speak, he has the power to break through all kinds of resistance, to penetrate to the core of self-consciousness, and to create community bonds among those to whom he comes. The fact that his thoughts are not man's may make it more difficult to establish contact—and, by the same token, easier.

Type 9. *A conversation in which human words become the*

*medium for a divine-human dialogue by telling the story of
Jesus of Nazareth in such a way that he becomes God's word
through the help of the Holy Spirit.* Non-Christian theists
commonly suppose that this adds new complications to the
already extended lines of communication, an unnecessary obstacle to more direct speech. Christians, however, recognize
in Jesus Christ the authentic, decisive, and adequate voice of
God, and judge all other conversation—whether with men or
with God—in the light of that message of which Jesus Christ
is the sole mediator. The church is composed of recipients
and ministers of this Word. To obey this Word is to become
servants or slaves of Christ. To tell this Word is to retell the
narrative of Jesus' humiliation and exaltation. This is a Word
of which men are *eye-witnesses* as well as narrators, for this
Word is a person who lived and died. This Word becomes
therefore a story of saving events. To witness to them is to
become story-tellers. The story convicts the minister of an
incomplete and sinful response on the part of both minister
and community; but the story also has power to overcome sin
and to create a communion of saints, faithful in their penitence
and in their prayer for forgiveness. The retelling of the story
and the relistening to it has the power to mediate God's
continuing conversation with his people through Christ and
his Holy Spirit. It is therefore the perennial task of every
minister to examine and reexamine how he listens and how
he tells this story of Jesus, this Gospel of God's salvation.

One may observe a curious telescoping of virtually all types
of conversation into one when a Christian congregation,
assembled for worship, listens to the words, "Here begins the
Scripture. . . ." The book is obviously one written in the
distant past for an ancient audience, both speakers and listeners being separated from us by death and by many cultural
and temporal changes. Yet it is read as a communication
from the church to this particular assembly. It is read by an
individual who is known as pastor by those who are listening.
As he reads, they will be linked by their memories to the
entire past, and by their hopes to the unknown future. The
Scripture lesson may sound wholly outdated and unrelated to

their immediate preoccupations. Yet ever and again the prayer is uttered and answered, "May the Lord bless to us this reading of his holy Word." The prayer is in order, because apart from the Lord's help, the difficulties of communication are altogether too great. Yet answers to the prayer, however rare, constitute evidence that each difficulty is an opportunity. The function of biblical hermeneutics is in part to reflect upon the previous episodes in this divine-human conversation and thus to turn present difficulties into opportunities.

Toward an Ecumenical Ecclesiology

J. Robert Nelson

In his essay J. Robert Nelson endeavors to stake out the dimensions of the enlarging field of common understanding about the church, and he does so by discussing six significant elements in an ecumenical concept of the church for today and tomorrow. Dr. Nelson is well aware of the frequently voiced objections to the present ecumenical convergence. Nonetheless he believes that that convergence—in doctrine, theology, and polity—will lead to an eventual union. "Never to a perfect, all-inclusive union, of course. . . . But the unity of the body of Christ in history is an element of faith, precisely because this visible unity is in the order of God's revealed purpose for mankind, namely, the reconciliation of all people in peace." Professor of Systematic Theology at Boston University School of Theology since 1965, Dr. Nelson is chairman of the Faith and Order Working Committee of the World Council of Churches, and from 1953 to 1957 was executive secretary for the Faith and Order Commission in Geneva. An ordained Methodist minister, he is the author of six books on church and unity, including *The Realm of Redemption* and *Criterion for the Church*. His most recent book is *No Man Is an Alien*. The Jesuit quarterly *Theological Studies** published his essay in its December 1970 number.

THE CONVERGING of most of the Christian churches does not need to be proved, but only illustrated and interpreted. Anyone who has even a modest knowledge of what has happened in the past two decades knows this. If during the *anno santo* of 1950, when Pope Pius XII announced the dogma of the bodily assumption into heaven of

---

* P.O. Box 1703, Baltimore, Md. 21203.

the Virgin Mary, a pious Dutch Catholic named Rip van Winkle had fallen into a twenty-year slumber, he would be utterly unable to believe what he saw and heard of the close relations of Christian churches. Whether he would welcome the new situation of ecumenical convergence would depend upon his disposition to agree with the course of theological change in these two decades. And if he were Professor van Winkle, whose soporific lectures had at last had the twenty-year effect upon himself, he would know upon awakening that he would have to test the value of the changes by the various criteria of ecclesiology, which is the understanding of the nature of the Church.

Some of the strongest causes of division in the past were the disagreements over the optimum form, order, ministry, worship, and purpose of the Church. Is it hierarchical control or local autonomy? Pope or council? Bishop or presbyter? Mass or Lord's Supper? Baptized infant or believer? Formal liturgy or free expression? National establishment or independence? Since these are the rocks and shoals over which ecclesial ships have foundered and broken in two, it is astonishing to see how the tides of agreement are rising and permitting safe passage.

It would be an illicit deception to pretend that unity and concord on the truth about the Church have already been achieved. We are describing the convergent trends, not the perfect coincidence of them. Without making unwarranted claims for unity, and fully cognizant of the continuing controversies over the issues of ecclesiology, we can point to trends which seem now to be undeviating. They are evident especially in four areas of inquiry: the Faith and Order conferences and studies, which began after 1920 and continue in the World Council of Churches and many national councils; the conversations and supporting studies which have been directed towards the uniting of Protestant churches; the theological preparation for the Second Vatican Council and the documents which were approved by it; and the great quantity of individual scholarship in the fields of Bible, history of doctrine, liturgy, canon law, sociology of religion, theology, and ecumenics. A truly prodigious amount of mental energy has been invested in the research, conference dialogue, and publication required for this unprecedented overhauling of ecclesiology in Christian history. Only to stake out the dimensions of the enlarging field of common understanding about the Church, we can discuss six significant elements in an ecumenical concept of the Church for today and tomorrow.

God's Purpose for Mankind

Primary and basic is the concern for all persons, considered both individually and in their social communities. The more we sense the reality of the oneness of the human race and express faith in it, the more passionately we question the divine purpose which impels us and awaits fulfillment. What is the meaning of man's historical existence? How does God's power operate within the course of that common history? Why is there such a continuing community as the Church, which is constituted by a distinct faith rather than by the natural affinities of race, tongue, or nationality? Does the existence of the Church have something to do with the destiny of all mankind, and not only with that of its own professed members?

In order to suggest some tentative, partially satisfying answers to these profound and ultimately insoluble questions, it has been necessary to discard some obsolete notions as well as to examine with caution some modern surrogates for them. A timeworn and now worn-out belief has been that the Church, like the floating zoo of Noah, was launched by God on the surly, insidious sea of history in order to be the lifeboat of the lucky few. The powerful imagery of the storm, shipwreck, and safe harbor has usually suggested that the Master of wind and waves had already decided arbitrarily which of the passengers and crew would be spared oblivion in the waters of chaos. So salvation, meaning eternal rescue, was equated with Church membership, and outside the Church there was no salvation.

A tempting substitute for this obsolete belief is the relativistic view that the Church of Jesus Christ does indeed embrace a minority of the race, but that it represents just one alongside of several religions held by the majority, any one of which is equally suitable as a means of salvation—whatever *that* may mean.

Does the Church have a monopoly on the shipping lanes leading to salvation? Or is it just one of the strong competitors in the maritime market? Neither of these metaphors can satisfy the mind of a Christian, unless he be one who is either blind to the realities of history or wholly determined in thought by historical relativism. Between these polarized positions is the area where an ecumenical convergence is taking place.

The general theory which dominates and informs this trend is the one derived from biblical theology: saving history, or the history of salvation. Probably the most notable Protestant protagonist of this motif is Oscar Cullmann of Basel. The foremost Catholic interpreter of it was the Second Vatican Council. It is not astonishing to one who compares the books of Cullmann with the texts of the Constitution on the Church and the two Decrees on Ecumenism and Mission when 'he learns of the special honor accorded to the Basel professor by Pope Paul VI and the theologians of the Council.[1]

Saving history has become widely known through discussions of it in countless writings of this century. It is commended as the biblical alternative to three main types of historical theory: the cyclical view of eternal return or endless repetition; the optimistic idea of constant progress by human achievement; and the nihilistic notion that history is aimless and meaningless. Of the Marxist theory it is often said that this is a secularized distortion of the biblical saving history.

History seems self-evidently to consist of perennial instances of men's use of political and economic power for exploitation, blindness to the plight of the distressed and oppressed, abuses of natural and human resources, hostile conflicts and deadly wars, and the rising and falling of nations and empires. Or a more cheerful analysis exposes the history of man's artistic expression, advances in technological skills, and the spread of religious and cultural institutions. All these are the ingredients of history. What sense do they make?

There is indeed a development of mankind, according to the concept of saving history. It is not explicable, however, in terms of any natural evolutionary process. It is chiefly a moral struggle among men, rather than a struggle against nature. In this drama of history God is not to be conceived as a kind of *deus ex machina*, plummeting from heaven to the human stage just in the nick of time to avert catastrophe. Rather, He is the God who is continually with man in joy and triumph as well as in deepest distress. Having given man the perilous blessing of freedom in creation, God does not abrogate man's use of it in order to prevent him from making drastic mistakes. Through the very events and conditions which are brought about by man's use of free choice and deliberate action, whether these be tragically destructive of life or happily beneficial, God enables him to learn the consequences of sin and to know the ways of righteousness which God requires.

How does this knowledge through history's significant events come to man? To all nations and peoples universally? To one people in particular? Or through the particularity of one people for the instruction of all mankind? It is the third answer which the Bible's implicit idea of saving history provides.

Just as the concept of peoplehood is being emphasized today by the Jews with new vigor, so it has been the presupposition of biblical faith since the exodus from bondage in Egypt. Yahweh was known to be a very particular God, inexplicably picking this remarkable tribe in the Eastern Mediterranean region to be His point of contact with the human race. He is the Creator and Lord of all people. So to gain communication and establish personal relationship with the universal race of man, winning their faith by stimulating them to make a free choice, God chose to open the secrets of His will to Israel in particular. The consistent themes of the

Old Testament show that His self-exposure was perceived by the prophets, priests, and historians of Israel. Insofar as they remained faithful to the covenant, the people of Israel were the corporate embodiment of the law of God as well as the bearers of promise and hope for mankind. Their vocation was not to conquer and rule, but to serve as the medium of God's Word to the nations and to prepare for the coming day of the Lord's righteousness. For believing and sensitive Jews this vocation remains intact and the expectation is undiminished.

Christianity appropriated saving history, however, as a matter of its own identity. It is primarily faith in Jesus, the savior of Israel itself and of all men. Christian faith still asserts that He was the anointed one, the Messiah, whom Israel expected as the fulfillment of its hopes, and thus as the light of God to the nations. If the insights of Israel were correct, then salvation meant accepting the way of faithfulness to God, submission to His will and laws, acceptance of suffering and the humilating effects of evil, expression of love and the extension of forgiveness to offenders, and using the gifts of creation for the glory of God and the life of peace, *shālōm*, among men. All these were taught, exemplified, embodied, and illuminated by Jesus Christ. Christian faith was posited and remains grounded upon the faith that Jesus fulfilled what Israel hoped for. Therefore He became the medium and mediator of God's saving truth and action to all mankind, precisely as the representative man of Israel.

The relation of Jesus Christ to human history is not, however, just that of a man to the race. Even as Yahweh relates to mankind through the people Israel, so God through Jesus relates Himself to mankind through a people, the *ekklēsia*, Church. The very being and person of Jesus, the nature of His ministry and life, the fact of His death, and the witness to His resurrection from death were not simply remembered by the Church as the virtues and deeds of the venerated founder. They were the collective elements of the event which, in place of any human contriving or long-range planning, brought the Church into existence. In the symbolic event of Pentecost it was infused by God's Spirit with enduring power. Through the experience of men and women, as brilliantly interpreted in the letters of Paul, the meaning and hope of human existence were now known in virtue of knowing the risen Christ, whose instrument of death became the sign of victory. In carrying this message from Jerusalem outward through the Empire to Jews, Greeks, Romans, and barbarians, the early missionaries were letting themselves be used as the bearers of the meaning of history, namely, peace with God and among men.

With respect to this great process by which God in Christ is renewing man, Paul could honestly declare: "All this is from God" (2 Cor. 5:18). It is the work of divine knowledge, power, and grace, not a great leap forward by human effort. The reconciliation and peace with God, and the consequent harmony with other men, come neither to individuals nor to peoples as the instantaneous consequences of God's gift. As Paul knew very well, and as countless large and small evidences of history have shown, there are long and exceedingly rough detours on the road of salvation. For the apostles, as the paradigms of Christian living, this meant "afflictions, hardships, calamities, beatings, imprisonments, tumults, labors, watching, hunger" (2 Cor. 6:4-6). These heroic words are not chosen for melodramatic effect; and it is hypocritical for Christians who seek comfort and security to flaunt them in order to make an impression on others. But such words and their cognates, when transposed from personal experience to the collective struggles, trials, and agonies of groups, peoples, and nations, are descriptive of the course of human life, into which the message of reconciliation and peace is brought by the Church.

The goal of saving history is not a tolerably just and peaceful social condition on earth; this is a penultimate goal, highly to be prized, of course. Neither is the purpose contained in the struggle as such: the efforts of the Church to discipline itself into obedience to God; its service and witness to human society; the contestation between the social forces seeking liberty and justice for all and those contending for the

power and privilege of a particular group, class, race, or
nation. The movement of saving history points beyond both
the inherent moral value of the struggle and the tolerably just
order of society to the ultimate goal. This is the reign of God,
that much-disputed biblical belief which is the undisputed
focal point of Jesus' life and message. He came proclaiming
the gospel of the kingdom, or reign, of God among men. It is
near, at hand, in your midst, and yet always coming, being
sought, and ultimately to be received and entered. The temp-
tation of Christians has always been to say: Lo, it is here, or
there! To identify, capture, domesticate, and manipulate for
their own purposes so profound and elusive a mystery as the
kingdom of God has invariably meant to convert it into a self-
sufficient ecclesiastical structure or to trade it off for a particular ordering of economics and politics in the secular realm.
But to despair of any human realization of the kingdom
within the bounds of time and space has meant to relegate it
to the transcendent dimension called heaven, of which the
mortal mind can scarcely hold a conception.

Because they cannot contain or control the reign of God as
a social order, Christians are faithless or of poor power of
discernment when they despair of ever knowing it in history.
If they have known Jesus Christ personally as fact and in
faith, and if they have experienced worship and service in the
Church at its best, they surely have clues to the meaning of
this divine rule. In contrast, however, they do not have war-
rant to claim that the Church and the reign of God are
coterminous and the same, so that history has little better to
show than the Church itself. Fortunately, this latter disposition of Roman Catholic thought has been abruptly altered in
the recent reform. In the convergence of Christian understanding, the Church participates now in the state of God's
righteous reign, even while it is enmeshed in historical circumstances which are contrary to His will. And it continues
in history as a community of hope, sincerely expecting that
God will continue to lead both the Church and all peoples
towards the realization of that kind of life which was seen in

Jesus Christ. This one man prefigures both the nature and shape of the Church as well as the ultimate destiny of humanity.

The Corporate and Popular Community

There is ecclesiological convergence, secondly, in the growing recognition of Orthodox, Catholics, and Protestants that the Church is both corporate and popular. These two adjectives should be taken in their literal sense. The word "corporate" means that the Church is a body, the *corpus Christi*, or body of Christ. And the word "popular" means that it is *populus*, a people of distinct character, "God's own people." The prominent mark of thinking about the Church in these two ways is the realism attached to the corporate and popular character. It is easy enough to say that the Christian community, the whole Church, is *like* a biological body, wherein all members have an appointed and necessary place. It is also evident that the Church is *comparable* to a people with a common identity, that identity being the Christian religion for the Church and a certain tribal history, language, culture, or nationality for the people. But injustice is done to the biblical intention for these two words if today we think of them just as convenient and appropriate comparisons. The biblical language is still understood today in a realistic sense: the Church is the body of Christ even as it *is* the people of God. Those who have argued the case for a "merely metaphorical" interpretation of the body of Christ in Paul's letters have some evidence to cite in the text, but not enough to convince most writers on the subject.[2] Those who interpret on behalf of the churches of the World Council of Churches as well as the scholars of the Roman Catholic Church use these two concepts with great frequency and realism.

It is a bit ironical that within the ecumenical discussions of the World Council there has been a tendency to set these two concepts against each other: either the body of Christ or the people of God is the appropriate way to designate the Church, so take your choice. Behind this tendency is a long history of distorted usage, stemming from the Reformation. The Christians of the "catholic" style (Roman, Anglican, and others) gave primary attention to the organic nature of the Church, as a living unity, a body. They saw the Church as a continuing, comprehensive community, into which infants were born and baptized, within which members were regularly and frequently nourished by Christ's body and blood in the Eucharist, and over which the bishops and priests as representatives of Christ and the apostles ruled with a pastoral and priestly power. Distinct from these were the Christians of "protestant" style, who thought of the Church as the people of God, called together for His service, and freely responding in the confession of faith and acceptance of the covenant. Their prophetic interpretations of the Word of God led them often into conflicts with society and governments, thus strengthening the sense of voluntarism in membership. The two sacraments were indeed used faithfully, but with less of a sacramental aura about them. And the priestly role of the minister was subordinated to his preaching and teaching function, which was directed mainly to the purpose of instructing and inspiring the pilgrim people on their struggling march through history.

These two categorical concepts of the Church, the "catholic" and "protestant," were rather formally recognized by the report of the Amsterdam 1948 assembly of the World Council. And some delegates of the churches with congregational polity argued in addition for a third type, a still freer and more democratic form of the people of God than the churches of Continental Protestantism.[3] The line between body of Christ and people of God seemed sharply drawn.

Only four years later, at the Third World Conference on Faith and Order at Lund (1952), the two concepts were given almost equal emphasis. Likewise, the distinction between "catholic" and "protestant" ecclesiology began to be blurred, alarming the staunchest defenders of both traditions. But Methodists, Lutherans, Presbyterians, and Baptists were speaking positively and realistically of the body of Christ, while Anglicans and some Orthodox, without abandoning the body concept, gave prominence to the people of God. Bringing Christ and the Christians together in historic conjunction, then, the Church could fittingly be called Christ's embodied people.

It remained for the Second Vatican Council to give the most explicit expression to this conjunction. Following in large measure the ecclesiological writings of Yves M.-J. Congar, the Constitution on the Church presents both concepts in parallel but interpenetrating chapters. If anything, it gives the greater emphasis to the people of God, which for modern Catholicism generally is a rather novel idea. Catholic reasoning about the Church's nature had long been dominated by the doctrine of the Mystical Body of Christ, especially since the Encyclical *Mystici corporis* (1943). This doctrine was heavily laden with hierarchical sacramental beliefs which had been built up during centuries of developing practice. The relatively simple insight of the New Testament, that the body of Christ meant the communion of faithful people in whose midst the risen Christ dwells, had been altered according to the institutional growth of the Roman Catholic Church. Papacy, curia, episcopacy, priesthood—these, in effect, were the loci of Christ's presence and the essential shape of His body, the Church. But what of the people who constitute the membership of the body? In this passing, obsolescent view, the people of God were the laity, and thus very distinctly separated in both office and in theological definition from the hierarchy.[4] It is really no wonder that the conservative bishops and theologians at the Second Vatican Council wanted to have, first, a chapter on the hierarchy and then one on the people of God, as they prepared the schema *De ecclesia*. The final draft, however, is the most vivid demonstration of the way converging ecumenical ecclesiological thought affected the Council. The final and proper order of the first four chapters, of course, was: the mystery of Christ's body, the Church; the people of God as fully inclusive; the hierarchy, with attention to episcopacy; and the laity. The validity of this order has been vindicated many times during the postconciliar years, as the laity have applied pressure to the parish priests, and the priests have put pressure on the bishops, and the bishops have pressed their representatives to the synod in the Vatican to press the pope, for the purpose of enabling all kinds of members of the Church to enjoy a more responsible participation in the affairs of the whole body.

There is no exact counterpart to *Lumen gentium* in non-Roman churches or the World Council of Churches. However, clear similarities of thought are found in the major reports of the world conferences on Faith and Order held at Lund in 1952 and Montreal in 1963. There is frequent juxta-position of the body-of-Christ and people-of-God motifs, with emphasis upon both the living presence of Christ and the priesthood of all the members, including the ordained ministry. These are not empty or abstract speculations of theologians, for it is the concrete, historical Church which is meant. The conventional notion that the Protestants regard the true Church to be "invisible," while the "visible" Church is of dubious authenticity, is now wholly indefensible. The delegates to Lund declared: "We are agreed that there are not two Churches, one visible and the other invisible, but one Church which must find visible expression on earth."[5] By an unusual coincidence, the Vatican Council fathers were moved to say precisely the same thing in paragraph 8 of *Lumen gentium*. The theological understanding behind both documents was the same: the one Church is like the one Jesus Christ, having a single reality (or person) and yet both the invisibly divine and the visibly human natures.

Furthermore, the ecclesiology of both Vatican II and the World Council reports is firmly based upon belief in what is called the "Christological analogy." This means that the Church on earth shares an identity with Jesus Christ, even while not wholly identical with Him. In the language of Karl Barth, the Church is "the earthly-historical form of existence of Jesus Christ."[6] His body is the Church, as organic community, of which He remains the living head. Or the Church is God's called and commissioned people in history, but Christ remains the Lord of both Church and world. Since the relation is one of analogy rather than of univocal identity, theologians say that the proper form, style, life, action, and witness of the Church must be determined by analogy to the person and ministry of Jesus Christ, as known to us in the Gospels. This is summed up in the monosyllabic expression of 1 John 4:17: ". . . as He is so are we in the world." Thus *Lumen gentium* borrows the traditional scheme of the three-fold office of Christ—Prophet, Priest, King—of which John Calvin had made much use, and shows how the Church's ministry is likewise prophetic, priestly, and regal or magisterial.[7]

This analogical consideration of the Church's being and task leads to very specific indications of its inescapable vocation. To play a variation on the familiar formula of Ignatius of Antioch, "Where Christ is, there is the catholic Church" means "As Jesus Christ was and did, so is and does the Church." Was He indeed the Son of God in the form of a slave? Then the Church must keep accepting the role of servant in society. Was He, in the words made popular by Bonhoeffer, the man for others? Then the Church must live for others rather than itself. As Jesus preached the gospel of love and embodied it by attitude and action, so the Church has the same mission in all times and places. As He spoke the prophetic words of judgment upon man's personal and social evils and injustices, so must the Church, in constant reference to Him as the authority, be a prophetic community. Jesus was often in prayer to the Father; so must the Church, in constant reference to Him as the authority, be a prophetic community. Jesus was often in prayer to the Father; so must be the Church. And even as He submitted to humiliation and death by crucifixion, only to be raised by God's creative power, so the Church should be ready to accept humiliation and the death of its forms and institutions, as obedience to God requires, in faith that God will always maintain His people by giving newness of life.

Truth is concrete. These true Christological patterns for the Church and its many parts are concrete and specific; for those who prefer comfort and ease, they are too readily translatable into programs of inner reform and outward service. It is often and rightly said that the current period of ferment and reform in the churches has been provoked by the circumstances of the whole human society, which means by secular conditions, events, ideas, and movements. But the more profound and basic reason why it is possible for churches to experience reform in the direction of an appropriate response to the world's needs is precisely because of the intimate relation of Jesus Christ to the Church and the Christological analogy which is built upon this. As He is so is the Church in the world: and what the Christ of the Gospels is *not* is complacent, introverted, craven, haughty, detached, wealthy, schizoid, or domineering.

In the converging ecclesiology, then, the Church is both Christocentric and Christomorphic: constantly deriving its life from Christ the center of its being, and always—except when deterred by sin—seeking ways of assuming the shape and style of His earthly life and ministry.

Ministry: Differences Making Less Difference

In nearly all religions there is some concept and office of ministry: priest, shaman, guru, rabbi, mufti, mullah, elder, pastor, bishop, and many more. In the various Christian churches the patterns of ministry have developed from a common New Testament source into a wide diversity. Members of the different communions have for generations become accustomed to their particular kinds of special or ordained ministers; and they have their distinctive expectations of ministers. These offices have been conditioned not only by varieties of theological and sacramental understanding, but also by the pressures of cultures and nations. An Ethiopian abuna, a Swedish Lutheran *kyrkoherde*, an Anglican country vicar, an Italian archbishop or curial *monsignore*, an Appalachian revivalist, a Russian archimandrite are all known generically as Christian ministers. But what irreconcilable differences of self-identity and function! No wonder that progress towards the unity of churches always seems to be hindered most gravely by the multiplicity of ministries. Even where there is a strong will to circumvent or transcend the barrier of the ministry, the discussions or negotiations often come to a deadlock.

There is encouragement, nevertheless, to be found in the clear evidence of ferment and change within the several church traditions. These changing ideas about the nature of the ministry are tending in the same direction. Instead of remaining as insurmountable walls of separation, the structures of ministry are actually becoming means of unitive convergence.

When the Vatican Council's Constitution on the Church is compared to such ecumenical statements about the ministry as the report of the Montreal Conference or the principles of the Consultation on Church Union, it would appear that any attribution of convergence is an expression of insupportable optimism. The significant chapters on the hierarchical structure (with special attention to the episcopate) and on the laity seem far removed from any kind of Protestant understanding. The contrast with the Montreal report is manifest.

The Montreal ecumenical report accepts a ministerial sequence like this: Christ's ministry—the apostles—the whole membership as a royal priesthood—the specialized and ordained ministries. Adhering to Catholic tradition, *Lumen gentium* treats the progression as follows: Christ's ministry—Peter(=papacy)—the apostles(=bishops)—priests—deacons—(religious—) laity. While the divergence is still great, the affinities are not without significance, especially because these affinities are being strengthened by much of the scholarly writing as well as the practical exercise having to do with ministry.

First among these is the recognition that the primacy of the ministry is not found in any particular officer of the Church (such as a primate!), but in Jesus Christ Himself. The service of the entire Church membership, as well as the function and authority of the ordained ministry, are derived from Christ. The ministry of the Church in the world, then, from the greatest saint or power figure to the least impressive and effective member, is actually the ministry of Christ. Great and small, and the Church over-all, are instruments of His ministry. This is an indispensable element of our belief that Jesus Christ as the risen Lord and Head of the body still lives. Because of Easter, He still exercises by the communicative power of the Holy Spirit His redeeming ministry; and he does it particularly, if perhaps not exclusively, through the members of His body, the Church. This means service in two dimensions: the mutual care of those identified with the community, and the sympathy, helpfulness, and sacrifice on behalf of anyone who stands in such need. This primacy of Christ's ministry is by no means a novel insight or belief; it is clearly derived from the New Testament. But for many Christians it has been obscured by the ascendant clericalism in the history of virtually all churches. The conventional distinction between the Roman Catholic and Orthodox churches as being priest-ridden and hierarchically dominated, on the one hand, and the Protestant churches exercising the priesthood of every faithful member, on the other, has had less and less validity in modern times. The former are not abandoning a hierarchical structure, of course. And most Protestant churches are still in fact controlled by clergymen, whether as pastors, bishops, or executive secretaries. The most powerful means for propelling the movement of declericalization, though, is just the sober reflection on the most appropriate means by which the living Christ's ministry can be mediated to mankind. Surely the answer is the whole people of God, in all their diversity of ability and locality.

But a second indication of convergence is notable in contemporary thinking about ministry. It is the unique place of the apostle. Simply in the examination of the process by which Christian faith becomes possible for any person, there is an irrefutable logic of historical sequence. How can we know anything at all about Jesus Christ? Through the witness of others in the Church, or through the New Testament, or books based upon the scriptural and historical records of faith. But the books and the personal faith are derived from knowledge of Christ in the New Testament. And how was this formed, if not by writing of the oral tradition of the earliest generation of Christians? And the source of their knowledge was the testimony of the ones who had experienced the risen Lord and known Him in the flesh: the apostles. If this seems too self-evident to be interesting, let us be reminded that apostleship as a theological as well as historical category has long been ignored by many Protestants. Either they have honored the memory of the apostles as first missionaries and also authors of the Gospels and letters, or else they have minimized the apostles in their polemical thinking against the Catholic doctrine of apostolic succession. Now it is becoming more evident that apostolicity means more than succession or even mission, both of which are included in the term. It means primarily the congruity of the Church in every generation with the faith, vocation, and worship of the apostolic community, and *through* this to the time of the event of Incarnation, to Jesus Christ.[8]

The apostles are thus in large measure acknowledged as the secondary basis of all ministry, as Christ is primary. In the ecumenical convergence it is being seen that an expanding agreement on the meaning of apostleship and apostolicity can assist the churches in coming to proximate agreements on the essential ministry.

Of course, this is where Roman Catholics and the "Catholic-minded" Protestants stand in opposition to Protestant thought in the World Council of Churches and elsewhere. *Lumen gentium*'s preoccupation with the episcopal hierarchy as derived immediately from the first apostles, and its subordination of priests and deacons to bishops, and further subordination of all the laity to the clergy constitute a dogmatic position which is neither congenial nor attractive to non-Catholics. On the other hand, as will soon be shown, there is now developing among many nonepiscopal churches a new appreciation for the office of bishop and for the principles of pastoral oversight, historic continuity, and manifest unity which are usually claimed for episcopacy.

Public attention since the Second Vatican Council has often been drawn to the new emphasis upon the comprehensive meaning of the people of God, as a designation of the Church, and also upon the newly heightened prerogative of the laity. No one can seriously dispute the value of these new perspectives in Catholic ecclesiology. Still, it is not unfair or untrue to observe that the publicity has been rather exaggerated. In the first place, it is difficult to accept at face value the Council's description of the Church as the people of God on pilgrimage, struggling to hold forth the Christomorphic life and the light of the gospel in a hostile world. The imagery is excellent; and in some times and places the Church has shown itself to be such a people of sojourners and strangers. For the most part, however, in lands of religious pluralism as well as in the lands of Catholic monopoly, it would require an unrestrained and generous imagination to conceive the Roman Catholic Church as such a pilgrim people. Its accommodations to political and economic institutions and to general cultural patterns are well known. So the possibilities of an effective ministry, especially a prophetic ministry, within the situation of cultural domestication are less available to a ministering laity than should be hoped.

The Vatican Council, moreover, has not emancipated the laity to the degree which the publicity of the issue seems to imply. *Lumen gentium*, having defined the laity as all those not in holy orders or a religious order, declares of their ministry: "They are in their own way made sharers in the priestly, prophetic, and kingly functions of Christ" (no. 31). Many good things are said in the chapter about the apostolate of the laity in the world of labor, business, recreation, technology, and education. And it stresses an important point, shared throughout the ecumenical movement by those who are trying to define the role of the laity, namely, that in virtue of "their baptism and confirmation, all are commissioned to that apostolate by the Lord Himself" (no. 33). Even so, the subordination of laity to clergy is rigorously maintained by the Constitution. In a manner which seems grossly condescending, it is admitted that laymen who have "knowledge, competence, and outstanding ability" may be "permitted and sometimes even obliged to express their opinions on those things that concern the good of the Church" (no. 37). To the laity of today, who are rather well aware of their own knowledge, competence, and outstanding ability, this grudging acknowledgment of their usefulness in the Church must seem egregiously irritating or dismaying. In the same paragraph this secondary status of the laymen is succinctly indicated in the admonition that they "promptly accept in Christian obedience the decisions of their pastors, since they are representatives of Christ as well as teachers and rulers in the Church."

Catholic theologians are by no means deficient in their estimate of the "royal priesthood" of all church members for the inner life and the external mission of the Church. Hans Küng is not typical of all, but is representative of the progressivists who recognize the need and the opportunities for freeing and developing the whole people of God for service in the world. Indeed, no more convincing description and rationale for the idea of the "priesthood of all believers," that hallmark of the Reformation, has been written lately than the section in Küng's book.[9] Movements for the enhancing of this concept, for the education and practical preparation of laymen, and the alteration of lay-clergy relationships at all levels of church life are underway in the Catholic Church, in parts of Orthodoxy, and many Protestant churches. Their potentiality for instilling new vigor in the churches and also for furthering the process of ecumenical convergence becomes increasingly apparent.

This prior and proper emphasis upon the priesthood of all the people eliminates, in the minds of a relatively few Protestants, the need for an ordained, or special, ministry. This is the most radical consequence of a prevailing confusion about the distinct meaning of ordination; but its effect is limited to individuals. It has not influenced the policy of Protestant church bodies as such. On the contrary, it can be said of most of these that the ecumenical discussions on ministry, and in particular the negotiations for church union, have produced a deepening sense of seriousness about the reality of ordination to the ministry of Word and sacrament. The blunt requirement of any fairly comprehensive union of denominations for a common ministry which is accepted by all concerned, and acknowledged as widely as possible throughout Christianity, compels the churches to revise their understanding of orders in the light of the contrary claims, or of biblical, historical, and theological investigations. None has stood still and immutable. In the reaches of the Anglican Communion, and especially in the counsels of the decennial Lambeth Conference of bishops, there has been a clear move towards more recognition of nonepiscopal ministries as truly used by the Holy Spirit to do in the churches what ministries are intended to do. This drift of thought and policy has even opened the way for the concelebration of the Eucharist by Anglican priests and ministers of those churches with which Anglicans are still negotiating for union.[10]

Even more remarkable is the trend of thought, real albeit unofficial, in Catholic theological circles respecting the orders of other churches. It is based upon the decision of the Vatican Council in its Degree on Ecumenism to refer to non-Catholic bodies as churches and ecclesial communities, rather than employing the previously familiar terms of avoidance, such as sect or society. Now, if a particular Methodist or Lutheran church is regarded by Vatican II as a church or ecclesial community—and the conciliar theologians draw no sharp distinction—then the ordained ministry of that church must have a certain validity in Catholic appraisal. Otherwise it would appear that the decision to acknowledge that church's ecclesial character was insincere or deceptive. The old epithet "absolutely null, utterly void" which was applied to Anglican orders[11] has not been formally repealed. But in actuality the movement of ecumenical discourse on church and ministry has already rendered the epithet itself virtually null and void. What this kind of thinking will eventually lead to, and whether it will cause the formal modification of canon law respecting the recognition of non-Catholic orders, is still a matter of conjecture.

Finally, there is a notable trend which is not for conjecture but is well established. It pertains to those official efforts to achieve union among several denominations, including the Anglican or Episcopal churches. Already accomplished in South India in 1947, these conversations and negotiations are in various stages of fruition in North India, Ceylon, Pakistan, New Zealand, Ghana, Nigeria, England, Canada, and the United States. For the most part, the other churches which may contract for union are the Methodist, Presbyterian, and Congregational. These have in virtually every case acceded to the plan of continuing the threefold ministry of bishop, prebyter (priest), and deacon in the united church.[12] Clearly this is a major change of ministerial concept and order for some of them. Already there is a twofold process of reconception discernible here. First, we note in some of the Protestant churches which have managed to survive for centuries without the benefit of bishops, and indeed have often fought against episcopacy, a growing appreciation for the office of a spiritual superintendent or pastoral overseer. While some decry this as a capitulation to Anglicanism or Catholicism, many see it as an honest recognition of the inherent value of such a minister in the spiritual life and temporal economy of the Church. Second, as though intending to remove the cause for legitimate attacks on episcopal prelacy and autocracy, some of the Episcopal churches are agreeing that a different kind of bishop is needed today, different from either the Renaissance prelate, the aristocratic Lord Bishop, or the contemporary general manager of church affairs. Again and again it is asserted that the bishop must be primarily a liturgical and pastoral leader, a teacher of the faith, a leader in the cause of Christian unity, and a spokesman and active contender for social justice and human welfare. These characterizations of the style, role, and responsibility of the bishop do not necessarily influence the theological doctrine of the historic episcopate or apostolic succession. But the nonepiscopal churches are at least ready to accept the historic episcopate within defined constitutional limits of power, and with at least as much latitude of doctrinal interpretation as now obtains within the Anglican communion itself. Thus there is a bending inward which foretells some future agreement on the reconception of the office of bishop in those churches which already have the episcopal order and in those which are disposed to accept it.

Of course, many Protestants are less than enthusiastic about the adoption of episcopacy in a united church of which they may become a part, because they are persuaded of its benefits by neither theological nor historical nor pastoral arguments. They look upon it as a nonnegotiable demand laid down by Anglicans, rather than an offer to share something which is either indispensable, or at least of much value, for the Church's realization of its best nature. For such Protestants, the commending of episcopacy as belonging either to the *esse*, the *bene esse*, or the *plene esse* is of little effect. Some hold an intransigently negative view of bishops because of a corporate memory of past abuses and conflicts, especially in Great Britain. Many who believe that church order should be determined strictly by the pattern of the New Testament church are convinced that the titles of bishop (*episkopos*) and elder (*presbyteros*) were interchangeable, and that neither corresponded in conception or function to the office of bishop as it later developed and is known today. And a good many Protestants resist episcopacy simply because they see it as an infringement upon the freedom in Christ and the rights of conscience of both individuals and congregations. So the convergence towards accord on episcopacy in Protestant church union plans, while manifestly genuine to a degree, is not without strong contestation.

Three observations about the present place of episcopacy in the Roman Catholic Church indicate that it too participates in the converging movement. First it must be noted that the Second Vatican Council continued to give strong emphasis to the doctrine of the apostolic succession in the Constitution on the Church as well as the Decree on the Bishops' Pastoral Office in the Church. There was no retreating from the traditional doctrine. However, secondly, the descriptions in both documents of the proper function, attitude, and responsibility of Catholic bishops is quite congenial with expectations of Protestants for their bishops, superintendents, church presidents, or whatever title they have. The Council admonishes bishops to follow in the triple office of Jesus Christ: prophet (teacher), priest, and king (shepherd, pastor), the same rubric which applies to the entire ministry of the Church. So the bishop is called to safeguard the unity of faith, instruct the faithful in love, care for the poor and sorrowing, preach untiringly the gospel, and fulfill his liturgical role as a priest. In brief, the full description of the episcopal office (*Lumen gentium*, nos. 23-27) is peculiarly Roman only in the way it is related by subordination to the papacy. Meanwhile, thirdly, the actual compliance with these conciliar recommendations is being effected by many progressive bishops in such ways that a revised image of the office is emerging. The credibility of the Vatican Council's depiction of episcopacy is obviously dependent upon the degree of success which bishops can have in the practical implementation of the theories of the doctrine. This means becoming detached and disassociated from the pattern of bishop as known in recent history, and adopting the new style: the style which is devoid of pretensions and pomposity, pastoral in both administration and personal relations, and courageous in the face of the numerous dehumanizing forces which modern societies have engendered.

Everyone knows that there are troops of other issues and problems affecting the Christian concept and practice of ministry today. It is a critical time of much contention and disaffection. But for that very reason it may prove to be a time of fruitful reappraisal and reconception. We have considered superficially only four aspects: Christ's enduring ministry, apostleship, the laity, and the episcopacy. In each we not only see some indications of the converging towards greater agreement among churches, with more mutual acknowledgment and acceptance of diverse ministries, but we also discern the emergence of patterns and styles of ministry which are suitable for the rapidly changing and emerging structures of human society in which the ministry or service of the Church must be exercised.

All Baptized into One Body

An intensified seriousness about the doctrine of holy baptism is most evident in the ecumenical conference reports and the publications of scholars. This is consequent upon at least three challenges: the fresh concern with biblical theology, the drive for Christian unity, and the dismay or near panic caused by the crumbling of long-established "Christian societies" in Europe and the Americas. We know full well that the practice of baptizing in Christ's name has become either so conventional in some lands or so pointless in others that baptism is dismissed by serious thinkers as nugatory. At the same time as this fall into apparent irrelevancy, however, baptism is extolled by some leading ecumenical thinkers, most notably the late Augustin Cardinal Bea, as the firm common ground of a vital Christian unity. It is the ostensible purpose of present inquiries and discussions both to enable the churches to build their unitive structures upon this one ground, and also to repristinate baptism as a strong factor in the renewing of the communal life, the worship, and the mission of the churches.[13]

However little many Christians today may think of baptism or disregard its importance, there can be no doubt that it was assumed by the New Testament church as a decisive mark of admission to the Christian fellowship and thus to the Spirit-empowered new life in Christ. In the earliest recorded preaching of the apostles, the expected reaction of persons to the hearing of the gospel of Christ was to repent of sins, confess faith, and be baptized (Acts 2:38). When addressing the first Christians in various cities, Paul kept reminding them of what their baptism meant: they were new persons, who had died and risen with Christ, and had been invested by Christ for a new life of love and service (Rom. 6:4; Col. 2:12, 3:3; Eph. 5:26). Even when contemporary Christians are obviously living in social situations which are entirely different from those of the first century, and when there are cultural and psychological factors which separate them from the first

Christian generation, there is no good reason why baptism cannot have the same decisive meaning for the present generation as for the first—if, that is, its primary meaning is recognized as such, and the secondary meanings are given subordinate place. The primary reference for each believer and for the community is simply the belonging to Jesus Christ. Baptism is the event by which we are made to know and to testify that, above all else in life, we belong to Christ and are His disciples. And since belonging to Christ means identifying with His people, His body, the Church, baptism is literally the incorporation into Christ, being embodied in Him.

In the current ecumenical dialogue there is an astonishing wideness of agreement on this primary Christological meaning of baptism. With increasing clarity it is being seen that baptism in the New Testament was much more than an adoption with slight variations of the Jewish proselyte baptism, or the washing rituals of pagan religions. The external cultic relations are certainly evident. But the internal meaning for faith is determined by the whole saving mission of Jesus Christ in life and death. The baptism of Jesus at the hands of John has for many Christians been a cause for perplexity. If John called people to repent because the judgment of God in the kingdom was coming, how could Jesus submit to the rite in the Jordan, since Jesus is regarded to have been without sin? Matthew's Gospel recognizes this difficulty for faith, and so in its account of this opening scene in Jesus' ministry the rugged prophet from the wilderness attempted to prevent Jesus from coming to him. But Jesus replied with the enigmatic words "Let it be so now; for thus it is fitting for us to fulfil all righteousness" (Mt. 3:13-17). Many commentators now agree that this answer was the indication of Jesus' assumption of the role of man's savior which had been predicated for Him. In the imagery and words of the Servant of God passages of Second Isaiah, it is the righteousness of the one vicarious servant which would bring "the many" of mankind to righteousness before God. Since John's baptism was a universal call to repentance, Jesus consciously responded, identifying Himself with sinful humanity as its representative. But this was the beginning, not the whole, of His baptism. Baptism for Jesus was His life and death of self-giving, from the River Jordan to the Jerusalem dump heap named Golgotha. This is clearly attested in Mark's Gospel, when Jesus answered the awkward question of James and John, His disciples. They asked for a place of privilege in the kingdom of heaven; but the reply they heard was a summons to suffering: "Are you able to drink the cup that I drink, or to be baptized with the baptism with which I am baptized?" (10:38). This was no talk of the ritual in water, but rather of the coming ordeal on the cross.

To be baptized, then, to be one with Jesus Christ, means to have a share in His suffering, even as He assumed the suffering for all mankind. This is what the symbolic words of John the Baptist pointed to, concerning the one coming after him who would baptize, not with water, but with Spirit and fire. By the Holy Spirit one is led in faith to know Christ and to be at one with Him; by the fire he becomes a witness for Christ and accepts the ordeals which may come on account of his faithfulness in a hostile world. Thus Spirit and fire are the marks of the baptism of the apostolic Church on Pentecost.

It is easy to see why baptism can be regarded as the bond or ground of unity of Christians, despite church divisions, when it is understood in this Christological and Christomorphic manner. Baptism is thus virtually the identifying mark of being a Christian. And the common faith which surrounds it is such as to provide for the mutual recognition of Christians who in other ways are not merely different but separated by doctrines and church structures.

If Christ, as the primary meaning, unites in baptism, there are secondary meanings which divide. Is baptism a sacrament, as the Eucharist is, or an ordinance or action of men? While the majority of churches presuppose the sacramental character of baptism, as a uniting of the Word of God with water and the Spirit-engendered faith, the Baptist churches and some others refuse to consider it as such. Neither did Karl Barth, the greatest theologian of the Reformed tradition since John Calvin. In the last of his numerous and ponderous books, Barth took his stand against a sacramental interpretation of baptism, and divided the baptism by Spirit from the baptism by water, only the former of the two being the work of God.[14] For this reason, Barth felt compelled to espouse the conviction of the Baptists: no baptizing of infants or uncomprehending children; baptism of professing believers only. There is consistency and cogency in Barth's theological argument. In obviating the need for a theological interpretation and defense of infant baptism, which has always been a notoriously difficult mental task, he has brought the baptismal rite with water, the work of the Spirit, and the conscious confession of faith into unambiguous unity. This interpretation is also practical, as well as intelligible, for those concerned about the Church in the "post-Constantinian era" of Western civilization, when it can no longer be assumed that infants are automatically gathered into the bosom of Mother Church. Moreover, it resolves the vexed theological question of the proper meaning of confirmation, as the complement to baptism in the process of Christian initiation. The crisis of confirmation for churches which still regard themselves as living within the Constantinian era is no less acute than that of baptism. One way to resolve the problem is the historic usage of the Greek Orthodox Church, whereby baptism of the infant and confirmation (chrismation) are brought immediately together, and then the wine of the Eucharist is administered to the little child. While resolving the one issue of confirmation as a complementary sacrament, however, this merely raises other problems concerning nurture, decision, and profession in the Church.

The ecumenical dialogue and the practices of the churches with regard to baptism, then, are now in much ferment. It is reported from time to time that some Anglican and Roman Catholic priests as well as Lutheran pastors have decided against the baptizing of infants, for reasons suggested above. At the same time, some of the churches which traditionally baptize believers only, and which are now engaged in church-union discussions with paedobaptist churches, are agreeing to a dual practice in the united church. In this way, while recognizing the primacy of identifying with Jesus Christ through the grace of God and the act of the Holy Spirit, they would admit for reasons of conscience either the baptism of infants or of believers. But they would not regard this as cause for a breach in the one church, even though they knowingly run the risk of tensions over strong disagreement.

Eucharist: Toward a Real, Not Merely Formal, Fellowship

These days one seldom hears the old expression "fencing the table." It summons up immediately the vivid and melancholy image of an altar or Communion table in the chancel of a church; surrounding it is a high fence of steel wire. At the single gate stands a minister, checking the tickets of those who seek admission to the Sacrament; while these enter to have a part in the Church's highest act of worship, those who were rejected stand outside, fingers clutching the wires, as they peer wistfully at the spectacle of Christ's broken body, and sensing that they *are* His broken body.

Apart from its undue sentimentality, this sad vision of the fenced table fails to be realistic for two reasons. First, in spite of canon laws and rubrics about who may properly be admitted to the Eucharist (call it Lord's Supper, Holy Communion, Mass, liturgy, etc.), priests and ministers do not stand guard against illicit intruders. Secondly, there just are not many Christians, when considered in proportion to the whole membership, who feel the anguish of those excluded ones outside the fence. Only the few sensitive folk have a feeling of dismay or pain because of the much-deplored scandal of divisions at the altar. Most Christians can live with it all right. Nevertheless, the hypersensitive few are right. Eucharistic schism *is* a scandal. Not only does it outrage the common belief in the unity of the body of Christ as a theological proposition, but it perpetuates a grave hindrance to the common and effective service and witness of the churches in the world.

Just as the sacramental apartheid should not be minimized, neither should the immediate and practical consequences of a unity of Communion between two or more denominations be accorded too much expectation. Consider, for instance, the two familiar denominations in America, the Presbyterian and Methodist. Between them exists a tacit and unchallenged state of intercommunion: members and ministers are welcome at each other's Communions. It is the relationship towards which many Catholics, Anglicans, and other so-called high-church ecumenists aspire. Undoubtedly it is a worthy and important aspiration. But to be utterly honest, it must be said that the Eucharistic openness of the Methodist and Presbyterian churches has hardly any bearing upon their relationships in the local area or the national scene. If they maintained dogmatic barriers to such fellowship in the Eucharist, it is dubious whether their co-operation and intimacy would be greater or less than at present. Why is this? For the plain reason that the Sacrament does not play a central role in the life of these two denominations. Despite the traditional teaching of each, respectively from Calvin and Wesley who both had the highest estimate for a regular celebration of Communion, these denominations, like some others, have without deliberate intention relegated the Sacrament to a peripheral position. This is the more obvious when comparison is drawn to the Orthodox, Catholic, Anglican, and Lutheran churches.

Holy Communion as an ecumenical concern thus has two dimensions. One is the need for drawing the churches into unrestricted fellowship so that they can celebrate the fulness of their unity in Christ. The other is to provide such interpretation of Eucharistic doctrine and to discover such new meaning in common that the centrality of the Sacrament will be truly efficacious for all the churches.

The convergence of which we speak has still left many members unmoved and uninterested; but for a significant number, and especially for those consciously involved in the ecumenical movement, it amounts to a virtual revolution. Indeed, there is, so to speak, a double convergence. One is in Eucharistic theology, the other in church practice as well as the practice of voluntary groups. The one is increasingly apparent in the formal conciliar studies and the scholarly reassessments of biblical and historical theology; the latter makes stories for the secular press as well as the religious. Liturgies are being revised, rubrics made more flexible, the sacred preciousness of the ritual is being modified for more relevance to people's secular concerns, and unprecedented statements of agreement are being registered among churches divided by centuries.

To begin a brief scanning of the points of agreement on the graph of convergence, the close connection of baptism and Eucharist should be pondered. Not only do these have the character of sacraments, according to the doctrines of the majority of churches, but for Catholicism and Orthodoxy they are pre-eminent among the sacraments, and for Protestantism they are the only two. There is persuasive and illuminative power in the currently popular interpretation of Christ Himself as the sacrament par excellence, the Church as the primordial sacrament of grace, and the two dominical sacraments of baptism and Eucharist derived from Christ and perpetuated in the Church. The power lies in the consistent emphasis of the reality of Christ in His community and through these particularly dramatic and universally symbolic means of grace. The implications of this scheme of connections are that Christ is the controlling principle in the individual's personal relation to God the Father, that He gives the Church the identity of a community of grace, and that baptism and Eucharist both convey His power to create and sustain new life for man.

Those who know the serenity, consolation, encouragement, love, and hope which come from Christ through faith can understand, as others cannot, why the Holy Communion is called Eucharist. It means simply thanksgiving. It is the rendering of gratitude to God for all He creates and for the redemption He grants to men and women. In this sense it is the offering of thanks not only through words of prayer, but through the giving of bread and wine. Jesus at the Last Supper identified these products of man's making as His body and blood, or by implication as Himself. Thus they are offered with prayer to God as emblematic of ourselves too. Our individual lives and the common life of the Church are sacrifices, even as the life of Jesus was a sacrifice offered to God on behalf of all. In the Sacrament our small sacrifices are conjoined with His great, unique, and once-for-all sacrifice. The intent is not to appease God—for He needs no appeasement—but to please Him by this ultimate act of thanksgiving and self-giving. On this first point, ancient as it is and forgotten by many as it has been, there is now a more general agreement than heretofore in modern Church history. To be sure, this interpretation of sacrifice is considered insufficient or unacceptable to those who believe confidently that the Eucharist is an objective and propitiatory sacrificial action wrought upon the altar by the priest as agent.

The second nexus of growing consensus is the understanding of the word "memorial." "Do this in remembrance of me" is one of the best known words of Jesus in His momentous experience with the disciples in the upper room in Jerusalem, even though it is regarded by scholars as a marginal addition to the text of Luke 22:20. Is the idea simply that Christians make a mental effort to remember Jesus as they worship? In the Anglican Book of Common Prayer the ritual, which is expressive of the Western liturgical tradition, includes a prayer of the priest in which he tells God that "the memorial which thy Son hath commanded us to make" has been made by the congregation. Does not this sound like the "mere memorialism" attributed to Huldrich Zwingli of Zurich's reformation, and continued in the "nonsacramentarian" churches of the left-wing Protestantism? During four centuries there have been heated arguments over the issue of whether the Eucharist involves just a corporate memory of Jesus, or whether in some sense Jesus Christ is truly present. This raises the related question of an alleged repetition of His atoning death in the Catholic celebration of the Mass. Considering the almost universal sense of reverence for the Eucharist's purpose of promoting reconciliation and peace, we recoil from the dreary and offensive spectacle of Christians fighting one another over its meaning. While some of this belligerency has been due to mean prejudice, however, it must be admitted that many Christians have contended against what they regarded as false interpretations precisely for the reason that they felt constrained to defend the Eucharist from either rationalistic or superstitious perversions of its sacramental character.

A fortunate escape from this past bitterness has been made possible by recent ecumenical studies of the Greek word *anamnēsis* (=memorial). The emerging consensus resolves some ancient issues of dispute. The concept of time has been revised in the light of its biblical meaning. In Eucharistic memorial the past and the future meet in the present moment, and the moment is always on the move. It means that the historical event of the life and death of Jesus Christ is recalled in such a way as to make it an experienced reality in the present. But also, the future fulfillment of personal life and of man's history is anticipated in faith, so that during the Eucharist—and constantly in the attitude of faith—we are already being encouraged and directed by the reign of God which is to come. So the Eucharist encourages no brooding about what is past, nor preoccupation with the present moment and its problems, nor flight of fancy and imagination into the refuge of the unknown future. The three dimensions of the experience of time and history converge in the awareness and recognition that God's love in Jesus Christ applies in all times and all circumstances of man's existence.

Only with such a concept of time, and only by faith in the resurrection of Christ and the continuing effect of the Holy Spirit, can there be meaningful discourse about the much-disputed "real presence" of Christ in the Eucharistic action. Just here the lines of Christian interpretation are coming together with astonishing rapidity. Negatively, it is agreed by thinkers of diverse Catholic and Protestant traditions that it is fruitless to press a distinction between the "material" and the "spiritual" presence of Christ. Likewise, it is clear that opposition to belief in the "real" presence must, if consistent, be based upon the tacit idea of an "unreal" presence; but this really means no presence at all. Opponents of "real" presence thus find themselves in the awkward position of affirming the presence of Christ in one's faith, prayer, loving service, and in preaching and teaching the gospel—but *not* in the Holy Communion! Moreover, since the presence of Christ is more generally being conceived in terms of personal relation between the faithful and the living Christ, the localization of His presence in the elements of bread and wine, consecrated through ritual action, is receiving less and less emphasis even among Catholic theologians.

"Transsignification" is the term suggested by some as preferable to "transubstantiation." Whereas the latter word has served Catholic theology for centuries, it belongs to a philosophical view of matter and spirit which is virtually obsolete. The former term expresses an insight more agreeable to a modern understanding of human existence in the world, which is being rapidly described and explained in scientific terms. Hence, the interpretation of the meeting of divine and human in the Eucharistic celebration—even after admitting freely the sheer mystery of the ultimate meaning—gains credibility in so far as it can be communicated to minds which think in existential, personal, and phenomenological categories. The idea of transsignification may sound new, but actually it is resonant of a biblical view of God's use of matter and of human spirit for the communication of grace. It accounts for the way by which something's nature or identity is determined more by its appointed use than by its physical make-up. For example, the nature of a national flag cannot be explained by the threads of its fabric or the dyes in the coloring, or even by the human inventiveness of its designer. It has a character of its own because of its use as a rallying center for patriotic feeling and action. And the intensity of its power to communicate or stimulate a feeling or idea is further dependent upon the time and circumstance in which it is used. Rolled and left in a closet, it is inert. Flying from a staff, but little noticed, it has moderate meaning. But carried into battle to the sound of bugle and gunfire, its significance is profoundly increased. By such an analogy, the use of bread and wine as the media for conveying the reality of Christ's presence, always within the limitations of human perception and understanding, may be transsignified by the requisite conditions: the gathering of the community, large or small; the attitude of faith on their part; the offering of prayer; the preaching of the gospel; and the consecration by the minister on behalf of the Church, followed by the solemn yet joyful eating and drinking together.[15]

These clues to Eucharistic meaning which emanate from the full concept of the word "remembrance" (*anamnēsis*) are complemented and made effective through the Church's prayer to the Holy Spirit. The familiar Greek word is *epiklēsis*, the "calling upon" the Spirit to make effective and real for the gathered people the presence of Jesus Christ, and thus to sanctify the communion of the people with Him. This is an aspect of the ritual which in some churches has been neglected. In the current ecumenical discussions it is stressed with particular vigor by the Eastern Orthodox; with good reason they contend for the importance of invoking the Spirit of God in the midst of this dramatic action by human beings. Without the Spirit it would be merely a drama.

Another aspect of the Eucharist on which almost universal ecumenical concord is being registered is its inherent power to knit people into personal *communion*. Of course, this is why it bears that alternate name to Eucharist: communion is the translation of the Greek *koinōnia*, meaning "mutual sharing" by all concerned. This sense of shared fellowship has long been emphasized by the Orthodox, on the one hand, with their doctrine of *sobornost*, and by such freely constituted churches as the Church of the Brethren and the Christian Churches (Disciples of Christ), on the other. But in some others the meaning and experience of communion have been lost for one of two seemingly opposite reasons. Either the excessive subjectivism has caused people to consider the Eucharist an occasion for sublime but individualistic experiences of pious devotion, or else the excessive objectivism has turned it into an operation performed by the priest, in relation to which the laymen can serve only as spectators. The correction of these differing distortions of the Sacrament is coming about, not by some radically new insight, but by recapturing the truth of the event which has belonged to it from the beginning. "The bread which we break," said St. Paul, "is it not a participation (*koinōnia*) in the body of Christ?" (1 Cor. 10:16). Obviously this recovery is important not only for the sake of a common understanding among the churches. Just as significant, in this age of increasing social forces which dehumanize and atomize people, is the Church's opportunity to provide for people a social situation in which the mutual expression of personal care is the reflection of the love of God which Christ makes manifest to any who will receive it.

Therefore, lastly, there is an expanding recognition of the power of the Eucharist for *mission*. Many still regard the Sacrament as an arcane ritual which the Church provides for the benefit of the relatively small number of faithful members. This is quite wrong. If the Christian doctrine of the Eucharist is so richly beneficial as it is claimed to be, then there is need to share the same faith in Christ with other persons, to the end that they also become participants in this dimension of life. The intentions, prayers, and preached words have to do with the needs of all men and women, just as the ministry and self-giving of Jesus Christ were for all. Holy Communion is not a sectarian event. It is literally ecumenical and secular, that is, for the whole world. This is one reason why there is much concern for the overcoming of barriers to communion among the various churches, so that the reality of reconciliation in Christ may be made manifest. The realization of intercommunion, and beyond that of full communion, is not sought for the sole purpose of vindicating theological notions about unity of the Church, but to advance the mission of the gospel to mankind.

A Fair and Representative Way of Governing

The quest for a more equitable system of consultation and government in the Roman Catholic Church is one of the most prominent consequences of the Second Vatican Council. The Council promised to reform the bureaucracy of the Roman Curia, rewrite canon law, and press the pope to accept a collegial relation to the bishops. The synod of bishops held in 1967 seemed to be an artful dodging of the Council's proposals; but in 1969, led by certain eminent cardinals of progressive outlook and strong courage, the likelihood of these reforms was secured. Collegiality, as the alternative to absolute papal monarchy, is nothing new to most Orthodox and Protestant churches. They simply use different names for the same kinds of instrument of polity: assemblies, conferences, synods, conventions, houses, etc. In all cases it is more and more agreed that the Church, made up of "priestly people," needs to have a governmental system in which, as they meet corporately, they may determine what actions and policies are most in keeping with the mind of Christ. Most Protestants would regard these instruments and forms of collegial government as the practical expedients which have developed through the centuries of church history. But the Roman Catholics in their search for an understanding and implementation of collegiality are guided by motives and expectations which are more than pragmatic. They seek an order which is truly integral to the being of the Body of Christ on earth, that is, a form of collegiality which is genuinely expressive of the *koinōnia* belonging to the nature and life of the Church. This same expectation is not wanting among Protestants, but they have no consistency of belief about it.

With regard to polity, it has been long established in the Faith and Order discussions about unity that the elements of three types of church structure must be maintained. These are the episcopal, the presbyterial, and the congregational. In essence these three connote, first, a concentration of power in the bishop's office; second, a centering of power in the group of elders from churches in a limited area, and third, the autonomy and perhaps independence of each local congregation. Convergence has already broken down the demarcations among these three. A genuinely collegial government, bringing together both freedom of representative expression and the recognized and constituted authority of church officers, requires the blending of all three. The value of this has been demonstrated already in the Church of South India, united in 1947, and it is well expected in current efforts to achieve union.

There has developed a different form of collegiality in recent years. It was unprecedented before the twentieth century, but now has become the distinctive form of church relationship and consultation in this time. It is the council of churches. Adequately to do the work which God's known will requires of His people in modern civilization, it has been necessary to bypass the continuing divisions of the denominations and various ecclesial families. Interconfessional committees, national Christian councils, co-operative working groups, and the councils of churches: these are the provisional, insufficient, but indispensable means of expressing the unity of the one Church. They are the temporary expedients rather than the permanent forms of unity. They deserve a more careful consideration of their nature and functions than is possible here.

An attempt has been made in this essay to show, in barely more than an outline, how the current ecumenical era has witnessed the converging of Christian thought on a wide variety of major doctrines, and in particular on elements of ecclesiology. On these fundamental matters the many churches are no longer in parallel.

Next comes the large question: Must the analogy of geometry be consistently sustained? That is, must the converging lines of Christian doctrine and practice eventually intersect or coincide? Is the union, or reunion, of all the churches inevitable? Desirable? Feasible?

One of the first influential Catholic ecumenists in America, Gustave Weigel, was already writing on the subject of convergence before the Second Vatican Council assembled. He wrote in 1961: "We are pursuing converging lines of thought, not identical, but converging. When will they meet? I am neither a prophet nor the son of a prophet. I refuse to answer the question."[16] Was he wise in refusing to venture an answer? Lacking in faith? Or did he really desire the unknown form of the Church of the future, toward which all the present convergence is pointing?

Certainly there are many Christians today who are becoming nervous and afraid of the future implications of the present converging. They want to slow down the process, to withdraw support, to return if possible to the familiar, more comfortable ways which they and their parents have known.

Some argue that converging so madly towards unity is endangering Christian liberty. They fear a so-called monolithic, totalitarian, uniform church, in which the unsolicited promptings of the Holy Spirit and the exercise of His diverse gifts would be stifled and stagnated by the weight of the homogeneous institution.

Others declare that the ultimate aim of convergence is insidious, because it will finally destroy the motivating power of the Church to accomplish their tasks. Using the quaint term of Vatican II's Decree on Ecumenism in a distorted sense, they urge a "fraternal rivalry" as meaning denominational competition. They think of the world as a vast market, or even a sports stadium, in which the rival churches sustain their vitality by striving to outstrip each other in mission, conversion, service, and institutional growth.

Still others, especially many younger persons who are quickly becoming the majority of both Church and mankind, are declaring that neither unity nor division of the Church is important enough to worry about anymore, since the Church itself is so unimportant for the well-being of mankind in coming years. So they could not care less for the ecumenical convergence, conferences and councils, common worship and co-ordinated committees.

All four of these objections—the longing to turn back, the concern for liberty and diversity, the estimate of fair competition, and the disdain for institutional churches—require serious attention. They can be either allayed or rejected in debate, where time permits. But not in this context.

Instead, we conclude optimistically with a testimony of hope for the future of the Church. The main issues on which

Christians are coming to agree are essential for the people of God. It is not, however, for the Church's interior health only, but for the renewed sense of diaconal mission to mankind on behalf of Jesus Christ, that this unitive movement is to be furthered and prized.

Is it justifiable, then, to believe that the convergence of doctrine, theology, and polity will lead to an eventual union? Yes! Never to a perfect, all-inclusive union, of course. There will surely be continuing parties, sects, and divisions. But the unity of the body of Christ in history is an element of faith, precisely because this visible unity is in the order of God's revealed purpose for mankind, namely, the reconciliation of all people in peace.

1. Oscar Cullmann, *Salvation in History* (New York, 1967). See *Ecumenical Experiences*, ed. Luis V. Romeu (London, 1965), p. 36.
2. Among numerous influential studies of these figures, apart from Roman Catholic works, see J. A. T. Robinson, *The Body* (London, 1951); Paul S. Minear, *Images of the Church in the New Testament* (Philadelphia, 1960); and Ernest Best, *One Body in Christ* (London, 1955).
3. *First Assembly of the World Council of Churches* (London, 1949), pp. 51–63.
4. See Jerome Hamer, *The Church Is a Communion* (New York, 1964).
5. *Report of the Third World Conference on Faith and Order* (London, 1953), p. 21.
6. *Church Dogmatics* 4/2 (Edinburgh, 1958), p. 633.
7. *Institutes of the Christian Religion* 2, 15.
8. See the definition of apostolicity agreed upon by the joint study commission of the World Council of Churches and the Vatican, published in *One in Christ*, 4 (1970), 458. An interpretation of apostolicity for American Protestant churches is found in the author's *Criterion for the Church* (New York, 1963).
9. Hans Küng, *Structures of the Church* (New York, 1964), chap. 5; also *The Church* (London, 1967), pp. 363–70.
10. See *The Lambeth Conference 1968: Resolutions and Reports* (London, 1968), p. 128.
11. By Leo XIII in *Apostolicae curae* (1896).

12. Consummation of the church unions in Pakistan and North India have been set for November 1970. For definition of the threefold ordained ministry, as well as the whole corporate ministry, of the proposed united church in the United States, see *A Plan of Union* (Princeton, 1970), chap. 7.

13. An excellent comprehensive study is Dale Moody's *Baptism: Foundation for Christian Unity* (Philadelphia, 1967).

14. *Church Dogmatics* 4/4 (fragment: Edinburgh, 1969).

15. This view of transsignification as well as the analogy of the symbolic reality of the flag are developed by E. Schillebeeckx, *Die eucharistische Gegenwart* (Düsseldorf, 1968; translated from the Dutch original, *Christus' tegenwoordigheid in de Eucharistie* [Bilthoven]). He cites fellow Catholic theologians I. de Baciocchi and P. Schoonenberg as well as Reformed theologians F. J. Leenhardt and M. Thurian in support of this view (pp. 70–81).

16. "Ecclesiology and Ecumenics," in *Problems before Unity* (Baltimore, 1962), p. 43.

New Theology No. 1

New Theology No. 2

Introduction

I: THE PROBLEM OF GOD AND THE GODLESS

Christianity Without Religion
> C. B. Armstrong

The Theology of True Secularity
> William O. Fennell

A New Linguistic Madness
> Langdon B. Gilkey

"Non-metaphysical" Christian Philosophy and Linguistic Philosophy
> James W. Woelfel

Whither the Doctrine of God Now?
> David Jenkins

II: NATURE AND LAW

Naturalism, Historicism, and Christian Ethics: Toward a Christian Doctrine of Natural Law
> Douglas Sturm

Autonomy and Reason in Judaism
> Alexander Carlebach

The Natural Law Teaching of the Eastern Orthodox Church
> Stanley S. Harakas

Teilhard de Chardin: A Philosophy of Procession
> E. R. Baltazar

III: THE CHURCHES IN RELATION

Judaism and Christianity: Then and Now
> Krister Stendahl

The Significance of the Ecumenical Councils
> William Nicholls

Ecclesiology and Roman Catholic Renewal
> George A. Lindbeck

IV: BIBLICAL TRENDS

A Survey of Recent Gospel Research
> Harvey K. Mc Arthur

Rudolf Bultmann and Post-Bultmann Tendencies
> P. Joseph Cahill, S.J.

V: EXTENSION OF THEOLOGY

A New Trio Arises in Europe
> John B. Cobb, Jr.

The Form of the Church in the Modern Diaspora
> M. Richard Shaull

Through Dooms of Love
> William Stringfellow

Christ and the Christ Figure in American Fiction
> Robert Detweiler

New Theology No. 3

New Theology No. 4

New Theology No. 5

Christian Hope and Human Futures

I: SECULAR THEOLOGY—CAUTIONARY WORDS

New Left Man Meets the Dead God
    Steve Weissman
Man and His World in the Perspective of Judaism: Reflections on Expo '67
    Emil L. Fackenheim
Did Jesus Believe in God? Some Reflections on Christian Atheism
    R. F. Aldwinckle

II: THE THEOLOGY OF HOPE—ENTHUSIASTIC WORDS

Hope in a Posthuman Era
    Sam Keen
Toward a Theology of Hope
    Carl E. Braaten
Appearance as the Arrival of the Future
    Wolfhart Pannenberg
Creative Hope

    Johannes B. Metz

III: THE ORIENTATION TOWARD THE FUTURE— TENTATIVE WORDS

God and the Supernatural
    Leslie Dewart
The Dehellenization of Dogma
    Bernard J. F. Lonergan, S.J.
The Future of Belief Debate
    Justus George Lawler

IV: ALTERNATIVE FUTURES

Ernst Bloch and "The Pull of the Future"
    Harvey Cox
The Absolute Future
    Michael Novak
Communists and Christians in Dialogue
    Roger Garaudy
Evolution, Myth, and Poetic Vision
    Walter J. Ong, S.J.

New Theology No. 6

Theology and Revolution

I: THE GROUNDWORK OF THEOLOGIANS

Biblical Theology Today
J. Christiaan Beker
From Anxiety to Responsibility: The Shifting Focus of Theological Reflection
Thomas W. Ogletree
Toward a Political Hermeneutics of the Gospel
Jürgen Moltmann

II: THE THEORY OF REVOLUTION: PRO AND CON

A Christian Looks at Revolution
George Celestin
Ecumenical Theology of Revolution
J. M. Lochman
Christian Faith as Scandal in a Technocratic World
Richard Shaull
A Theology of Rebellion
Rolland F. Smith
Marx and Religion: An Impossible Marriage
Louis Dupré

III: THE PRACTICE OF REVOLUTION: THEOLOGICAL REFLECTION

a. Race
The Afro-American Past
Vincent Harding
Martin Luther King—Unsung Theologian
Herbert Warren Richardson
b. Peace and Conscience
The Foundation and Meaning of Christian Pacifism
Hans-Werner Bartsch
Revolutionary Faithfulness
R. W. Tucker
Vietnam: Crisis of Conscience
Robert McAfee Brown
c. The Church
Gospel and Revolution
16 Bishops of the 3rd World
England's Troubles and the Catholic Left
Desmond Fennell
The Free Church Movement in Contemporary Catholicism
Rosemary Ruether

New Theology No. 7

New Theology No. 8